P9-DVU-291

DATE DUE

DE 7 '99			
NO 13 '01			
DE 4 '01			
DE 19 '01			
NR 25 '02			
AP 21 '08			

DEMCO 38-296

THE END
OF
THE WORLD

The Four Horsemen of the Apocalypse *by Albrecht Dürer, 1497-1499*

THE END
OF
THE WORLD

Edited by Lewis H. Lapham
with Peter T. Struck

St. Martin's Press   New York

Riverside Community College
OCT '99   Library
4800 Magnolia Avenue
Riverside, CA 92506

D 24 .E53 1998

The end of the world

THOMAS DUNNE BOOKS.
An imprint of St. Martin's Press.

THE END OF THE WORLD. Copyright © 1997 by Lewis H. Lapham. All rights reserved.
Printed in the United States of America. No part of this book may be used or reproduced in any manner whatsoever without written permission except in the case of
brief quotations embodied in critical articles or reviews. For information, address
St. Martin's Press, 175 Fifth Avenue, New York, N.Y. 10010.

Acknowledgement of permission to reprint copyrighted materials can be found
starting on page 289.

ISBN 0-312-19264-9

First published in the United States by History Book Club

First Edition: December 1998

10 9 8 7 6 5 4 3 2 1

TABLE OF CONTENTS

PART II: THE FALL OF NATIONS

PART III: THE TWENTIETH CENTURY: THE END IN A VOID

LIST OF ILLUSTRATIONS

INTRODUCTION

CLIO STRIKES BACK

by Simon Schama

Where is Rubens when you really need him? Who else, after all, could paint the allegory I have in mind: *The Captivity of History*? At the center would be the pathetic figure of Clio, the Muse of History, seriously undernourished (for Rubens) and in chains, languishing atop a pile of books, inscribed, "Macaulay," "Parkman," "Gibbon"; while worms gnaw through the pages and mice nibble at ancient bindings. At her right would be a scowling figure, bloated and bespectacled, pushing a mute into Clio's abandoned trumpet with one hand, and in the other holding the keys to her fetters. Inscribed on his armor are the words "Social Studies," and he is supported by three grim and wasted furies, on whose drab apparel are stencilled the names "Relevance," "Thematics," and "Correctness," and who trample together the corpse of a Dead White Male. Behind them, a grieving matron, Mnemosyne, the guardian of Memory, reaches imploringly towards a great cave wherein are imprisoned the twins Narrative and Chronology. But the entrance to the cave is guarded by a snarling many-headed hound whose collar bears the words "Adoption Committee" as well as a massive wall of industrially-produced Text Books, the size of cinder blocks. In the background, a great mountain is carved with the colossal heads of Herodotus, Thucydides, and Tacitus. Boulders in the shape of teardrops appear to depend from their cheeks.

The scene is not, however, completely tragic. In the right background, a shaft of light breaks the black bank of clouds, revealing a winged figure, flying towards the scene, bearing a spear sharpened like the quill of a pen, and the words "Popular History" inscribed on her helmet.

She'll have her work cut out for her. But popular history, both in written and visual documentary form, is now the most powerful and eloquent means by which the American public engages with the record of the past. In fact it's nothing short of a miracle that the hunger for history in the reading public remains strong (witness the best-selling success of authors like Stephen Ambrose, Doris Kearns Goodwin and David McCullough), despite the best efforts of curricula to destroy it. The most important thing we could do by way of instilling a passion for history in our children would be to abolish Social Studies outright, and liberate its constituent elements into their proper and separate disciplines, restoring their proper names: History, the study of the Past; Geography, the study of Place; Politics, the study of Power. Short of this miracle of enlightened courage actually occurring, the next best thing we can do is to nourish our own historical imagination by reading the best work of the past and present, and passing on that passion to our children as an indispensable element of their growth to maturity. For as Cicero pointed out, cultures that lack history, be they ever so powerful, remain in the condition of an infant, ignorant of whence they have come, and thus, of whither they go.

There are many things that history is not, or should not be. The first is a fix-it manual for contemporary dilemmas. Of course, *without* historical understanding, there is no hope of intelligent encounter with our problems. That was why Thucydides wrote his account of the Peloponnesian Wars. But lazy historical analogy must never be the crutch of political convenience. Insisting that Saddam Hussein is "just like Hitler" dilutes the singular enormity of both their crimes; seeing Bosnia as a "Vietnam waiting to happen" betrays historical ignorance of both conflicts. Nor should history be identity fodder, feeding the craving of particular social or ethnic groups for collective self-esteem, or for the habitual perpetuation of grievance. It should never flinch from documenting injustice, of course, or from offering an account of the journey of a culture through time, but as soon as its purposes are driven by retribution, it becomes the tame creature of ethnic orthodoxy, in short, propaganda. History as the vehicle of collective self-admiration, be it imposed from Patriotic Correctness (as in the scandalous censorship inflicted on the Smithsonian's Hiroshima exhibition) or from Political Correctness, never has the ring of truth, because the quality of self-criticism that must be meat and drink to vivid and persuasive history has been muffled.

So what, then, should history *be?* At its best history is a way of understanding ourselves, fathoming the human condition, through an intense and close-up engagement with our ancestors, be they ever so remote as the ancient Persians or as close as the Doughboys of World War I. This should never be confused with ancestor-worship, since history's incorruptible virtue is that it more often produces nasty surprises (see Thucydides) than consolatory pieties. To make that engagement serious and persuasive, effectively written history must have the power to tear the reader from his own time and place and deposit him into an utterly different, even alien world with the narrator as his only guide and scout. That world might be Jefferson's Virginia, the Mughal court of the Emperor Akhbar or the Hawaii of Kamehameha I; but for the duration of the book, it should become more real and immediate to the reader than the commuter train or the corporate meeting. The past should get under our skin, working its way stealthily into our cultural bloodstream, its transformation of our knowledge of who we are having the stealthy potency of poetry or philosophy.

Then again, of course, history can deliver sudden bolts of unexpected illumination. In the late 1960s I was working in the old national archive of the Netherlands in The Hague, doing research for my first book on the impact, mostly sad, of the French Revolution on the Dutch Republic. Sheets of rain were, as usual, falling down the windows: pale golden light from the archive lamps making the documents glow; the Readers' Room enveloped in the dustiness of old paper and parchment and pencil shavings that, even in the age of the laptop, is the natural element of all true historians. A folder of documents was brought to my table: the records of a Dutch soldier-politician who had been killed during a military campaign. In the batch was a packet still bearing the unbroken seal of the Batavian Republic (the official name of the revolutionized Netherlands). Nothing as serious as seal-breaking can be entrusted to mere historians, so it was the Reading Room superintendent who got to crack the red wax. Spilled on to my table, the contents saw the first light of day since they had been sealed in

1799 and sent on their way to the soldier's wife. Unbeknownst to him she had herself died, cause unknown, and the packet made its way unopened to the parliamentary archive from which I pulled it a century-and-a-half later.

What emerged from the yellowing envelope were the elements of a life: public and private; civic and impassioned. There were proofs of a high-minded article the soldier had written on constitutional reform; a silhouette confirming his position as a member of the Batavian National Assembly—in effect his I.D.— and subscription tickets to a chamber concert (Haydn) in The Hague, which the length of the campaign had precluded his attending. There was a letter to his wife, brimming with devotion and affection and shadowed by the candidly expressed fear of battle. There seemed, though, to be something else at the bottom of the envelope. When I shook it, a tiny folded paper, secured with string, fell out. This time I avoided the superintendent's eye and opened it myself. Inside was a lock of golden hair, tied with a ribbon of shockingly bright blue; a blue that remained unfaded by time; a blue of the summertime sky over the Frisian islands. The hair, surely, must have been cut from the soldier's wife's head. But what, then, was it doing in a packet of his possessions sent back to his home? Some questions—the most compelling—never get answered. I held the silky lock in my hand and suddenly caught a strong scent that cut through the powdery staleness of my archive. Furtively, behind my concealing hand, I brushed the hair against my nostrils. The effect was startling, the musky aroma of some animal gland; the heaviness of rosewater; no light floral notes here—they would wait until the reinvention of the perfume industry in the nineteenth century. For a fleeting minute or two I inhaled the intimacy of a late eighteenth-century marriage. Then it was gone, drifting off into the murky air of 1968.

Such little epiphanies shape an historian's life: the delicate touch of the fingertips of Clio. But there's no need for her to be always that coy. Within the pages of *History*, she'll take the hands of its readers and, unchained at last, lead them into the endless palace of marvels that is our common past.

There have been and there will be many and divers destructions of mankind, of which the greatest are by fire and water, and lesser ones by countless other means.

—Plato

broadcasts updating the approach of weird storms, in the statistical abstracts forecasting the collapse of the international monetary system, the corruption of the genetic codes or the disappearance of the Atlantic salmon. The prophecies become more dreadful as they become more numerous, and the publishers of oracular texts multiply the sum of alarm with titles that announce, among other calamities, "The End of Architecture," "The Death of Intimacy," "The End of Nature," "The Death of Economics," "The End of Science," and "The Death of Meaning." Along similar but more picturesque lines, the producers of Hollywood disaster films supply continuous montages of earthquake and fire, and the authors of best-selling novels imagine the once-pastoral landscape of western civilization overrun by ancient reptiles or post-modern insects.

The foretelling of the end of the world is as old as the wind in the trees, and against the siege of dire prophecy the reading of history provides a reliable defense. The world as large numbers of people have known it—the Romans at Pompeii in 79 A.D., the Confederate States of America at Richmond in 1865, the Jews in Berlin in 1938—has come to an end many, many times, and writers as unlike one another as Mary Chestnut and Pliny the Younger have had occasion to remark on the spectacle. Usually it turns out that the soothsayers have been misinformed, and what becomes clear in the pages of this book is the striking difference in tone between the voices drumming up the threat of imminent damnation and the voices bearing witness to the event.

The prophets speak in metaphors and imagine the end of the world as the work of invisible forces giving instructive form to eternal abstractions— divine wrath (Joachim de Fiore, The Book of Revelations); the dissolution of atoms (Lucretius); the word of God (the Gospels, Jonathan Edwards); the nature of politics (Ibn Khaldun); biology (Mary Shelley, Charles Darwin); mathematics (Malthus); the second law of thermo-dynamics (Henry Adams); the structure of civilization (Oswald Spengler); politico economic theory (Francis Fukuyama); volcanoes (The Rapture Index). The evolving shape of the Beast of the Apocalypse inspires corresponding changes of descriptive adjective; the poetic image becomes the scientific treatise, physics replaces

FOREWORD

THE WRECK OF TIME (I)

About suffering they were never wrong,
The Old Masters: how well they understood
Its human position; how it takes place
While someone else is eating or opening a window
Or just walking dully along . . .

In Brueghel's Icarus, for instance: how everything turns away
Quite leisurely from the disaster; the ploughman may
Have heard the splash, the forsaken cry,
But for him it was not an important failure; the sun shone
As it had to on the white legs disappearing into the green
Water; and the expensive delicate ship that must have seen
Something amazing, a boy falling out of the sky,
Had somewhere to get to and sailed calmly on.

—W. H. Auden, *"Musée des Beaux Arts"*

For the better part of a decade the heralds of apocalypse have been placarding the walls of the news and entertainment media with the s͏c͏ules of misfortune certain to coincide with the end of the millennium. portents of doom appear every week in press bulletins monitoring the dis tion of the ozone layer or the proliferation of nuclear weapons, on telev metaphysics, and the verses of Isaiah give way to Rachel Carson's list of lost birds.

Put to the trials of history, the end of the world doesn't fulfill the promise of its advance billing. Although terrible, the work is never complete, and no matter how broad the flood or how ravenous the flames, the living outnumber the dead—maybe not in the immediate vicinity of the Lisbon waterfront or the Hindenburg Trench, but within reach of a new generation salvaged, like all generations, from the wreck of time.

More often than not the catastrophe turns out to have been made by man, not God, and instead of taking the form of a divine wind, the forces at hand appear in the person of the Emperor Vespasian or Heinrich Himmler. The judgments of immortal heaven descend from the scars of mortal passion, the furious energies of destruction released not by an immutable or universal law but on the volatile whims of lust, ambition and greed. The barbarians who come clattering through the gates mounted on Mongol horses or German tanks don't take the trouble to distinguish between the just and the unjust, and the cities ablaze in the gulf of time—among them Troy, Carthage, Jerusalem, London, San Francisco, Nanking, Berlin, Hiroshima and Phnom Penh—make a mockery of the supposition that God will reward the righteous and punish the wicked.

As long ago as 416 B.C., an Athenian army occupying the island of Melos introduced the theme of conquest elaborated through a long series of historical variation not only by the Roman emperors and the Medici popes but also by Napoleon, Adolf Hitler and Harry S. Truman. Having first made sure of their military victory, the Athenians presented the citizens of Melos with the choice of abandoning their loyalty to Sparta or accepting a sentence of death.

"As practical men," said the Athenians, "you know and we know that the question of justice arises only between parties equal in strength, and the strong do what they can, and the weak submit."

Thucydides reports the conversation in his *History of the Peloponnesian War,* and it can be read as a gloss on the modern foreign policies that assign the larger measures of justice to the heavier concentrations of cash. The law of nations becomes the rule of money, and the trans-national corporations intimidate the world's parliaments with the force of capital in much the same way that the Greek city states in the 5th Century B.C. bullied one another with the force of arms.

Although the 20th century has been ranked as the most violent known to the history of mankind—an opinion supported by the evidence of two world wars, the chimneys of Auschwitz and the nuclear fires of Hiroshima and Nagasaki—the ferocity of man's heart has never lacked for a means of murderous expression. The Roman legions didn't encumber themselves with the nuisance of taking prisoners, preferring instead to slaughter or sell into slavery the entire population of a conquered city. At Jerusalem in 70 A.D. they eviscerated the women and children suspected of having swallowed gold coins, and the Roman general, Titus, set aside 2500 captives to be burned alive or fed to wild animals at the festival games celebrating his brother's birthday. During the first half of the 13th century, Pope Innocent III gave his blessing to the Albigensian Crusade, a program of systematic terror sustained for nearly fifty years against the townspeople of the Languedoc. The Pope denounced them as heretics for their questioning of the primacy of Rome, and to the command of the Papal armies he assigned Arnaud Amalric, the ruling abbot of the Cistercians. When the abbot's troops burned the city of Beziers in 1231 and made prisoners of its 15,000 inhabitants, they asked their commander how they were to distinguish between those still faithful to Holy Church and those who had strayed into the paths of perdition. Improvising the theory that in the 20th century became known as the doctrine of Mutual Assured Destruction, Amalric replied, "Kill them all! God will recognize his own."

On the last day of what was once a world, the rain of hailstones or artillery fire falls on the hastily reawakened professions of faith in the Virgin Mary or the Great Spirit of the Lakota Sioux, and again it is the ancient Greeks who first draw a clear distinction between the forces at the disposal of the temporal and spiritual power. The Athenian envoys on Melos offered their ultimatum with the advice that the inhabitants "avoid the mistake that most men make, who might save themselves by human means, and then, when visible hopes desert them, in their extremity turn to the invisible."

But in their extremity most men do make the mistake (if only because they have little choice in the matter), and the records speak not only to the ruin of cities but also to the fantastic dreams of improbable rescue. The Romans besieged by Alaric's Visigoths in the summer of 410 revived their worship of Minerva and Capitoline Jove, obsolete pagan gods whom they had ignored for 200 years. On the night before the Turks sacked Constantinople in 1453, the Byzantine emperor, Constantine Palaeologus, accompanied by priests and a choir of the faithful, made a solemn embassy to the altar of Hagia Sophia and there assigned the defense of his kingdom to the bones of a saint. When the Turks broke through the doors of the church the next morning, they found 10,000 people praying in a sanctuary sweet with the smell of incense and fear.

Most of the writers present at the end of a world make the expected observations about the speed of events (a single afternoon in Paris in September 1870; "thirty seconds' twitching of the earth's crust" at Lisbon in November 1775; one tenth of a millionth of a second at Hiroshima in August 1945) and about the extravagant prices paid for the means of escape (ships at Constantinople, horses at Richmond). Their more surprising remarks bear out the lesson in suffering that Auden saw in Brueghel's painting of Icarus falling into an imaginary sea. Even in the midst of vast destruction and the forsaken cries of an immense multitude, the sun shines and somewhere else on the horizon the human spirit sails calmly on. Rome suffered its most brutal scourging not at the hands of 5th-century Goths but in the year 1527, when both Titian and Michelangelo were painting the brilliant portrait of the high Renaissance. In San Francisco in 1906 Jack London notices "no hysteria, no disorder" among the people engulfed by "the advancing flames"; John Reed in St. Petersburg in 1917 sees the crowds that engulf the Winter Palace flowing through the streets "like a black river," and yet, "on that night not a single holdup occurred, not a single robbery,"; in a foul-smelling trench in World War I, knowing himself present in "the gloom and disaster of the thing called Armageddon," Siegfried Sassoon discovers that a man can yet "stand up and defy gross darkness"; Count Harry Kessler wanders through the streets of Berlin in January 1919, observing that despite the incessant machine gun fire, the sidewalk vendors were selling "malt goodies and soap" and that in the brightly-lit café Vaterland, "the band was playing, the tables were full, and the lady in the cigarette booth smiled as winsomely at her customers as in the sunniest days of peace."

Although the book in hand duly takes note of man's proverbial inhumanity to man, it also speaks to the human capacity for regeneration and so balances the weight of the contemporary superstitions bidding up the market in freaks and wonders. Nearly three years remain on the game clock of the 20th century, but the bearers of bad news already have swarmed onto the field waving the banners of destruction and blowing the triumphs of doom. Amidst the clatter of foreseeable headlines we can expect them to continue to predict catastrophes matched to the fears of the audiences they have been paid to alarm—politicians talking about the trade and moral deficits, economists worrying about the depleted reserves of oil and deutsche marks, movie producers depicting the future as an increasingly barren heath largely inhabited by robots—and in the fog of so many evil omens the reader may find in the consolations of history a remedy against the counsels of despair.

Many of the passages in the book have been abbreviated without use of ellipsis, but the words in all instances remain faithful to the original texts, and none of the meanings have been changed. The notion of a collection of scenes from the end of the world I borrowed from the late Otto Friedrich, who published his own book on the subject in 1986, teaching me that the premonitions of disaster can be dispelled by the telling of a true story—not because the words can re-elect Abraham Lincoln or rebuild the walls of Troy but because they increase the common stores of energy and hope.

L.H.L.

PART I

THE RUINS OF EMPIRES

Shurrupak, 3000 B.C.

To the best of our knowledge, the first documented destruction of the world took place in Mesopotamia at the beginning of the third millennium B.C. The following passage from the Epic of Gilgamesh *(retold much later as the Noah story in the book of* Genesis*) purports to be the eyewitness account of Utnapishtim the Faraway, the only survivor of the deluge, as told to Gilgamesh, a Mesopotamian king. Archaeological evidence discovered in this century confirms the occurrence of a great flood that obliterated many of the richest cities in the Mesopotamian plain.*

Utnapishtim said to him, "Why do you come here, wandering over the wilderness in search of the wind?"

Gilgamesh said to him, "Despair is in my heart and my face is the face of one who has made a long journey. Why should I not wander over the pastures? My friend, my younger brother who seized and killed the Bull of Heaven and overthrew Humbaba in the cedar forest, my friend who was very dear to me and endured dangers beside me, Enkidu, my brother whom I loved, the end of mortality has overtaken him. I wept for him seven days and nights till the worm fastened on him. Because of my brother I am afraid of death; because of my brother I stray through the wilderness. His fate lies heavy upon me. How can I be silent, how can I rest? He is dust and I shall die also and be laid in the earth for ever. Oh, father Utnapishtim, you who have entered the assembly of the gods, I wish to question you concerning the living and the dead, how shall I find the life for which I am searching?"

Utnapishtim said, "There is no permanence. Do we build a house to stand for ever, do we seal a contract to hold for all time? Do brothers divide an inheritance to keep for ever, does the flood-time of rivers endure? It is only the nymph of the dragon-fly who sheds her larva and sees the sun in his glory. From the days of old there is no permanence. The sleeping and the dead, how alike they are, they are like a painted death. What is there between the master and the servant when both have fulfilled their doom? When the Anunnaki, the judges, come together, and Mammetun the mother of destinies, together they decree the fates of men. Life and death they allot but the day of death they do not disclose."

Then Gilgamesh said to Utnapishtim the Faraway, "Tell me truly, how was it that you came to enter the company of the gods and to possess everlasting life?" Utnapishtim said to Gilgamesh, "I will reveal to you a mystery, I will tell you a secret of the gods."

"You know the city Shurrupak, it stands on the banks of Euphrates? That city grew old and the gods that were in it were old. There was Anu, lord of the firmament, their father, and warrior Enlil their counsellor, Ninurta the helper, and Ennugi watcher over canals; and with them also was Ea. In those days the world teemed, the people multiplied, the world bellowed like a wild bull, and the great god was aroused by the clamour. Enlil heard the clamour and he said to the gods in council, 'The uproar of mankind is intolerable and sleep is no longer possible by reason of the babel.' So the gods agreed to exterminate mankind. Enlil did this, but Ea warned me in a dream. He whispered their words to my house of reeds, 'Reed-house, reed- house! Wall, O wall, hearken reed-house, wall reflect; O man of Shurrupak, son of Ubara-Tutu; tear down your house and build a boat, abandon possessions and look for life, despise worldly goods and save your soul alive. Tear down your house, I say, and build a boat. These are the measurements of the barque as you shall build her: let her beam equal her length, let her deck be roofed like the vault that covers the abyss; then take up into the boat the seed of all living creatures.'

[TABLET]

| CENTIMETERS | 1 | 2 | 3 | 4 | 5 | 6 | 7 | 8 | 9 | 10 |
| INCHES | | 1 | | 2 | | 3 | | 4 |

The flood tale from the Epic of Gilgamesh, *the oldest recorded destruction of the world, was translated from this Akkadian-language tablet, found in 1853 at Nineveh, in Mesopotamia, in the library of the Assyrian king Ashurbanipal (reigned 668 B.C.-627 B.C.).*

"When I had understood I said to my lord, 'Behold, what you have commanded I will honour and perform, but how shall I answer the people, the city, the elders?' Then Ea opened his mouth and said to me, his servant, 'Tell them this: I have learnt that Enlil is wrathful against me, I dare no longer walk in his land nor live in his city; I will go down to the Gulf to dwell with Ea my lord. But on you he will rain down abundance, rare fish and shy wild-fowl, a rich harvest-tide. In the evening the rider of the storm will bring you wheat in torrents.'

"In the first light of dawn all my household gathered round me, the children brought pitch and the men whatever was necessary. On the fifth day I laid the keel and the ribs, then I made fast the planking. The ground-space was one acre, each side of the deck measured one hundred and twenty cubits, making a square. I built six decks below, seven in all, I divided them into nine sections with bulkheads between. I drove in wedges where needed, I saw to the punt-poles, and laid in supplies. The carriers brought oil in baskets, I poured pitch into the furnace and asphalt and oil; more oil was consumed in caulking, and more again the master of the boat took into his stores. I slaughtered bullocks for the people and every day I killed sheep. I gave the shipwrights wine to drink as though it were river water, raw wine and red wine and oil and white wine. There was feasting then as there is at the time of the New Year's festival; I myself anointed my head. On the seventh day the boat was complete.

"Then was the launching full of difficulty; there was shifting of ballast above and below till two thirds was submerged. I loaded into her all that I had of gold and of living things, my family, my kin, the beast of the field both wild and tame, and all the craftsmen. I sent them on board, for the time that Shamash had ordained was already fulfilled when he said, 'In the evening, when the rider of the storm sends down the destroying rain, enter the boat and batten her down.' The time was fulfilled, the evening came, the rider of the storm sent down the rain. I looked out at the weather and it was terrible, so I too boarded the boat and battened her down. All was now complete, the battening and the caulking; so I handed the tiller to Puzur-Amurri the steersman, with the navigation and the care of the whole boat.

"With the first light of dawn a black cloud came from the horizon; it thundered within where Adad, lord of the storm was riding. Then the gods of the abyss rose up; Nergal pulled out the dams of the nether waters, Ninurta the war-lord threw down the dykes, and the seven judges of hell, the Anunnaki, raised their torches, lighting the land with their livid flame. A stupor of despair went up to heaven when the god of the storm turned daylight to darkness, when he smashed the land like a cup. One whole day the tempest raged, gathering fury as it went, it poured over the people like the tides of battle; a man could not see his brother nor the people be seen from heaven. Even the gods were terrified at the flood, they fled to the highest heaven, the firmament of Anu; they crouched against the walls, cowering like curs. Then Ishtar the sweet-voiced Queen of Heaven cried out like a woman in travail: 'Alas the days of old are turned to dust because I commanded evil; why did I command this evil in the council of all the gods? I commanded wars to destroy the people, but are they not my people, for I brought them forth? Now like the spawn of fish they float in the ocean.' The great gods of heaven and of hell wept, they covered their mouths.

"For six days and six nights the winds blew, torrent and tempest and flood overwhelmed the world, tempest and flood raged together like warring hosts. When the seventh day dawned the storm from the south subsided, the sea grew calm, the flood was stilled; I looked at the face of the world and there was silence, all mankind was turned to clay. The surface of the sea stretched as flat as a roof-top; I opened a hatch and the light fell on my face. Then I bowed low, I sat down and I wept, the tears streamed down my face, for on every side was the waste of water. I looked for land in vain, but fourteen leagues distant there appeared a mountain, and there the boat grounded; on the mountain of Nisir the boat held fast, she held fast and did not budge. One day she held, and a second day on the mountain of Nisir she held fast and did not budge. A third day, and a fourth day she held fast on the mountain and did not budge; a fifth day and a sixth day she held fast on the mountain. When the seventh day dawned I loosed a dove and let her go. She flew away, but finding no resting-place she returned. Then I loosed a swallow, and she flew away but finding no resting-place she returned. I loosed a raven, she saw that the waters had retreated, she ate, she flew around, she cawed, and she did not come back. Then I threw everything open to the four winds, I made a sacrifice and poured out a libation on the mountain top. Seven and again seven cauldrons I set up on their stands, I heaped up wood and cane and cedar and myrtle. When the gods smelled the sweet savour, they gathered like flies over the sacrifice. Then, at last, Ishtar also came, she lifted her necklace with the jewels of heaven that once Anu had made to please her. 'O you gods here present, by the lapis lazuli round my neck I shall remember these days as I remember the jewels of my throat; these last days I shall not forget. Let all the gods gather round the sacrifice, except Enlil. He shall not approach this offering, for without reflection he brought the flood; he consigned my people to destruction.'

"When Enlil had come, when he saw the boat, he was wroth and swelled with anger at the gods, the host of heaven, 'Has any of these mortals escaped? Not one was to have survived the destruction.' Then the god of the wells and canals Ninurta opened his mouth and said to the warrior Enlil, 'Who is there of the gods that can devise without Ea? It is Ea alone who knows all things.' Then Ea opened his mouth and spoke to warrior Enlil, 'Wisest of gods, hero Enlil, how could you so senselessly bring down the flood?

> Lay upon the sinner his sin,
> Lay upon the transgressor his transgression,
> Punish him a little when he breaks loose,
> Do not drive him too hard or he perishes;
> Would that a lion had ravaged mankind
> Rather than the flood,
> Would that a wolf had ravaged mankind
> Rather than the flood,
> Would that famine had wasted the world
> Rather than the flood,
> Would that pestilence had wasted mankind
> Rather than the flood.

It was not I that revealed the secret of the gods; the wise man learned it in a dream. Now take your counsel what shall be done with him.'

"Then Enlil went up into the boat, he took me by the hand and my wife and made us enter the boat and kneel down on either side, he standing between us. He touched our foreheads to bless us saying, 'In time past Utnapishtim was a mortal man; henceforth he and his wife shall live in the distance at the mouth of the rivers.' Thus it was that the gods took me and placed me here to live in the distance, at the mouth of the rivers."

SODOM, 2000 B.C.

The towns of Sodom and Gomorrah most likely were situated on the southern coast of the Dead Sea, near the present-day border between Israel and Jordan. The book of Genesis, which was put into its present form around 950 B.C., makes of the ruin of Sodom a proof of God's judgment upon the unrepentant wickedness of mankind. Presumably destroyed by an earthquake c. 2000 B.C., Sodom and Gomorrah were never rebuilt, nor have their ruins ever been found.

And there came two angels to Sodom at even; and Lot sat in the gate of Sodom: and Lot seeing them rose up to meet them; and he bowed himself with his face toward the ground; and he said, Behold now, my lords, turn in, I pray you, into your servant's house, and tarry all night, and wash your feet, and ye shall rise up early, and go on your ways. And they said, Nay; but we will abide in the street all night. And he pressed upon them greatly; and they turned in unto him, and entered into his house; and he made them a feast, and did bake unleavened bread, and they did eat.

But before they lay down, the men of the city, even the men of Sodom, compassed the house round, both old and young, all the people from every quarter: And they called unto Lot, and said unto him, Where are the men which came in to thee this night? bring them out unto us, that we may know them. And Lot went out at the door unto them, and shut the door after him, And said, I pray you, brethren, do not so wickedly. Behold now, I have two daughters which have not known man; let me, I pray you, bring them out unto you, and do ye to them as is good in your eyes: only unto these men do nothing; for therefore came they under the shadow of my roof.

And they said, Stand back. And they said again, This one fellow came in to sojourn, and he will needs be a judge: now will we deal worse with thee, than with them. And they pressed sore upon the man, even Lot, and came near to break the door. But the men put forth their hand, and pulled Lot into the house to them, and shut to the door. And they smote the men that were at the door of the house with blindness, both small and great: so that they wearied themselves to find the door.

And the men said unto Lot, Hast thou here any besides? son in law, and thy sons, and thy daughters, and whatsoever thou hast in the city, bring them out of this place: For we will destroy this place, because the cry of them is waxen great before the face of the LORD; and the LORD hath sent us to destroy it.

And Lot went out, and spake unto his sons in law, which married his daughters, and said, Up, get you out of this place; for the LORD will destroy this city. But he seemed as one that mocked unto his sons in law.

And when the morning arose, then the angels hastened Lot, saying, Arise, take thy wife, and thy two daughters, which are here; lest thou be consumed in the iniquity of the city.

And while he lingered, the men laid hold upon his hand, and upon the hand of his wife, and upon the hand of his two daughters; the LORD being merciful unto him: and they brought him forth, and set him without the city.

And it came to pass, when they had brought them forth abroad, that he said, Escape for thy life; look not behind thee, neither stay thou in all the plain; escape to the mountain, lest thou be consumed.

And Lot said unto them, Oh, not so, my LORD: Behold now, thy servant hath found grace in thy sight, and thou hast magnified thy mercy, which thou hast shewed unto me in saving my life; and I cannot escape to the mountain, lest some evil take me, and I die: Behold now, this city is near to flee unto, and it is a little one: Oh, let me escape thither, (is it not a little one?) and my soul shall live.

And he said unto him, See, I have accepted thee concerning this thing also, that I will not overthrow this city, for the which thou hast spoken. Haste thee, escape thither; for I cannot do anything till thou be come thither. Therefore the name of the city was called Zoar.

The sun was risen upon the earth when Lot entered into Zoar.

Then the LORD rained upon Sodom and upon Gomorrah brimstone and fire from the LORD out of heaven; And he overthrew those cities, and all the plain, and all the inhabitants of the cities, and that which grew upon the ground.

But his wife looked back from behind him, and she became a pillar of salt.

And Abraham gat up early in the morning to the place where he stood before the LORD: And he looked toward Sodom and Gomorrah, and toward all the land of the plain, and beheld, and, lo, the smoke of the country went up as the smoke of a furnace.

And it came to pass, when God destroyed the cities of the plain, that God remembered Abraham, and sent Lot out of the midst of the overthrow, when he overthrew the cities in the which Lot dwelt.

ATLANTIS, 1500 B.C.

The tale of the destruction of the mythical city of Atlantis, for which Plato (c. 428 B.C.-348/47 B.C.) is our only ancient source, possibly derives from reports of a massive volcanic eruption that took place on the island of Thera in the Aegean Sea around 1500 B.C. Greek settlements within a radius of 70 miles were shattered by a series of earthquakes and tidal waves.

Solon said that when he was questioning such of their priests [in Egypt] as were most versed in ancient lore about their early history, he discovered that neither he himself nor any other Greek knew anything at all, one might say, about such matters.

And on one occasion, when he wished to draw them on to discourse on ancient history, he attempted to tell them the most ancient of our traditions, concerning Phoroneus, who was said to be the first man, and Niobe; and he went on to tell the legend about Deucalion and Pyrrha after the Flood, and how they survived it, and to give the genealogy of their descendants; and by recounting the number of years occupied by the events mentioned he tried to calculate the periods of time. Whereupon one of the priests, a prodigiously old man, said, "O Solon, Solon, you Greeks are always children: there is not such a thing as an old

Greek." And on hearing this he asked, "What mean you by this saying?" And the priest replied, "You are young in soul, every one of you. For therein you possess not a single belief that is ancient and derived from old tradition, nor yet one science that is hoary with age. And this is the cause thereof: There have been and there will be many and divers destructions of mankind, of which the greatest are by fire and water, and lesser ones by countless other means.

"For in truth the story that is told in your country as well as ours, how once upon a time Phaethon, son of Helios, yoked his father's chariot, and, because he was unable to drive it along the course taken by his father, burnt up all that was upon the earth and himself perished by a thunderbolt,—that story, as it is told, has the fashion of a legend, but the truth of it lies in the occurrence of a shifting of the bodies in the heavens which move round the earth, and a destruction of the things on the earth by fierce fire, which recurs at long intervals. At such times all they that dwell on the mountains and in high and dry places suffer destruction more than those who dwell near to rivers or the sea; and in our case the Nile, our Saviour in other ways, saves us also at such times from this calamity by rising high. And when, on the other hand, the Gods purge the earth with a flood of waters, all the herdsmen and shepherds that are in the mountains are saved, but those in the cities of your land are swept into the sea by the streams; whereas in our country neither then nor at any other time does the water pour down over our fields from above, on the contrary it all tends naturally to well up from below.

"Hence it is, for these reasons, that what is here preserved is reckoned to be most ancient; the truth being that in every place where there is no excessive heat or cold to prevent it there always exists some human stock, now more, now less in number. And if any event has occurred that is noble or great or in any way conspicuous, whether it be in your country or in ours or in some other place of which we know by report, all such events are recorded from of old and preserved here in our temples; whereas your people and the others are but newly equipped, every time, with letters and all such arts as civilized States require; and when, after the usual interval of years, like a plague, the flood from heaven comes sweeping down afresh upon your people, it leaves none of you but the unlettered and uncultured, so that you become young as ever, with no knowledge of all that happened in old times in this land or in your own.

"Certainly the genealogies which you related just now, Solon, concerning the people of your country, are little better than children's tales; for, in the first place, you remember but one deluge, though many had occurred previously; and next, you are ignorant of the fact that the noblest and most perfect race amongst men were born in the land where you now dwell, and from them both you yourself are sprung and the whole of your existing city, out of some little seed that chanced to be left over; but this has escaped your notice because for many generations the survivors died with no power to express themselves in writing. For verily at one time, Solon, before the greatest destruction by water, what is now the Athenian State was the bravest in war and supremely well organized also in all other respects. It is said that it possessed the most splendid works of art and the noblest polity of any nation under heaven of which we have heard tell." Upon hearing this, Solon said that he marvelled, and with the utmost eagerness requested the priest to recount for him in order and exactly all the facts about those citizens of old.

The priest then said: "I begrudge you not the story, Solon; nay, I will tell it, both for your own sake and that of your city, and most of all for the sake of the Goddess who has adopted for her own both your land and this of ours, and has nurtured and trained them,—yours first by the space of a thousand years, when she had received the seed of you from Gê and Hephaestus, and after that ours. And the duration of our civilization as set down in our sacred writings is 8000 years. Of the citizens, then, who lived 9000 years ago, I will declare to you briefly certain of their laws and the noblest of the deeds they performed.

"Many, in truth, and great are the achievements of your State, which are a marvel to men as they are here recorded; but there is one which stands out above all both for magnitude and for nobleness. For it is related in our records how once upon a time your State stayed the course of a mighty host, which, starting from a distant point in the Atlantic ocean, was insolently advancing to attack the whole of Europe, and Asia to boot. For the ocean there was at that time navigable; for in front of the mouth which you Greeks call, as you say, 'the pillars of Heracles,' [Gibraltar] there lay an island which was larger than Libya [Africa] and Asia together; and it was possible for the travellers of that time to cross from it to the other islands, and from the islands to the whole of the continent over against them which encompasses that veritable ocean. For all that we have here, lying within the mouth of which we speak, is evidently a haven having a narrow entrance; but that yonder is a real ocean, and the land surrounding it may most rightly be called, in the fullest and truest sense, a continent. Now in this island of Atlantis there existed a confederation of kings, of great and marvellous power, which held sway over all the island, and over many other islands also and parts of the continent; and, moreover, of the lands here within the Straits they ruled over Libya as far as Egypt, and over Europe as far as Tuscany. So this host, being all gathered together, made an attempt one time to enslave by one single onslaught both your country and ours and the whole of the territory within the Straits. And then it was, Solon, that the manhood of your State showed itself conspicuous for valor and might in the sight of all the world. For it stood pre-eminent above all in gallantry and all warlike arts, and acting partly as leader of the Greeks, and partly standing alone by itself when deserted by all others, after encountering the deadliest perils, it defeated the invaders and reared a trophy; whereby it saved from slavery such as were not as yet enslaved, and all the rest of us who dwell within the bounds of Heracles it ungrudgingly set free. But at a later time there occurred portentous earthquakes and floods, and one grievous day and night befell them, when the whole body of your warriors was swallowed up by the earth, and the island of Atlantis in like manner was swallowed up by the sea and vanished; wherefore also the ocean at that spot has now become impassable and unsearchable, being blocked up by the shoal mud which the island created as it settled down."

TROY, 1250 B.C.

A confederation of Greek cities in the 13th century B.C. sent their armies across the Aegean Sea to make war on the city of Troy. After ten years of hard fighting, the Greeks breached Troy's walls and killed or enslaved

combatants and non-combatants alike. Twelve centuries after the fact,
Virgil (70 B.C.-19 B.C.) imagines the hero of his epic, the Aeneid, *telling*
the story of the city's destruction, and that of Priam and Hecuba, the
Trojan king and queen.

Perhaps you now will ask the end of Priam.
When he has seen his beaten city ruined—
the wrenching of the gates, the enemy
among his sanctuaries—then in vain
the old man throws his armor, long unused,
across his shoulders, tottering with age;
and he girds on his useless sword; about
to die, he hurries toward the crowd of Greeks.

Beneath the naked round of heaven, at
the center of the palace, stood a giant
shrine; at its side an ancient laurel leaned
across the altar stone, and it embraced
the household gods within its shadow. Here,
around that useless altar, Hecuba
together with her daughters—just like doves
when driven headlong by a dark storm—huddled;
and they held fast the statues of the gods.
But when she saw her Priam putting on
the armor he had worn when he was young,
she cried: "Poor husband, what wild thought drives you
to wear these weapons now? Where would you rush?
This is no time for such defense and help,
not even were my Hector here himself.
Come near and pray: this altar shall yet save
us all, or you shall die together with us."
When this was said she took the old man to her
and drew him down upon the sacred seat.

But then Polites, one of Priam's sons
who had escaped from Pyrrhus' slaughter, down
long porticoes, past enemies and arrows,
races, wounded, across the empty courts.
But after him, and hot to thrust, is Pyrrhus;
now, even now he clutches, closing in;
he presses with his shaft until at last
Polites falls before his parents' eyes,
within their presence; he pours out his life
in streams of blood. Though in the fist of death,
at this, Priam does not spare voice or wrath:
"If there is any goodness in the heavens
to oversee such acts, for this offense
and outrage may you find your fitting thanks
and proper payment from the gods, for you
have made me see the murder of my son,
defiled a father's face with death. Achilles —
you lie to call him father—never dealt
with Priam so—and I, his enemy;
for he had shame before the claims and trust
that are a suppliant's. He handed back
for burial the bloodless corpse of Hector
and sent me off in safety to my kingdom."
The old man spoke; his feeble spear flew off —
harmless; the hoarse bronze beat it back at once;
it dangled, useless now, from the shield's boss.
And Pyrrhus: "Carry off these tidings; go
and bring this message to my father, son
of Peleus; and remember, let him know
my sorry doings, how degenerate
is Neoptolemus. Now die." This said,
he dragged him to the very altar stone,

with Priam shuddering and slipping in
the blood that streamed from his own son. And Pyrrhus
with his left hand clutched tight the hair of Priam;
his right hand drew his glistening blade, and then
he buried it hilt-high in the king's side.
This was the end of Priam's destinies,
the close that fell to him by fate: to see
his Troy in flames and Pergamus laid low—
who once was proud king over many nations
and lands of Asia. Now he lies along
the shore, a giant trunk, his head torn from
his shoulders, as a corpse without a name.

JERUSALEM (I), 587 B.C.

*In 587 B.C., after an 18-month siege, the Babylonians under
Nebuchadnezzar marched into Jerusalem, ravaged the city, and reduced
the temple to rubble. Sometime during the tumultuous decades that followed, an unknown poet inserted the following account, known as the
"Isaiah Apocalypse," into the book of the prophet Isaiah.*

Behold, the LORD maketh the earth empty, and maketh it waste,
and turneth it upside down, and scattereth abroad the inhabitants
   thereof.
And it shall be, as with the people, so with the priest;
as with the servant, so with his master;
as with the maid, so with her mistress;
as with the buyer, so with the seller;
as with the lender, so with the borrower;

as with the taker of usury, so with the giver of usury to him.
The land shall be utterly emptied, and utterly spoiled:
for the LORD hath spoken this word.
The earth mourneth and fadeth away,
the world languisheth and fadeth away,
the haughty people of the earth do languish.
The earth also is defiled under the inhabitants thereof;
because they have transgressed the laws,
changed the ordinance,
broken the everlasting covenant.
Therefore hath the curse devoured the earth,
and they that dwell therein are desolate:
therefore the inhabitants of the earth are burned,
and few men left.
The new wine mourneth,
the vine languisheth,
all the merryhearted do sigh.
The mirth of tabrets ceaseth,
the noise of them that rejoice endeth,
the joy of the harp ceaseth.
They shall not drink wine with a song;
strong drink shall be bitter to them that drink it.
The city of confusion is broken down:
every house is shut up, that no man may come in.
There is a crying for wine in the streets;
all joy is darkened,
the mirth of the land is gone.
In the city is left desolation,
and the gate is smitten with destruction.
When thus it shall be in the midst of the land
among the people,
there shall be as the shaking of an olive tree,
and as the gleaning grapes when the vintage is done.

The treacherous dealers have dealt treacherously;
yea, the treacherous dealers have dealt very treacherously.
Fear, and the pit, and the snare,
are upon thee, O inhabitant of the earth.
And it shall come to pass, that he who fleeth from the noise of the fear
    shall fall into the pit;
and he that cometh up out of the midst of the pit
shall be taken in the snare:
for the windows from on high are open,
and the foundations of the earth do shake.
The earth is utterly broken down,
the earth is clean dissolved,
the earth is moved exceedingly.
The earth shall reel to and fro like a drunkard,
and shall be removed like a cottage;
and the transgression thereof shall be heavy upon it;
and it shall fall, and not rise again.
And it shall come to pass in that day,
that the LORD shall punish
the host of the high ones that are on high,
and the kings of the earth upon the earth.
And they shall be gathered together,
as prisoners are gathered in the pit,
and shall be shut up in the prison,
and after many days shall they be visited.
Then the moon shall be confounded,
and the sun ashamed,
when the LORD of hosts shall reign
in mount Zion, and in Jerusalem,
and before his ancients gloriously.

MELOS, 416 B.C.

In the summer of 416 B.C., an Athenian army occupied Melos, a small island with leanings toward Sparta, the principal rival of Athens in the wars that divided the Greek city states in the 5th century B.C. The Athenian envoys then dictated the terms of submission. Thucydides (died c. 400 B.C.) here records the last exchange of views before every Melian man was executed, and the women and children sold for slaves.

ATHENIANS

If you have met us in order to make surmises about the future, or for any other purpose than to look existing facts in the face and to discuss the safety of your city on this basis, we will break off the conversations; otherwise, we are ready to speak.

MELIANS

In our position it is natural and excusable to explore many ideas and arguments. But the problem that has brought us here is our security, so, if you think fit, let the discussion follow the line you propose.

ATHENIANS

Then we will not make a long and unconvincing speech, full of fine phrases, to prove that our victory over Persia justifies our empire, or that we are now attacking you because you have wronged us. Let each of us say what we really think and reach a practical agreement. You know and we know, as practical men, that the question of justice arises only between parties equal in strength, and that the strong do what they can, and the weak submit.

MELIANS

As you ignore justice and have made self-interest the basis of discussion, we must take the same ground, and we say that in our opinion it is in your interest to maintain a principle which is for the good of all—that anyone in danger should have just and equitable treatment and any advantage, even if not strictly his due, which he can secure by persuasion. This is your interest as much as ours, for your fall would involve you in a crushing punishment that would be a lesson to the world.

ATHENIANS

Leave that danger to us to face. At the moment we shall prove that we have come in the interest of our empire and that in what we shall say we are seeking the safety of your state; for we wish you to become our subjects with least trouble to ourselves, and we would like you to survive in our interests as well as your own.

MELIANS

It may be your interest to be our masters: how can it be ours to be your slaves?

ATHENIANS

By submitting you would avoid a terrible fate, and we should gain by not destroying you.

MELIANS

Would you not agree to an arrangement under which we should keep out of the war, and be your friends instead of your enemies, but neutral?

ATHENIANS

No: your hostility injures us less than your friendship. That, to our subjects, is an illustration of our weakness, while your hatred exhibits our power.

MELIANS

But do you see no safety in our neutrality? Will you not make enemies of all neutral Powers when they see your conduct and reflect that some day you will attack them? Will not your action strengthen your existing opponents, and induce those who would otherwise never be your enemies to become so against their will?

ATHENIANS

No. The mainland states, secure in their freedom, will be slow to take defensive measures against us, and we do not consider them so formidable as independent island powers like yourselves, or subjects already smarting under our yoke. These are most likely to take a thoughtless step and bring themselves and us into obvious danger.

MELIANS

Surely then, if you are ready to risk so much to maintain your empire, and the enslaved peoples so much to escape from it, it would be criminal cowardice in us, who are still free, not to take any and every measure before submitting to slavery?

ATHENIANS

No, if you reflect calmly: for this is not a competition in heroism between equals, where your honour is at stake, but a question of self-preservation, to save you from a struggle with a far stronger Power.

MELIANS

Still, we know that in war fortune is more impartial than the disproportion in numbers might lead one to expect. If we submit at once, our position is desperate; if we fight, there is still a hope that we shall stand secure.

ATHENIANS

Hope encourages men to take risks; men in a strong position may follow her without ruin, if not without loss. But when they stake all that they have to the last coin (for she is a spendthrift), she reveals her real self in the hour of failure, and when her nature is known she leaves them without means of self-protection. You are weak, your future hangs on a turn of the scales; avoid the mistake most men make, who might save themselves by human means, and then, when visible hopes desert them, in their extremity turn to the invisible—prophecies and oracles and all those things which delude men with hopes, to their destruction.

MELIANS

Still we trust that Heaven will not allow us to be worsted by Fortune, for in this quarrel we are right and you are wrong. Besides, we expect the support of Lacedaemon [Sparta] to supply the deficiencies in our strength, for she is bound to help us as her kinsmen, if for no other reason, and from a sense of honour. So our confidence is not entirely unreasonable.

ATHENIANS

You said that you proposed to discuss the safety of your city, but we observe that in all your speeches you have never said a word on which any reasonable expectation of it could be founded. Your strength lies in deferred hopes; in comparison with the forces now arrayed against you, your resources are too small for any hope of success. You will show a great want of judgment if you do not come to a more reasonable decision after we have withdrawn. Surely you will not fall back on the idea of honour, which has been the ruin of so many when danger and disgrace were staring them in the face. How often, when men have seen the fate to which they were tending, have they been enslaved by a phrase and drawn by the power of this seductive word to fall of their own free will into irreparable disaster, bringing on themselves by their folly a greater dishonour than fortune could inflict! If you are wise, you will avoid that fate. The greatest of cities makes you a fair offer, to keep your own land and become her tributary ally: there is no dishonour in that. The choice between war and safety is given you; do not obstinately take the worse alternative. The most successful people are those who stand up to their equals, behave properly to their superiors, and treat their inferiors fairly. Think it over when we withdraw, and reflect once and again that you have only one country, and that its prosperity or ruin depends on one decision.

The Athenians now withdrew from the conference; and the Melians, left to themselves, came to a decision corresponding with what they had maintained in the discussion, and answered, "Our resolution, Athenians, is unaltered. We will not in a moment deprive of freedom a city that has existed for seven hundred years; we put our trust in the fortune by which the gods have preserved it until now, and in the help of men, that is, of the Lacedaemonians; and so we will try and save ourselves. Meanwhile we invite you to allow us to be friends to you and foes to neither party, and to retire from our country after making such a treaty as shall seem fit to us both."

Such was the answer of the Melians. The Athenians broke up the conference saying, "To judge from your decision, you are unique in regarding the future as more certain than the present and in allowing your wishes to convert the unseen into reality; and as you have staked most on, and trusted most in, the Lacedaemonians, your fortune, and your hopes, so will you be most completely deceived."

[PREMONITION]

CARTHAGE, 146 B.C.

Phoenician sailors from present-day Lebanon founded Carthage on the North African coast in the 9th century B.C. The city achieved wealth and influence in the western Mediterranean and the Romans soon formed the opinion that for Rome to rise, Carthage must fall. The two states fought three wars over a period of 125 years. In the third and final war, the Romans sent an army instructed to accept the city's surrender, depopulate it, and then raze it so that no stone would sit on top of any other. The account is that of Polybius (c. 200 B.C.-c. 118 B.C.), an historian in the employ of the Roman general, Scipio.

Scipio, beholding [Carthage], which had flourished 700 years from its foundation and had ruled over so many lands, islands, and seas, as rich in arms and fleets, elephants, and money as the mightiest empires, but far surpassing them in hardihood and high spirit (since, when stripped of all its ships and arms, it had sustained famine and a mighty war for three years), now come to its end in total destruction—Scipio, beholding this spectacle, is said to have shed tears and publicly lamented the fortune of the enemy. After meditating by himself a long time and reflecting on the inevitable fall of cities, nations, and empires, as well as of individuals, upon the fate of Troy, that once proud city, upon the fate of the

Assyrian, the Median, and afterwards of the great Persian empire, and, most recently of all, of the splendid empire of Macedon [Alexander the Great's possessions], either voluntarily or otherwise the words of the poet escaped his lips:

> The Day shall come in which our sacred Troy
> And Priam, and the people over whom
> Spear-bearing Priam rules, shall perish all. [*Iliad* 6.448-9]

Being asked by Polybius in familiar conversation (for Polybius had been his tutor) what he meant by using these words, Polybius says that he did not hesitate frankly to name his own country, for whose fate he feared when he considered the mutability of human affairs. And Polybius wrote this down just as he heard it.

Atoms in the Void

We know very little of the Roman poet Lucretius except that sometime during the 1st century B.C., he wrote a long narrative poem, On the Nature of Things, *giving poetic voice to the ideas of the Greek philosopher Epicurus. Lucretius believed that the gods were unconcerned with human affairs, and concluded that the impermanent world is nothing more than a jumble of atoms tossed into a temporary form that will one day dissolve.*

And since the time when the world came into being, since the first birthday of sea and earth, and since the arising of the sun, many bodies have been added from without, many seeds have been added around, which the great All has brought together in its tossing; that from these sea and land might increase, and the habitation of the sky might amplify its expanse and uplift its dwellings high over the earth, and the air might rise up. For all bodies are distributed abroad by blows from all places each to its own thing and pass back to their own kinds:

liquid goes to liquid, earth grows by earthy elements, fires forge out fires and air air, until up to the extreme limit of growth, nature, the maker of all things, has brought them through with finishing touch; as happens when no more is now given into the arteries of life than what flows out and passes away. At this point the life of all things must come to a stand, at this point nature by her power curbs back growth. For whatever you see growing with merry increase, and gradually climbing the steps of mature life, assimilates to itself more bodies than it discharges, so long as food is easily absorbed into all the veins, and so long as the things are not so widely spread open as to let go many elements and to spend away more than their age feeds on. For certainly we must own ourselves convinced that many elements flow out and pass away from things; but still more must be passed in, until they have touched the pinnacle of growth. After that by minute degrees age breaks the strength and mature vigour, and melts into decay. And indeed when growth ceases, the larger a thing is and the wider it is, the more particles it now scatters abroad on all sides and lets go from itself, nor is food easily sent abroad into all its veins, nor is this enough, in proportion to the abundant streams that it streams out, to enable as much to spring up and to be brought up in its place. With good reason therefore the things pass away, when by the flowing off they have become thinned, and all fall by blows from without, inasmuch as by great age food fails at last, nor is there anything which bodies buffeting from without cease to break up and to subdue with fatal blows.

So therefore the walls of the mighty world in like manner shall be stormed all around, and shall collapse into crumbling ruin. For it is food that must repair all by renewing, food must support, food sustain everything, but in vain, since the veins cannot contain enough and nature does not supply as much as is necessary. Even now indeed the power of life is broken, and the earth exhausted scarce produces tiny creatures, she who once produced all kinds and gave birth to the huge bodies of wild beasts. For it is not true, as I think, that the races of mortal creatures were let down from high heaven by some golden chain upon the fields, nor were they sprung from sea or waves beating upon the rocks, but the same earth generated them which feeds them now from herself. Besides, she of her own accord first made for mortals the bright corn and the luxuriant vineyards, of herself she gave forth sweet fruits and luxuriant pasturage, which now scarce grow great when increased by our toil; and we exhaust our oxen and the strength of our farmers, we wear out the ploughshare, and then are scarce fed by our fields: so do they grudge their fruits and increase our toil. Now the ancient ploughman shaking his head sighs many a time that his great labour has all come to nothing, and comparing times present with times past often praises the fortunes of his father. Sadly also the cultivator of the degenerate and shrivelled vine rails at the progress of time and continually criticizes the age, and grumbles how the old world, full of piety, supported life with great ease on a narrow domain, though the man's portion of land was formerly much smaller than it is now; nor does he comprehend that all things gradually decay, and go to the reef of destruction, outworn by the ancient lapse of years.

ROME (I), 49 B.C.

When Julius Caesar in 49 B.C. led his army across the Rubicon River from Gaul into Italy, he set in motion the final sequence of events that destroyed the Roman republic and established, twenty-two years later under the rule of Caesar Augustus, the Roman Empire. The poet Lucan (39 A.D.-65 A.D.), who was devoted to the ideals of the republic and died for his part in the rebellion against the emperor Nero, imagines Caesar's crossing in his epic poem, The Civil War.

Now swiftly Caesar had surmounted the icy Alps and in his mind conceived immense upheavals, coming war. When he reached the water of the little Rubicon, clearly to the leader through the murky night appeared a mighty image of his country in distress, grief in her face, her white hair streaming from her tower-crowned head; with tresses torn and shoulders bare she stood before him and sighing said: "Where further do you march? Where do you take my standards, warriors? If lawfully you come, if as citizens, this far only is allowed." Then trembling struck the leader's limbs, his hair grew stiff, and weakness checked his progress, holding his feet at the river's edge. At last he speaks: "O Thunderer, surveying great Rome's walls from the Tarpeian Rock; O Phrygian house-gods of Iulus' clan and mysteries of Quirinus, who was carried off to heaven; O Jupiter of Latium, seated in lofty Alba, and hearths of Vesta; O Rome, the equal of the highest deity, favor my plans. Not with impious weapons do I pursue you—here am I, Caesar, conqueror by land and sea, your own soldier everywhere. The man who makes me your enemy, it is he will be the guilty one."

The ruddy Rubicon flows forth from a tiny spring and in summer's burning heat moves with meager waters; through the valley's depths it snakes and separates the Gallic fields from the farmers of Ausonia, a fixed boundary. But at that time winter was strengthening it, its waters had been swollen by rainy Cynthia with laden crescent for three nights running and by the Alpine snows melted in the moist blasts of Eurus. First the cavalry is drawn up aslant the stream to take the waters' force, then the remaining throng passes through the unresisting waters of the river broken now—an easy ford. When Caesar had crossed the flood and reached the opposite bank, on Hesperia's forbidden fields he took his stand and said: "Here I abandon peace and desecrated law; Fortune, it is you I follow. Farewell to treaties from now on; I have relied on them for long enough; now war must be our referee."

Caesar's massive forces with their gathered might made him confident to venture higher: he extends through all of Italy; he occupies the nearest towns. And empty rumour, speedy messenger of quickening war, augmented genuine fears; it invaded people's minds with pictures of calamity to come and unlocked countless tongues to utter false assertions. They picture him not as they remember him: in their thoughts he seems greater, wilder, more pitiless from the conquest of the enemy. Then follow close behind, they say, the peoples from between the Rhine and Elbe, uprooted from ancestral home in northern lands; fierce foreign races are ordered to sack Rome—with a Roman looking on. So by his panic each gives strength to rumour, and they fear ungrounded evils of their own invention.

The multitude is not alone in panicking, struck by empty terror, but the Senate, too, yes even the Fathers leapt up from their seats, and as they flee assign to the consuls the dreaded declaration of war. Then, uncertain where to go for safety, where to run from danger, wherever impulse of flight sweeps them on, they drive the people rushing headlong. You might suppose that impious fire-brands had ignited houses, that homes were swaying, tottering, shaken by imminent collapse: so the throng rushed through the city heedlessly, as if the sole salvation for their battered fortunes were to leave the ancestral walls. Now none could be detained by his father weak with age, nor a husband by his wife's laments, nor by ancestral Gods for long enough to utter prayers for preservation so uncertain; none lingered on the threshold and then left, after looking his fill maybe for the last time on beloved Rome: the multitude raced on, unstoppable.

Then preventing any hope even for the future lifting up their frightened minds, came proof manifest of fate still worse to come, and menacing gods filled earth and sky and sea with prodigies. Dark nights witnessed unfamiliar stars, the sky ablaze with flames, meteors flying aslant through heaven's empty space, the tail of fear-inspiring star, the comet, herald of a shift in power on earth. Lightning flashed repeatedly in the deceptive cloudless sky, its fire presenting different shapes in the dense air, now, with lengthened light, a spear, now, with light spread out, a torch. Lesser stars which usually proceed on course through the empty hours of the night appeared at noon. Black Charybdis wrenched from the depths a blood-red sea and the savage dogs howled dolefully. They say the Native Gods shed tears, the hearth-gods by their sweat confirmed Rome's hardship, offerings tumbled in their temples, ill-omened birds darkened the day, and wild beasts boldly left their woods at night's approach and made their dens in the midst of Rome. Then tongues of animals took readily to human sounds, and people's offspring were unnatural in shape of limbs and number—the mother was terrified by her own baby. Then those inspired by fierce Bellona slash their arms and chant the gods' intent; the Galli whirl their bloodied locks and howl dread omens to the people. Urns full of bones laid to rest emitted groans. Trumpets of war resounded; black night gave a shout as loud as cohorts clashing, though the breeze was still. From the Campus the shade of Sulla was seen to rise and uttered dreadful oracles, and the farmers fled as Marius burst his tomb and raised his head by Anio's chill waters.

THE KINGDOM COME

According to the Gospel of Mark, written in the 60s A.D., Jesus of Nazareth stood on the porch of the Temple in Jerusalem and said the following to his disciples, shortly before his death about 30 A.D.

And as he went out of the temple, one of his disciples saith unto him, Master, see what manner of stones and what buildings are here!

And Jesus answering said unto him, Seest thou these great buildings? there shall not be left one stone upon another, that shall not be thrown down.

And as he sat upon the mount of Olives over against the temple, Peter and James and John and Andrew asked him privately, Tell us, when shall these things be? and what shall be the sign when all these things shall be fulfilled?

And Jesus answering them began to say, Take heed lest any man deceive you: For many shall come in my name, saying, I am Christ; and shall deceive many. And when ye shall hear of wars and rumours of wars, be ye not troubled: for such things must needs be; but the end shall not be yet. For nation shall rise against nation, and kingdom against kingdom: and there shall be earthquakes in divers places, and there shall be famines and troubles: these are the beginnings of sorrows.

But take heed to yourselves: for they shall deliver you up to councils; and in the synagogues ye shall be beaten: and ye shall be brought before rulers and kings for my sake, for a testimony against them. And the gospel must first be published among all nations. But when they shall lead you, and deliver you up, take no thought beforehand what ye shall speak, neither do ye premeditate: but whatsoever shall be given you in that hour, that speak ye: for it is not ye that speak, but the Holy Ghost. Now the brother shall betray the brother to death, and the father the son; and children shall rise up against their parents, and shall cause them to be put to death. And ye shall be hated of all men for my name's sake: but he that shall endure unto the end, the same shall be saved.

But when ye shall see the abomination of desolation, spoken of by Daniel the prophet, standing where it ought not, (let him that readeth understand), then let them that be in Judaea flee to the mountains: And let him that is on the housetop not go down into the house, neither enter therein, to take any thing out of his house: And let him that is in the field not turn back again for to take up his garment. But woe to them that are with child, and to them that give suck in those days!

And pray ye that your flight be not in the winter. For in those days shall be affliction, such as was not from the beginning of the creation which God created unto this time, neither shall be. And except that the Lord had shortened those days, no flesh should be saved: but for the elect's sake, whom he hath chosen, he hath shortened the days. And then if any man shall say to you, Lo, here is Christ; or, lo, he is there; believe him not: For false Christs and false prophets shall rise, and shall shew signs and wonders, to seduce, if it were possible, even the elect.

But take ye heed: behold, I have foretold you all things. But in those days, after that tribulation, the sun shall be darkened, and the moon shall not give her light, And the stars of heaven shall fall, and the powers that are in heaven shall be shaken. And then shall they see the Son of man coming in the clouds with great power and glory. And then shall he send his angels, and shall gather together his elect from the four winds, from the uttermost part of the earth to the uttermost part of heaven.

Now learn a parable of the fig tree; When her branch is yet tender, and putteth forth leaves, ye know that summer is near: So ye in like manner, when ye shall see these things come to pass, know that it is nigh, even at the doors. Verily I say unto you, that this generation shall not pass, till all these things be done. Heaven and earth shall pass away: but my words shall not pass away.

But of that day and that hour knoweth no man, no, not the angels which are in heaven, neither the Son, but the Father. Take ye heed, watch and pray: for ye know not when the time is. For the Son of man is as a man taking a far journey, who left his house, and gave authority to his servants, and to every man his work, and commanded the porter to watch. Watch ye therefore: for ye know not when the master of the house cometh, at even, or at midnight, or at the cock-crowing, or in the morning: Lest coming suddenly he find you sleeping. And what I say unto you I say unto all, Watch.

ROME (II), 64 A.D.

*Of all the Roman emperors, none was more reviled than Nero (37 A.D.-
68 A.D.). He fell so low in the opinion of his subjects that many accused
him, on doubtful evidence, of setting the most destructive fire Rome had
ever seen, in order to clear the way for his own architectural fancies. The
flames raged for a week and destroyed or severely damaged ten of Rome's
14 regions. The following account, published well after Nero's death, is
taken from the writings of Suetonius (c. 70 A.D.-c. 140 A.D.).*

Nero showed neither discrimination nor moderation in putting to death whom-
soever he pleased on any pretext whatever. To mention but a few instances,
Salvidienus Orfitus was charged with having let to certain states as headquarters
three shops which formed part of his house near the Forum; Cassius Longinus, a
blind jurist, with retaining in the old family tree of his house the mask of Gaius
Cassius, the assassin of Julius Caesar; Paetus Thrasea with having a sullen mien,
like that of a preceptor. To those who were bidden to die he never granted more
than an hour's respite, and to avoid any delay, he brought physicians who were
at once to "attend to" such as lingered; for that was the term he used for killing
them by opening their veins. It is even believed that it was his wish to throw living men to be torn to pieces and devoured by a monster of Egyptian birth, who
would crunch raw flesh and anything else that was given him. Transported and
puffed up with such successes, as he considered them, he boasted that no prince
had ever known what power he really had, and he often threw out unmistakable
hints that he would not spare even those of the senate who survived, but would
one day blot out the whole order from the State and hand over the rule of the
provinces and the command of the armies to the Roman knights and to his freedmen. Certain it is that neither on beginning a journey nor on returning did he kiss
any member or even return his greeting; and at the formal opening of the work
at the Isthmus the prayer which he uttered in a loud voice before a great throng
was, that the event might result favourably "for himself and the people of Rome,"
thus suppressing any mention of the senate.

But he showed no greater mercy to the people or the walls of his capital. When someone in a general conversation said:

When I am dead, be earth consumed by fire,

he rejoined "Nay, rather while I live," and his action was wholly in accord. For under cover of displeasure at the ugliness of the old buildings and the narrow, crooked streets, he set fire to the city so openly that several ex-consuls did not venture to lay hands on his chamberlains although they caught them on their estates with tow and firebrands, while some granaries near the Golden House, whose room he particularly desired, were demolished by engines of war and then set on fire, because their walls were of stone. For six days and seven nights destruction raged, while the people were driven for shelter to monuments and tombs. At that time, besides an immense number of dwellings, the houses of leaders of old were burned, still adorned with trophies of victory, and the temples of the gods vowed and dedicated by the kings and later in the Punic and Gallic wars, and whatever else interesting and noteworthy had survived from antiquity. Viewing the conflagration from the tower of Maecenas and exulting, as he said, in "the beauty of the flames," he sang the whole of the "Sack of Troy," in his regular stage costume. Furthermore, to gain from this calamity too all the spoil and booty possible, while promising the removal of the debris and dead bodies free of cost he allowed no one to approach the ruins of his own property; and from the contributions which he not only received, but even demanded, he nearly bankrupted the provinces and exhausted the resources of individuals.

To all the disasters and abuses thus caused by the prince there were added certain accidents of fortune; a plague which in a single autumn entered thirty thousand deaths in the accounts of Libitina; a disaster in Britain, where two important towns were sacked and great numbers of citizens and allies were butchered; a shameful defeat in the Orient, in consequence of which the legions in Armenia were sent under the yoke and Syria was all but lost. It is surprising and of special note that all this time he bore nothing with more patience than the curses and abuse of the people, and was particularly lenient towards those who assailed him with gibes and lampoons.

JERUSALEM (II), 70 A.D.

Of all the cities in the East, Jerusalem proved the most difficult for the Romans to subdue. In the last battle of a six-year campaign, several Roman legions and their allies, a force of nearly 100,000 men, burned the Jewish Temple and slaughtered a half-million people. The cramped, narrow streets of the walled city literally ran with blood. Josephus (37/38 A.D.-c. 100 A.D.), a Jewish aristocrat who took the Roman side, published his account of the campaign under the title The Jewish War. *The Roman general, Titus, was proclaimed emperor two years after the labors here described.*

By now the soldiers were setting fire to the gates. The silver melted and ran, quickly exposing the woodwork to the flames, which were carried from there in a solid wall and fastened on to the colonnades. When the Jews saw the ring of fire, they lost all power of body and mind; such was their consternation that not a finger was raised to keep out or quench the flames; they stood looking on in utter helplessness. Yet their dismay at the present destruction made them no wiser for the future, but as if the Sanctuary itself was already in flames they whipped up their rage against the Romans. All that day and the following night the flames were in possession: the colonnades could not be fired all at once but only bit by bit.

The next day Titus ordered a section of his army to put out the fire, and to make a road close to the gates to facilitate the approach of the legions. Then he summoned a council of war and invited opinions on the question of the Sanctuary. Some insisted that they should enforce the law of war: there would be continual revolts while the Sanctuary remained as a rallying-point for Jews all over the world. Others argued that if the Jews evacuated it and no armed man was allowed on it, it should be spared, but if they climbed on it for military purposes it should be burnt down; it would in that case be a fortress, not a sanctuary, and from then on the impiety would be blamable not on the Romans but on those who forced their hands. Titus replied that even if the Jews did climb on it for military purposes, he would not make war on inanimate objects instead of men, or, whatever happened, burn down such a work of art: it was the Romans who would lose thereby, just as their empire would gain an ornament if it was preserved.

Titus retired to Antonia, intending to launch a full-scale attack at dawn the next day and surround the Sanctuary completely. It had, however, been condemned to the flames by God long ago: by the turning of time's wheel the fated day had now come, the 10th of Loös, [Aug.-Sept.] the day which centuries before had seen it burnt by the king of Babylon. But it was the Jews themselves who caused and started this conflagration. When Titus had retired, the partisans remained quiet for a time, then again attacked the Romans, the garrison of the Sanctuary clashing with those who were putting out the fire in the inner court, and who routed the Jews and chased them as far as the Sanctuary. Then one of the soldiers, without waiting for orders and without a qualm for the terrible consequences of his action but urged on by some unseen force, snatched up a blazing piece of wood and climbing on another soldier's back hurled the brand through a golden aperture giving access on the north side to the chambers built round the Sanctuary. As the flames shot into the air the Jews sent up a cry that matched the calamity and dashed to the rescue, with no thought now of saving their lives or husbanding their strength—for that which hitherto they had guarded so devotedly was disappearing before their eyes.

A runner brought the news to Titus as he was resting in his tent after the battle. He leapt up as he was and ran to the Sanctuary to extinguish the blaze. His whole staff panted after him, followed by the excited legions with all the shouting and confusion inseparable from the disorganized rush of an immense army. Caesar [Titus] shouted and waved to the combatants to put out the fire; but his shouts were unheard as their ears were deafened by a greater din, and his gesticulations went unheeded amidst the distractions of battle and bloodshed. As the legions charged in, neither persuasion nor threat could check their impetuosity: passion alone was in command. Crowded together round the entrances many were trampled by their friends, many fell among the still hot and smoking ruins of the colonnades and died as miserably as the defeated. As they neared the Sanctuary they pretended not even to hear Caesar's commands and urged the men in front to throw in more firebrands. The partisans were no longer in a position to help; everywhere was slaughter and flight. Most of the victims were peaceful citizens, weak and unarmed, butchered wherever they were caught. Round the Altar the heap of corpses grew higher and higher, while down the Sanctuary steps poured a river of blood and the bodies of those killed at the top slithered to the bottom. The soldiers were like men possessed and there was no holding them, nor was there any arguing with the fire. Caesar therefore led his staff inside the building and viewed the Holy Place of the Sanctuary with its furnishings, which went far beyond the accounts circulating in foreign countries, and fully justified their splendid reputation in our own. The flames were not yet effecting an entry from any direction but were feeding on the chambers built round the Sanctuary; so realizing that there was still time to save the glorious edifice, Titus dashed out and by personal efforts strove to persuade his men to put out the fire, instructing Liberalius, a centurion of his bodyguard of spearmen, to lay his staff across the shoulders of any who disobeyed. But their respect for Caesar and their fear of the centurion's staff were powerless against their fury, their detestation of the Jews, and an uncontrollable lust for battle. Most of them were also spurred on by the expectation of loot, being convinced that the interior was bursting with money and seeing that everything outside was of gold. But they were forestalled by one of those who had gone in. When Caesar dashed out to restrain the troops, that man pushed a firebrand into the hinges of the gate. Then from within a flame suddenly shot up, Caesar and his staff withdrew, and those outside were free to start what fires they liked. Thus the Sanctuary was set on fire in defiance of Caesar's wishes.

Grief might well be bitter for the destruction of the most wonderful edifice ever seen or heard of, both for its size and construction and for the lavish perfection of detail and the glory of its holy places; yet we find very real comfort in the thought that Fate is inexorable, not only towards living beings but also towards buildings and sites. We may wonder too at the exactness of the cycle of Fate: she kept, as I said, to the very month and day which centuries before had seen the Sanctuary burnt by the Babylonians. From its first foundation by King Solomon to its present destruction, which occurred in the second year of Vespasian's reign, was a period of 1,130 years, 7 months and 15 days; from its rebuilding in the second year of King Cyrus, for which Haggai was responsible, to its capture under Vespasian was 639 years and 45 days.

While the Sanctuary was burning, looting went on right and left and all who were caught were put to the sword. There was no pity for age, no regard

for rank; little children and old men, laymen and priests alike were butchered;
every class was held in the iron embrace of war, whether they defended themselves or cried for mercy. Through the roar of the flames as they swept relent-
lessly on could be heard the groans of the falling: such were the height of the
hill and the vastness of the blazing edifice that the entire city seemed to be on
fire, while as for the noise, nothing could be imagined more shattering or more
horrifying. There was the war-cry of the Roman legions as they converged; the
yells of the partisans encircled with fire and sword, the panic flight of the people cut off above into the arms of the enemy, and their shrieks as the end
approached. The cries from the hill were answered from the crowded streets;
and now many who were wasted with hunger and beyond speech found
strength to moan and wail when they saw the Sanctuary in flames. Back from
Peraea and the mountains round about came the echo in a thunderous bass.

Yet more terrible than the din were the sights that met the eye. The Temple
Hill, enveloped in flames from top to bottom, appeared to be boiling up from
its very roots; yet the sea of flame was nothing to the ocean of blood, or the
companies of killers to the armies of killed: nowhere could the ground be seen
between the corpses, and the soldiers climbed over heaps of bodies as they
chased the fugitives.

The Romans, judging it useless to spare the outbuildings now that the
Sanctuary was in flames, set fire to them all—what remained of the colonnades
and all the gates except two, one on the east end, the other on the south, both
of which they later demolished. They also burnt the treasuries which housed
huge sums of money, huge quantities of clothing, and other precious things; here,
in fact, all the wealth of the Jews was piled up, for the rich had dismantled their
houses and brought the contents here for sake keeping. Next they came to the
last surviving colonnade of the outer court. On this women and children and a
mixed crowd of citizens had found a refuge—6,000 in all. Before Caesar could
reach a decision about them or instruct his officers, the soldiers, carried away by
their fury, fired the colonnade from below; as a result some flung themselves out
of the flames to their death, others perished in the blaze: of that vast number
there escaped not one. Their destruction was due to a false prophet who that
very day had declared to the people in the City that God commanded them to

go up into the Temple to receive the signs of their deliverance. A number of hireling prophets had been put up in recent days by the party chiefs to deceive the people by exhorting them to await help from God, and so to reduce the number of deserters and buoy up with hope those who were above fear and anxiety. Man is readily persuaded in adversity: when the deceiver actually promises deliverance from the miseries that envelop him, then the sufferer becomes the willing slave of hope. So it was that the unhappy people were beguiled at that stage by cheats and false messengers of God, while the unmistakable portents that foreshadowed the coming desolation they treated with indifference and incredulity, disregarding God's warnings as if they were moonstruck, blind and senseless.

Next day the Romans drove the terrorists from the Lower City and burnt the whole place as far as Siloam. They were glad enough to see the town destroyed but got precious little loot, as the whole area had been cleaned out by the partisans before they withdrew to the Upper City. These men felt no remorse for the mischief they had done—they boasted as if they were proud of it: when they saw the City burning, they laughed heartily and said they were happily awaiting the end; for, with the people slaughtered, the Sanctuary burnt to the ground, and the town blazing, they were leaving nothing to the enemy. Yet to the very last Josephus never wearied of appealing to them to spare what was left of the City, though however much he might say against their savagery and impiety, however much advice he might give them for their own good, he got nothing but ridicule in return. As they could not very well surrender because of their oath and were unable now to fight the Romans on equal terms, they were like caged animals, so used to killing that they thirsted for blood. They scattered through the outskirts of the City and lay in wait among the ruins for would-be deserters. Many in fact were caught, and as hunger had left them too weak even to run away, all were butchered and their bodies thrown to the dogs. But any kind of death was more bearable than starvation, so that although they had no hope now of mercy from the Romans, they still fled to them, falling into the murderous hands of the partisans with their eyes open. Not one spot in the whole City was empty: every single one had its corpse, the victim of hunger or faction.

The last hope that bolstered up the party chief and their terrorist gangs lay in the underground sewers. If they took refuge in them they did not expect to be

[PLAN]

THE TEMPLE

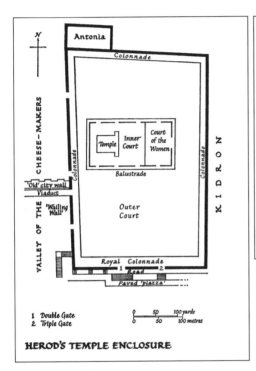

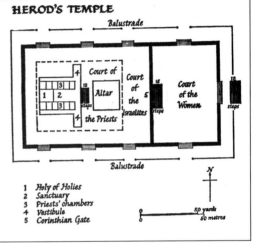

The Temple in Jerusalem, destroyed by the Romans in 70 A.D., and before them by the Babylonian King Nebuchadnezzer in 587 B.C.

tracked down, and their intention was to come out and make good their escape after the final capture of the City and the subsequent departure of the Romans. But this was only an idle dream: they were not fated to escape from either God or the Romans. At the time, however, they had such faith in their bolt-holes that they lit more fires than did the Romans. Those who fled from the burning buildings into the sewers they killed without hesitation and plundered; if they found anyone with food they snatched it away and swallowed it, dripping with the wretched man's blood. By now they were actually fighting each other for the loot; and I have little doubt that if capture had not forestalled it, their utter bestiality would have made them get their teeth into the very corpses.

During this same period a priest named Jeshua, son of Thebuthi, obtained from Caesar a sworn guarantee of safety on condition that he should hand over some of the sacred treasures. He came out and handed over from the Sanctuary wall two lampstands closely resembling those kept in the Sanctuary, as well as tables, basins, and cups, all of solid gold and very heavy. He also handed over the curtains, the vestments of the high priests with the precious stones, and many other articles required for the Temple services. In addition the Temple treasurer Phineas, when taken prisoner, produced the tunics and girdles of the priests and a large supply of purple and scarlet kept in store for repairing the great curtain, together with cinnamon in bulk, cassia, and quantities of other spices, which were blended and daily burnt as incense to God. He handed over many of the other treasures too, with Temple ornaments in abundance, thus earning though a prisoner the pardon granted to deserters.

Masters now of the walls, the Romans set up their standards on the towers and with clapping and singing celebrated their victory, having found the end of the war much easier than the beginning. They had surmounted the last wall without losing a man—it seemed too good to be true—and when they found no one to oppose them, they could make nothing of it. They poured into the streets sword in hand, cut down without mercy all who came within reach, and burnt the houses of any who took refuge indoors, occupants and all. Many they raided, and as they entered in search of plunder, they found whole families dead and the rooms full of the victims of starvation: horrified by the sight, they emerged empty-handed. Pity for those who had died in this way was matched by no such feeling for the living: they ran every man through whom they met and blocked the narrow streets with corpses, deluging the whole City with gore so that many of the fires were quenched by the blood of the slain. At dusk the slaughter ceased, but in the night the fire gained the mastery, and on the 8th of Gorpiaios [Sept.-Oct.] the sun rose over Jerusalem in flames—a city that during the siege had suffered such disasters that if she had enjoyed as many blessings from her foundation, she would have been the envy of the world, and a city that deserved these terrible misfortunes on no other account than that she produced a generation such as brought about her ruin.

As the soldiers were now growing weary of bloodshed and survivors were still appearing in large numbers, Caesar gave orders that only men who offered armed resistance were to be killed, and everyone else taken alive. But as well as those covered by the orders the aged and infirm were slaughtered: men in their prime who might be useful were herded into the Temple and shut up in the Court of the Women. To guard them Caesar appointed one of his freedmen, and his friend Fronto to decide each man's fate according to his deserts. Those who had taken part in sedition and terrorism informed against each other, and Fronto executed the lot. Of the youngsters he picked out the tallest and handsomest to be kept for the triumphal procession; of the rest, those over seventeen were put in irons and sent to hard labour in Egypt, while great numbers were presented by Titus to the provinces to perish in the theatres by the sword or by wild beasts; those under seventeen were sold. During the days in which Fronto was sorting them out starvation killed 11,000 of the prisoners, some because the guards hated them too bitterly to allow them any food, others because they would not accept it when offered; in any case there was not even enough corn to fill so many mouths.

All the prisoners taken from beginning to end of the war totalled 97,000; those who perished in the long siege 1,100,000 [probably closer to 600,000]. Of these the majority were Jews by race but not Jerusalem citizens: they had come together from the whole country for the Feast of Unleavened Bread and had suddenly been caught up in the war, so that first the overcrowding meant death by pestilence, and later hunger took a heavier toll.

But now fate had decreed that one prison should confine the whole nation and that a city solid with men should be held fast in war's embrace. No destruction ever wrought by God or man approached the wholesale carnage of this war. Every man who showed himself was either killed or captured by the Romans, and then those in the sewers were ferreted out, the ground was torn up, and all who were trapped were killed. There too were found the bodies of more than 2,000, some killed by their own hand, some by one another's, but most by starvation. So foul a stench of human flesh greeted those who charged in that many turned back at once. Others were so avaricious that they pushed on, climbing over the piles of corpses; for many valuables were found in the passages and all scruples were silenced by the prospect of gain. The Romans now fired the outlying districts of the town and demolished the walls. So fell Jerusalem in the second year of Vespasian's reign, on the 8th of Gorpiaios, captured five times before and now for the second time utterly laid waste. Shishak king of Egypt, followed by Antiochus, then Pompey, and after that Sosius and Herod together, captured the City but spared it. Earlier on the king of Babylon [Nebuchadnezzar] had stormed it and laid it waste 1,468 years and 6 months from its foundation. From King David, the first Jew to reign in it, to the destruction by Titus was 1,179 years. But neither its long history, nor its vast wealth, nor its people dispersed through the whole world, nor the unparalleled renown of its worship sufficed to avert its ruin.

There was no one left for the soldiers to kill or plunder, not a soul on which to vent their fury; for mercy would never have made them keep their hands off anyone as long as action was possible. So Caesar now ordered them to raze the whole City and Sanctuary to the ground, leaving the towers that overtopped the others, and the stretch of wall enclosing the City on the west—the wall to serve as protection for the garrison that was to be left, the towers to show later generations what a proud and mighty city had been humbled by the gallant sons of Rome. All the rest of the fortifications encircling the City were so completely levelled with the ground that no one visiting the spot would believe it had once been inhabited. This then was the end to which the mad folly of revolutionaries brought Jerusalem, a magnificent city renowned to the ends of the earth.

POMPEII, 79 A.D.

The prosperous provincial town of Pompeii was situated on the Bay of Naples, at the mouth of the river Sarno and the foot of Mount Vesuvius, 130 miles southeast of Rome. The younger Pliny (61/62 A.D.-c. 113 A.D.) lived nearby because his uncle, a famous Roman natural scientist and friend of the emperor Titus, was stationed at a nearby military post. The following account is taken from letters he wrote to a friend. Pompeii remained buried under sixteen feet of pumice and ash until its ruins were accidentally rediscovered in 1748.

On 24 August [79 A.D.], in the early afternoon, my mother drew [my uncle's] attention to a cloud of unusual size and appearance. He had been out in the sun, had taken a cold bath, and lunched while lying down, and was then working at his books. He called for his shoes and climbed up to a place which would give him the best view of the phenomenon. It was not clear at that distance from which mountain the cloud was rising (it was afterwards known to be Vesuvius); its general appearance can best be expressed as being like a pine rather than any other tree, for it rose to a great height on a sort of trunk and then split off into branches, I imagine because it was thrust upwards by the first blast and then left unsupported as the pressure subsided, or else it was borne down by its own weight so that it spread out and gradually dispersed. Sometimes it looked white, sometimes blotched and dirty, according to the amount of soil and ashes it carried with it. My uncle's scholarly acumen saw at once that it was important enough for a closer inspection, and he ordered a boat to be made ready, telling me I could come with him if I wished. I replied that I preferred to go on with my studies, and as it happened he had himself given me some writing to do.

For several days past there had been earth tremors which were not particularly alarming because they are frequent in Campania: but that night the shocks were so violent that everything felt as if it were not only shaken but overturned. My mother hurried into my room and found me already getting up to wake her if she were still asleep. We sat down in the forecourt of the house, between the buildings and the sea close by.

By now it was dawn, but the light was still dim and faint. The buildings round us were already tottering, and the open space we were in was too small for us not to be in real and imminent danger if the house collapsed. This finally decided us to leave the town. We were followed by a panic-stricken mob of people wanting to act on someone else's decision in preference to their own (a point in which fear looks like prudence), who hurried us on our way by pressing hard behind in a dense crowd. Once beyond the buildings we stopped, and there we had some extraordinary experiences which thoroughly alarmed us. The carriages we had ordered to be brought out began to run in different directions though the ground was quite level, and would not remain stationary even when wedged with stones. We also saw the sea sucked away and apparently forced back by the earthquake: at any rate it receded from the shore so that quantities of sea creatures were left stranded on dry sand. On the landward side a fearful black cloud was rent by forked and quivering bursts of flame, and parted to reveal great tongues of fire, like flashes of lightning magnified in size.

Soon afterwards the cloud sank down to earth and covered the sea; it had already blotted out Capri and hidden the promontory of Misenum from sight. Then my mother implored, entreated, and commanded me to escape as best I could—a young man might escape, whereas she was old and slow and could die in peace as long as she had not been the cause of my death too. I told her I refused to save myself without her, and grasping her hand forced her to quicken her pace. She gave in reluctantly, blaming herself for delaying me. Ashes were already falling, not as yet very thickly. I looked round: a dense black cloud was coming up behind us, spreading over the earth like a flood. "Let us leave the road while we can still see," I said, "or we shall be knocked down and trampled underfoot in the dark by the crowd behind." We had scarcely sat down to rest when darkness fell, not the dark of a moonless or cloudy night, but as if the lamp had been put out in a closed room. You could hear the shrieks of women, the wailing of infants, and the shouting of men; some were calling their parents, others their children or their wives, trying to recognize them by their voices. People bewailed their own fate or that of their relatives, and there were some who prayed for death in their terror of dying. Many besought the aid of the gods, but still more imagined there were no gods left, and that the universe was plunged into eternal darkness for evermore. There were people, too, who added to the real perils by inventing fictitious dangers: some reported that part of Misenum had collapsed or another part was on fire, and though their tales were false they found others to believe them. A gleam of light returned, but we took this to be a warning of the approaching flames rather than daylight. However, the flames remained some distance; then darkness came on once more and ashes began to fall again, this time in heavy showers. We rose from time to time and shook them off, otherwise we should have been buried and crushed beneath their weight. I could boast that not a groan or cry of fear escaped me in these perils, had I not derived some poor consolation in my mortal lot from the belief that the whole world was dying with me and I with it.

At last the darkness thinned and dispersed into smoke or cloud; then there was genuine daylight, and the sun actually shone out, but yellowish as it is during an eclipse. We were terrified to see everything changed, buried deep in ashes like snowdrifts. We returned to Misenum where we attended to our physical needs as best we could, and then spent an anxious night alternating between hope and fear. Fear predominated, for the earthquakes went on, and several hysterical individuals made their own and other people's calamities seem ludicrous in comparison with their frightful predictions. But even then, in spite of the dangers we had been through and were still expecting, my mother and I had still no intention of leaving until we had news of my uncle.

When daylight returned on the 26th—two days after the last day he had seen—[my uncle's] body was found intact and uninjured, still fully clothed and looking more like sleep than death.

Of course these details are not important enough for history, and you will read them without any idea of recording them; if they seem scarcely worth even putting in a letter, you have only yourself to blame for asking for them.

[CARTOON]

RUFUS

The volcanic shower of pumice that smothered Pompeii in 79 A.D. preserved it in a pristine state, like an insect in amber. This graffito is one among hundreds of cartoons etched into Pompeii's frescoed walls. The caption reads "RUFUS EST" ("This is Rufus").

REVELATION

By the time John wrote the Book of Revelation, around 90 A. D., he had been exiled from Jerusalem by the Roman emperor to the small, rocky island of Patmos, in the middle of the Aegean Sea. The place called Armageddon is the hill of Megiddo in the northern section of what is now Israel.

And I heard a great voice out of the temple saying to the seven angels, Go your ways, and pour out the vials of the wrath of God upon the earth. And the first went, and poured out his vial upon the earth; and there fell a noisome and grievous sore upon the men which had the mark of the beast, and upon them which worshipped his image.

And the second angel poured out his vial upon the sea; and it became as the blood of a dead man: and every living soul died in the sea.

And the third angel poured out his vial upon the rivers and fountains of waters; and they became blood. And I heard the angel of the waters say, Thou art righteous, O Lord, which art, and wast, and shalt be, because thou hast judged thus. For they have shed the blood of saints and prophets, and thou hast given them blood to drink; for they are worthy. And I heard another out of the altar say, Even so, Lord God Almighty, true and righteous are thy judgments.

And the fourth angel poured out his vial upon the sun; and power was given unto him to scorch men with fire. And men were scorched with great heat, and blasphemed the name of God, which hath power over these plagues: and they repented not to give him glory.

And the fifth angel poured out his vial upon the seat of the beast; and his kingdom was full of darkness; and they gnawed their tongues for pain, And blasphemed the God of heaven because of their pains and their sores, and repented not of their deeds.

And the sixth angel poured out his vial upon the great river Euphrates; and the water thereof was dried up, that the way of the kings of the east might be prepared. And I saw three unclean spirits like frogs come out of the mouth of the dragon, and out of the mouth of the beast, and out of the mouth of the false prophet. For they are the spirits of devils, working miracles, which go forth unto the kings of the earth and of the whole world, to gather them to the battle of that great day of God Almighty.

Behold, I come as a thief. Blessed is he that watcheth, and keepeth his garments, lest he walk naked, and they see his shame. And he gathered them together into a place called in the Hebrew tongue Armageddon.

And the seventh angel poured out his vial into the air; and there came a great voice out of the temple of heaven, from the throne, saying, It is done.

And there were voices, and thunders, and lightnings; and there was a great earthquake, such as was not since men were upon the earth, so mighty an earthquake, and so great. And the great city was divided into three parts, and the cities of the nations fell: and great Babylon came in remembrance before God, to give unto her the cup of the wine of the fierceness of his wrath. And every island fled away, and the mountains were not found. And there fell upon men a great hail out of heaven, every stone about the weight of a talent: and men blasphemed God because of the plague of the hail; for the plague thereof was exceeding great.

ROME (III), 410 A.D.

When the Visigothic king Alaric broke through its walls, Rome was the preeminent city in the Western world. The event left the city and the remnants of its empire open to marauding barbarians for nearly a thousand years. The account is that of Procopius (c. 500 A.D.-after 560 A.D.), a Byzantine historian writing a hundred years after the fact.

There were many Gothic nations in earlier times, just as also at the present, but the greatest and most important of all are the Goths, Vandals, Visigoths, and Gepaedes. All these, while they are distinguished from one another by their names, as has been said, do not differ in anything else at all. For they all have white bodies and fair hair, and are tall and handsome to look upon, and they use the same laws and practice a common religion. For they are all of the Arian faith, and have one language called Gothic; and, as it seems to me, they all came originally from one tribe.

But the Visigoths, separating from the others, removed from there and at first entered into an alliance with the [eastern] Emperor Arcadius, but at a later time (for faith with the Romans cannot dwell in barbarians), under the leadership of Alaric, they became hostile to both [eastern and western] emperors, and, beginning with Thrace, treated all Europe as an enemy's land. Now the [western] Emperor Honorius had before this time been sitting in Rome, with never a thought of war in his mind, but glad, I think, if men allowed him, to remain quiet in his palace. But when word was brought that the barbarians with a great army were not far off, but somewhere among the Taulantii, he abandoned the palace and fled in disorderly fashion to Ravenna, a strong city lying just about at the end of the Ionian Gulf, while some say that he brought in the barbarians himself, because an uprising had been started against him among his subjects; but this does not seem to me trustworthy, as far, at least, as one can judge of the character of the man. And the barbarians, finding that they had no hostile force to encounter them, became the most cruel of all men. For they destroyed all the cities which they captured, especially those south of the Ionian Gulf, so completely that nothing has been left to my time to know them by, unless, indeed, it might be one tower or one gate or some such thing which chanced to remain. And they killed all the people, as many as came in their way, both old and young alike, sparing neither women nor children. Wherefore even up to the present time Italy is sparsely populated. They also gathered as plunder all the money out of all Europe, and, most important of all, they left in Rome nothing whatever of public or private wealth when they moved on to Gaul. But I shall now tell how Alaric captured Rome.

After much time had been spent by him in the siege, and he had not been able either by force or by any other device to capture the place, he formed the following plan. Among the youths in the army whose beards had not yet grown, but who had just come of age, he chose out three hundred whom he knew to be of good birth and possessed of valor beyond their years, and told them secretly that he was about to make a present of them to certain of the patricians in Rome, pretending that they were slaves. And he instructed them that, as soon as they got inside the houses of those men, they should display much gentleness and moderation and serve them eagerly in whatever tasks should be laid upon them by their owners; and he further directed them that not long afterwards, on an appointed day at about midday, when all those who were to be their masters would most likely be already asleep after their meal, they should all come to the gate called Salarian and with a sudden rush kill the guards, who would have no previous knowledge of the plot, and open the gates as quickly as possible. After giving these orders to the youths, Alaric straightway sent ambassadors to the members of the senate, stating that he admired them for their loyalty toward their emperor, and that he would trouble them no longer, because of their valor and faithfulness, with which it was plain that they were endowed to a remarkable degree, and in order that tokens of himself might be preserved among men both noble and brave, he wished to present each one of them with some domestics. After making this declaration and sending the youths not long afterwards, he commanded the barbarians to make preparations for the departure, and he let this be known to the Romans. And they heard his words gladly, and receiving the gifts began to be exceedingly happy, since they were completely ignorant of the plot of the barbarian. For the youths, by being unusually obedient to their owners, averted suspicion, and in the camp some were already seen moving from their positions and raising the siege, while it seemed that the others were just on the point of doing the very same thing. But when the appointed day had come, Alaric armed his whole force for the attack and was holding them in readiness close by the Salarian Gate; for it happened that he had encamped there at the beginning of the siege. And all the youths at the time of the day agreed upon came to this gate, and, assailing the guards suddenly, put them to death; then they opened the gates and received Alaric and the army into the city at their leisure. And they set fire to the houses which were next to the gate, among which was also the house of Sallust, who in ancient times wrote the history of the Romans, and the greater part of this house has stood half-burned up to my time; and after plundering the whole city and destroying most of the Romans, they moved on. At that time they say that the Emperor Honorius in Ravenna received the message from one of the eunuchs, evidently a keeper of the poultry, that Rome had perished. And he cried out and said, "And yet it has just eaten from my hands!" For he had a very large cock, Rome by name; and the eunuch comprehending his words said that it was the city of Rome which had perished at the hands of Alaric, and the emperor with a sigh of relief answered quickly. "But I, my good fellow, thought that my fowl Rome had perished." So great, they say, was the folly with which this emperor was possessed.

[CHAPTER HEADINGS]

SAINT AUGUSTINE ON THE SACK OF ROME

At the time Alaric sacked Rome, the empire had been officially Christian for about a hundred years, and some followers of the old Roman religion interpreted the disaster as punishment adminstered by Rome's traditional gods, angry because their places had been usurped by a provincial god from Palestine. St. Augustine (354-430), Bishop of Hippo and Doctor of the Church, provided the necessary sophistry for the counter-opinion. The Goths were made out to be God's servants, solid citizens of Christendom, punishing the Romans for their moral lassitude. Such a reading required Augustine to explain the atrocities and account for the sufferings inflicted on pagan and Christian alike. The chapter headings are taken from Augustine's first book of the City of God.

All homicide is not murder

By what judgment of God the enemy's lust was allowed to sin against the bodies of the chaste

Of the violence which may be done to the body by another's lust, while the
mind remains inviolate

The end of this present life must come, whether sooner or later

Blessings and disasters often shared by good and bad

The saints lose nothing by being deprived of temporal goods

In the sack of Rome, the cruelties conformed to the conventions of war; the
acts of clemency were due to the power of Christ's name

Those who complain of the Christian era really wish to wallow in shameful
self-indulgence

[POEMS]

IRELAND BEFORE THE VIKINGS

*Near the year 800 A.D., after four centuries of diligence, Saint Patrick's
mission was close to completed. Óengus of Clonenagh (fl. late 8th c.)
found reason to celebrate the triumph of the Irish Church. He wrote on
the eve of the Viking raids; within a matter of a very few years, the greater
part of Ireland's monasteries were in ashes.*

Old haunts of the heathen
Filled from ancient days
Are but deserts now
Where no pilgrim prays.

Little places taken
First by twos and threes
Are like Rome reborn,
Peopled sanctuaries.

Heathendom has gone down
Though it spread everywhere;
God the Father's kingdom
Fills heaven and earth and air.

THE VIKING TERROR
Anonymous, 10th c.

There's a wicked wind tonight,
Wild upheaval in the sea;
No fear now that the Viking hordes
Will terrify me.

JERUSALEM (III), 1099

On a sweltering afternoon in July of 1099, the armies of the First Crusade (13,000 Europeans, many of them in full body armor) scaled the walls of Jerusalem and killed virtually every person they saw. The chronicle is that of Fulcher of Chartres (c. 1059–c. 1127), a French chaplain in the employ of Baldwin of Flanders.

After the machines were prepared, namely, the battering-rams and the sows, they again prepared to assail the city. In addition to other kinds of siege craft, they constructed a tower from small pieces of wood, because large pieces could not be secured in those regions. When the order was given, they carried the tower piecemeal to a corner of the city. Early in the same morning, when they had gathered the machines and other auxiliary weapons, they very quickly erected the tower in compact shape not far from the wall. After it was set up and well covered by hides on the outside, by pushing it they slowly moved it nearer to the wall.

Then a few but brave soldiers, at a signal from the horn, climbed on the tower. Nevertheless the Saracens defended themselves from these soldiers and, with slings, hurled firebrands dipped in oil and grease at the tower and at the soldiers, who were in it. Thereafter death was present and sudden for many on both sides.

From their position on Mount Zion, Count Raymond and his men likewise made a great assault with their machines. From another position, where Duke Godfrey, Robert, Count of the Normans, and Robert of Flanders, were situated, an even greater assault was made on the wall. This was what was done on that day.

On the following day, at the blast of the trumpets, they undertook the same work more vigorously, so that by hammering in one place with the battering-rams, they breached the wall. The Saracens had suspended two beams before the battlement and secured them by ropes as a protection against the stones hurled at them by their assailants. But what they did for their advantage later turned to their detriment, with God's providence. For when the tower was moved to the wall, the ropes, by which the aforesaid beams were suspended, were cut by falchions, and the Franks constructed a bridge for themselves out of the same timber, which they cleverly extended from the tower to the wall.

Already one stone tower on the wall, at which those working our machines had thrown flaming firebrands, was afire. The fire, little by little replenished by the wooden material in the tower, produced so much smoke and flame that not one of the citizens on guard could remain near it.

Then the Franks entered the city magnificently at the noonday hour on Friday, the day of the week when Christ redeemed the whole world on the cross. With trumpets sounding and with everything in an uproar, exclaiming: "Help, God!" they vigorously pushed into the city, and straightway raised the banner on the top of the wall. All the heathen, completely terrified, changed their boldness to swift flight through the narrow streets of the quarters. The more quickly they fled, the more quickly were they put to flight.

Count Raymond and his men, who were bravely assailing the city in another section, did not perceive this until they saw the Saracens jumping from the top of the wall. Seeing this, they joyfully ran to the city as quickly as they could, and helped the others pursue and kill the wicked enemy.

Then some, both Arabs and Ethiopians, fled into the Tower of David; others shut themselves in the Temple of the Lord and of Solomon, where in the halls a very great attack was made on them. Nowhere was there a place where the Saracens could escape the swordsmen.

On the top of Solomon's Temple, to which they had climbed in fleeing, many were shot to death with arrows and cast down headlong from the roof. Within this Temple about ten thousand were beheaded. If you had been there, your feet would have been stained up to the ankles with the blood of the slain. What more shall I tell? Not one of them was allowed to live. They did not spare the women and children.

After they had discovered the cleverness of the Saracens, it was an extraordinary thing to see our squires and poorer people split the bellies of those dead Saracens, so that they might pick out besants [gold coins] from their intestines, which they had swallowed down their horrible gullets while alive. After several days, they made a great heap of their bodies and burned them to ashes, and in these ashes they found the gold more easily.

> With drawn swords, our people ran through the city;
> Nor did they spare anyone, not even those pleading for mercy.
> The crowd was struck to the ground, just as rotten fruit
> Falls from shaken branches, and acorns from a wind-blown oak.

Letter to the Faithful

Joachim of Fiore (c. 1135-1201/02), an Italian Cistercian monk, believed the end of the world to be as near at hand as the next storm or the next harvest. He pressed his millennialist theories on Holy Roman Emperor Henry VI, as well as on Richard the Lion Hearted, who met him at Messina in the winter of 1190/91, while en route to the Third Crusade.

Brother Joachim called Abbot of Fiore advises all Christ's faithful whom this letter reaches to watch and pray so that they do not enter into temptation (Matt. 26:41). When the Lord spoke to the prophet Ezechiel whom he set up as a watchman over the house of Israel at the time of the removal to Babylon, after he commanded him to write down many things he warned him: "If I say to a wicked man 'You will surely die,' and you do not make it known to him, he will indeed die in his iniquity, but I will require his blood from your hand" (Ezech. 3:18). Since what at that time was entrusted to one person in particular, in these days holds for all who seem to have received more information than others.

This is how it looked to me in the case of the divine plan I seem to understand in the true scriptures, especially since some monks have most urgently advised me that I have an obligation not to keep silent about the wrath of the Judge so soon to be revealed from heaven upon all the wickedness and injustice of men who are unwilling to do penance for their sins. If I am permitted to speak out to urge and excite hearts to be on guard I do not hesitate to say with the Apostle Paul, "I am innocent of the blood of all of you" (Acts 20:26). For some time I wished to cast anchor in the harbor of silence in deference to my priors, so as not to seem to stir up scandal or bickering in Christ's Church, especially because of those who run about more than others shouting, "Thus saith the Lord," when He has not commissioned them. But now: "Hear, O young men, and pay heed, you old men" (Joel 1:2). I will not speak in riddles so that you cannot understand because of the depth of the obscure speech, but I will both openly declare what happened from our fathers' days and will also incorporate what is to follow in our times so that even the little children can understand it plain and simple. You have read in the Apostle Paul what you see has been fulfilled for him and what you know has been truly foretold. He says, "In the last days dangerous times will come, and men will be lovers of themselves, covetous, puffed up, proud, blasphemers, disobedient to parents, ungrateful, wicked, without either affection or peace, calumniators, incontinent, unmerciful, without kindness, traitors, shameless, arrogant, lovers of pleasure more than God, making a pretense of piety, but rejecting its power. Stay clear of them" (2 Tim. 3:1-5).

All these statements, I say, and ones similar to what Paul said have been fulfilled. As a result, there is no place for those who seek the Lord, and the angel has been abandoned by those who fear him.

Death cries out from the East, destruction from the West. The multitude of the Greeks has become Sodom, the Latins have become Gomorrah, with the Greeks publicly proclaiming Egypt's crime, the Latins Babylon's disorder. All have plotted together at the same time against God, and all, as the prophet says, "have abandoned God, have blasphemed the Holy One of Israel, and have gone backward in retreat" (Isa. 1:4). "They have transgressed the laws, they have changed the order of justice, they have broken the everlasting covenant" (Isa. 24:5). "All peoples, now listen attentively; give ear, all who dwell on earth. He who has fled from fear will fall into the pit, and he who shall be freed from the pit will be taken by the snare, because the flood gates of heaven are open and the foundations of the earth will be shaken. The earth shall be completely shattered and totally crushed; like a drunken man it shall be violently shaken and shall be borne away like a tent of a single night. Its iniquity shall weigh it down, and it will fall and not be able to rise again" (Ps. 48:2; Jer. 48:43-4; Isa. 24:19-21).

Take this to heart, apostate children (Isa. 30:1); think on it and be afraid. Perhaps you may do penance for having rejected God's word and abandoned the bosom of the Chaste Mother who is now lowly and despised and preferred the Whore who rules over the kings of the earth. Hear the judgment that the Lord will perform in your days, a judgment He has not made from days of old, from the birth of time. Lo, the pagan nations will plot together and the kings of the earth gather and assemble against you, daughter of Babylon. They will fight against you like the fury of the sea and will root your offspring from the earth. All you citizens will be swept from the earth. All these things will come about as we have read; they will be fulfilled as has been written.

There is nothing more to be awaited for the execution of the judgment, because surely the sentence has been put off till now not for the sake of the wicked but for the meek. For when there were fifty just people in the city of Sodom the Lord spared the city for the sake of the fifty who lived there (Gen. 18:26 ff). And He spared it for the sake of the forty and thirty, and up till the time that ten were found He was eager to spare it. But when only Lot was found in the city of the vicious, Almighty God did not wish to bear such a vast mass of crime for the sake of one just man, but led him out of the city. As Peter says, "He snatched the just man Lot from unholy contact with the wicked" (2 Pet. 2:7). God knows how to snatch good men from temptation. He punished all who lived by the fearful chastisement of his condemnation; but Noah, that just man, was preserved in the ark when the remaining crowd of wicked were destroyed by the flood's waters.

What are we doing? We were seeking fifty, and hardly one is to be found. Whoever that person is who is signified by Lot, or whoever is designated by Noah, he should know that Babylon's judgment threatens in every way possible. Let him hear the Lord's voice as it mercifully cries out from heaven and says: "Go out from her, my people, so as not to share in her sins and so as not to partake of her punishments. For her sins have reached up to heaven and the Lord has remembered her iniquities" (Apoc. 18:4-5). Depart from her through confession and penance. Either ascend the mountain of contemplation, if you can, or if this seems difficult, keep yourself in the humility of the active life which is denoted by Segor, though it be small and lowly.

Forget the saying that "now it will not be today as it was yesterday and the day before" (1 Macc. 9:44). Truly, it will not be as it has been thus far for some of the sterile branches, but "the ax is already laid to the root of the tree and every tree that does not bear fruit will be cut down and thrown into the fire" (Matt. 3:10). This will not take place in the days of your grandchildren or in the old age of your children, but in your own days, few and evil. "This generation will not pass away until all these things have been accomplished" (Matt. 24:34). After this the Lord will console the remnants of his people and will relieve the oppression of his inheritance. He will restore his leaders as they were in the beginning and his counselors as they were of old, and He will descend upon them like a river of peace (Isa. 48:18) and like a tower glorifying those who give praise. Do penance now and be converted and live, "lest He at sometime seize upon your souls like a lion, while there is no one to redeem you or save you" (Ps. 7:3). The End.

Beziers, 1209

At the beginning of the 13th century, Pope Innocent III ordered a punitive military campaign against the Albigensian heretics of Languedoc, and on July 21, 1209, the papal legate arrived at Beziers with a crusading army of tens of thousands of men, the better part of them vagabonds. The besieged citizens made the fatal mistake of attempting a sortie against the attackers while leaving their gates unprotected. From the Crusade Against the Albigensians *by Guillaume de Tudèle (fl. 1210), translated by Joshua Phillips.*

It was at the feast of Mary Magdalene that the abbot of Cîteaux led his great army. All around Beziers, they camped on the plain. I now believe that torments and grief were being prepared for the inhabitants, because even the army of Menelaus, from whom Paris stole Helen, never pitched so many tents at the port under Mycenae nor such rich pavilions in the open at night as the French army did then. Besides the Count of Brienne, there was no baron in France who did not serve his military time there.

They spent the entire week skirmishing. Furthermore, listen to what these wretches [from Beziers], who are simpler and madder than hares, did: with their great white banners they went running past the French army, screaming at the top of their lungs; they thought to frighten them in the way one chases birds from a field of oats, by screaming, shouting and shaking their flags in the broad daylight of morning.

When the king of the vagabonds [the Crusader peasant army] saw the people of the city skirmishing against the French army and when he saw them wail and scream and kill and tear apart a French crusader after having thrown him to the bottom of a bridge, he called all his beggars together and assembled them. With a loud voice he cried, "To the assault!" As soon as this was said, they all went and armed themselves with clubs; I believe they had nothing more. There were more than 15,000 without shoes. In their shirts and breeches, they started to surround the city in order to batter the walls; they threw themselves into the ditches and began to chip away, while others broke down the doors and burst them apart. Seeing this, the people of the city were frightened and the French army cried, "Everyone, to arms!" Then you would have seen quite a press to enter the city! With great force, they made the people inside quit the walls. The besieged took their wives and their children to the church and had the bells rung: they had no other refuge.

The inhabitants of the city saw the crusaders coming and the king of the vagabonds who was going to invade them. They saw the beggars leap from all around into the ditches and break the walls and open the doors and they saw the French troops arm themselves in great haste. They knew in their hearts that they could not hold out. They took refuge as quickly as possibly in the grand monastery; the priests and the clerics went to array themselves and have the bells rung as if they were going to say a mass for the dead at a funeral. In the end they could not prevent the beggars from entering. These beggars seized houses at their pleasure for each man could have chosen ten houses if he so desired. The vagabonds were inflamed; death did not frighten them. They killed and massacred everyone they could find. And they seized great riches. They would have been rich forever, if they could have kept what they took. But before too long, they had to give it all up, because the barons of France wanted to claim possession of these things even though they had been taken by the vagabonds.

The crusaders killed all of those who had taken refuge in the monastery. Nothing could save them, neither the cross nor the altar, nor the crucifix. And these mad mendicant vagabonds massacred the clerics, and the women and children, such that I believe not a single one escaped. May God receive their souls in paradise. For I believe that such a savage massacre has not been thought of nor accomplished since the time of the Saracens. The churls installed themselves in the houses they took, which were decorated and full of riches. But the French [nobles], when they saw that, very nearly went mad. Outside, they beat them down with cudgels, like dogs.

The vagabonds and their king thought they were going to enjoy what they had taken and be rich from it for ever. When it was taken from them, they all cried in one voice, "Burn it! Burn it!" The miserable, foul beggars. So they brought torches. The city caught fire and fear spread. The whole city was burning, far and wide. When they smelled the fire, everyone retreated. And so all the great rooms and houses burned. Many cassocks burned there, many helmets, many padded doublets which were made in Chartres, in Blaye, or in Edesse and numerous good dresses that had to be left. And the whole monastery which master Gervais had built also burnt. It cracked in the middle due to the heat and two sections of it collapsed.

Lords, what the French and Normans had from Beziers was marvelously grand. They would have been rich their entire lives from it had it not been for the vagabonds and their king with the miserable beggars who burned the city, the women and children, the young and the old, and the priests who held themselves arrayed in their ornaments in the monastery. Three days they had remained in the verdant plains; on the fourth day, cavaliers and sergeants set out on a march through the unified land, where nothing stopped them, their standards raised and flapping in the wind

FLORENCE, 1348

The epidemic of bubonic plague known as "The Black Death" reached southern Italy from the Crimea in October 1347; moving implacably north and west over the next three years the infection killed upwards of 25 million people, roughly a third of the population of Europe. The ratio between the living and the dead coincided with the number foretold in Revelation ("the third part of men killed") at the sounding of the Last Trump. Florence at the time

*was the largest and most important city in medieval Italy, and Boccaccio
(1313-1375) describes the dying of 50,000 of its citizens (one in every two) in
his introduction to the first book of the* Decameron.

The era of the fruitful Incarnation of the Son of God had arrived at the year
1348 when the deadly plague reached the noble city of Florence, of all Italian
cities the most excellent. Whether it was owing to the action of the heavenly bodies or whether, because of our iniquities, it was visited upon us mortals for our
correction by the righteous anger of God, this pestilence, which had started some
years earlier in the Orient, where it had robbed countless people of their lives,
moved without pause from one region to the next until it spread tragically into
the West. It was proof against all human providence and remedies, such as the
appointment of officials to the task of ridding the city of much refuse, the ban-
ning of sick visitors from outside, and a good number of sanitary ordinances;
equally unavailing were the humble petitions offered to the Lord by pious souls
not once but countless times, whether in the course of processions or otherwise.
As the said year turned to spring, the plague began quite prodigiously to display
its harrowing effects. Here it did not develop as it had done in the East, where
death was inevitable in anyone whose symptoms were a loss of blood through
the nose. Its first sign here in both men and women was a swelling in the groin
or beneath the armpit, growing sometimes in the shape of a simple apple, sometimes in that of an egg, more or less: a bubo was the name commonly given to
such a swelling. Before long this deadly bubo would begin to spread indifferent-
ly from these points to crop up all over; the symptoms would develop then into
dark or livid patches that many people found appearing on their arms or thighs
or elsewhere; these were large and well separated in some cases, while in others,
they were a crowd of tiny spots. And just as the bubo had been, and continued
to be, a sure indication of fatal disease, so were these blotches for those on whom
they appeared. No physician's prescriptions, no medicine seemed of the slightest
benefit as a cure for this disease. Whether it was that the nature of the malady
would not permit it, or because doctors were unable to discover its origins and
therefore could not apply the proper remedy, not only did few people recover
but indeed nearly all the sick would succumb within three days of the above-

mentioned symptoms' first appearance; some died sooner, some later, and the majority with no fever, nothing.

And the plague gathered strength as it was transmitted from the sick to the healthy through normal intercourse, just as fire catches on to any dry or greasy object placed too close to it. Nor did the trouble stop there: not only did the healthy incur the disease and with it the prevailing mortality by talking to or keeping company with the sick—they had only to touch the clothing or anything else that had come into contact with or been used by the sick and the plague evidently was passed to the one who handled those things. You will be quite amazed by what I am about to tell you: were it not that many people witnessed it and I saw it with my own eyes, I would never have dared believe it, still less set it down in writing, even if I had had it on the most reliable authority. So potent was the contagion as it was passed on that it was transmitted not only between one person and the next: many a time it quite clearly went further than that, and if some animal other than a human touched an object belonging to a person who was sick or had died of the plague, the animal was not merely infected with it but fell dead in no time at all. As I have just mentioned, I saw this for myself one day in particular: the rags of a pauper who had died of the plague had been tossed out into the street and two pigs happened upon them; they nosed about them with their snouts, as pigs do, then took them in their jaws and shook them this way and that; it was not long before they fell into convulsions, as if they had swallowed poison, and then dropped dead on top of the rags they had so haplessly snatched up.

This sort of thing, as well as many another that was similar to it if not worse, produced in the survivors all manner of terrors and suspicions all tending to the same solution, and a very heartless one it was: they would keep their distance from the plague-victims, and from their chattels too, thus hoping to preserve their own skins. There were some who inclined to the view that if they followed a temperate life-style and eschewed all extravagance they should be well able to keep such an epidemic at bay. So they would form into a group and withdraw on their own to closet themselves in a house free of all plague-victims; here they would enjoy the good life, partaking of the daintiest fare and the choicest of wines—all in the strictest moderation—and shunning all debauchery; they would refrain from speaking to anyone or from gleaning any news from outside that related to deaths or plague-victims—rather did they bask in music and such other pleasures as were at their disposal. Others found the contrary view more enticing, that the surest remedy to a disease of this order was to drink their fill, have a good time, sing to their hearts' content, live it up, give free rein to their appetites—and make light of all that was going on. This was their message, this their practice so far as they were able; day and night would find them in one tavern or another, soaking up the booze like sponges, and carousing all the more in other people's houses the moment word got out that that's where the fun was to be had. This was easy enough to do because everyone had let his property go, just as he had let himself go, as if there was to be no tomorrow. Most houses therefore lay open to all comers, and people would walk in off the streets and make themselves at home just as if they owned the place. And while they pursued this brutish behavior they still took every care to avoid all contact with the sick.

Now with our city in such a sorry state, the laws of God and men had lost their authority and fallen into disrespect in the absence of magistrates to see them enforced, for they, like everyone else, had either succumbed to the plague or lay sick, or else had been deprived of their minions to the point where they were powerless. This left everyone free to do precisely as he pleased. There were many others who adhered to a middle way between these two, neither following the frugal regimen of the first group nor letting themselves go in the drunken, dissolute lifestyle of the second. They partook of their fill but no more and, instead of shutting themselves away, they would go about holding flowers to their noses or fragrant herbs, or spices of various kinds, in the belief that such aromas worked wonders for the brain (the seat of health), for the atmosphere was charged with the stench of corpses, it reeked of sickness and medication. Others there were who were totally ruthless and no doubt chose the safest option: there was in their view no remedy to equal that of giving the plague a very wide berth. On this premise any number of men and women deserted their city and with it their homes and neighbourhoods, their families and possessions, heedless of anything but their own skins, and made for other people's houses or for their country estates at any rate, as though the wrath of God, in visiting the plague on men to punish their iniquity, was never going to reach out to where they were; as though it was meant to harry only those remaining within their city walls, as though not a soul was destined to remain alive in the city, as though its last hour had come.

Barely a handful were accorded the benefit of seeing their dear ones in floods of compassionate tears: far from it, the new order called for quips and jollity more suited to a festive gathering. The womenfolk had largely suppressed their natural pity and become well practiced in this new frivolity to assure their own survival. Seldom were there more than ten or a dozen neighbours to escort the body of the deceased to church. Nor would the corpse be borne on the shoulders of prominent and distinguished citizens: the bier would be taken in charge by a tribe of pallbearers, people of the commonest sort who liked to call themselves undertakers and who fulfilled the function against payment in cash. They would bend their hastening steps, not to the church appointed by the deceased before his death, but to the nearest one, more often than not, preceded by maybe a half-dozen clerics holding the odd candle—sometimes with none at all. With the help of the pallbearers they would drop the corpse into the nearest available tomb that had space, without too much effort being wasted on a lengthy or solemn requiem.

Which is not to suggest that these obsequies were attended by any tears, any display or candles, any company: things had reached the point where the dying received no more consideration than the odd goat would today. What was inescapably apparent was that if the occasional minor disaster that occurs in the normal course had failed to teach patience to the wise, the sheer scale of the prevailing evil had taught even the simplest soul a degree of placid resignation. As there was not sufficient consecrated ground in which to bury the vast number of corpses that arrived at every church day after day and practically hour by hour, least of all while any effort had been made to give each person his own burial plot in accordance with age-old custom, enormous pits were dug in the graveyards, once saturation point had been reached, and the new arrivals were dropped into these by the hundred; here they were packed in layers, the way goods are stowed in a ship's hold, and each layer would get a thin covering of earth until the pit was filled up.

Before I go into yet more detail about the afflictions our city underwent in those days, I should only add that if the townsfolk were having such a ghastly time of it, the neighboring countryfolk were spared none of the rigors. To say nothing of the market-towns, which were like the city if on a smaller scale, in the remote villages and out in the fields the laborers, poor penniless wretches, and their households died like brute beasts rather than human beings; night and day, with never a doctor to attend them, no sort of domestic help, they would pass away, some indoors, others out on the roads or among their crops. As a result they, like the townsfolk, became feckless in their habits, neglecting their affairs and their possessions; indeed, far from encouraging their animals, their fields, their earlier labours to bear fruit, they all bent their best efforts to dissipating whatever came to hand, as though they were simply awaiting the day on which they could see they were going to die. Which is why the oxen, the donkeys, the sheep and goats, the pigs and hens, even the faithful hounds were driven off and went wandering at leisure through the fields where the harvest stood abandoned, not gleaned, not gathered in. Many of them behaved like perfectly rational beings, browsing to their hearts' content all day and at nightfall returning replete to their quarters without any herdsmen in attendance.

Leaving the countryside and returning to the city, what more is there to say but that, what with the inordinate wrath of Heaven and doubtless also to some extent the cruelty of men, between March and July more than a hundred thousand human beings are in all certainty believed to have lost their lives within the walls of Florence: this as a result partly of the sheer inexorability of the plague, partly of the terror possessing the survivors, which prevented them from attending and ministering to the sick in their need? Before the plague struck, who would have believed the city even numbered that many inhabitants? Oh think of all the great palaces, the fine houses and gorgeous mansions that once boasted full households, now bereft of their masters and mistresses, abandoned by all, down to the humblest menial! Imagine all those memorable family names, those vast estates and egregious fortunes left without a legitimate heir! How many gallant men, how many fair women and bright young people whom anybody would have pronounced among the fittest—even physicians as eminent as Galen, Hippocrates, and Aesculapius would have—sat down to breakfast with their families and friends only to find themselves dining that night with their forbears in the next world!

It gives me no pleasure to go raking over all these tribulations, and I propose to make no mention of whatever may suitably be passed over in silence.

WHY EMPIRES FALL

The span of Ibn Khaldûn's life (1332-1406) coincided with the most precarious years of the waning Muslim caliphates. A historian and philosopher uprooted more than a dozen times from cities in Europe, Africa, and the Middle East, Khaldûn was forced from a succession of governmental and academic positions by invasions of Turks and Mongols, in the meantime writing his massive Introduction to History.

Any royal authority must be built upon two foundations. The first is might and group feeling, which finds its expression in soldiers. The second is money, which supports the soldiers and provides the whole structure needed by royal authority. Disintegration befalls the dynasty at these two foundations.

A dynasty can be founded and established only with the help of group feeling. There must be a major group feeling uniting all the group feelings subordinate to it. This (major group feeling) is the family and tribal group feeling peculiar to the ruler. When the natural luxury of royal authority makes its appearance in the dynasty, and when the people who share in the group feeling of the dynasty are humiliated, the first to be humiliated are the members of the ruler's family and his relatives who share with him in the royal name. They are much more humiliated than anyone else. They become sick at heart when they see the ruler firmly established in royal authority. His envy of them then changes to fear for his royal authority. Therefore, he starts to kill and humiliate them and to deprive them of the prosperity and luxury to which they had become in large measure accustomed. They perish, and become few in number.

The ruler thus isolates himself from his family and helpers, those who have natural affection for him. Eventually, they no longer have the coloring of their group feeling. They forget the affection and strength that used to go with it. The authority of the ruling dynasty continues gradually to shrink. The dynasty then often splits into two or three dynasties, depending on its original strength.

Men with a cause, for which they make propaganda, eventually secede. They gain control over border areas and remote regions. There, they are able to make propaganda for their cause and achieve royal authority. As a result, the dynasty splits. As the dynasty shrinks more and more, this process often continues until the center is reached. The inner circle, thereafter, weakens, because luxury undermines it. Occasionally, it lingers on, because it has coloured the souls of its subject people with the habit of subservience and submission for so many long years that no one alive can think back to its beginning and origin. They cannot think of anything except being submissive to the ruler. Therefore, he can dispense with group strength. In order to establish his power, hired soldiers and mercenaries are sufficient. The submissiveness generally found in the human soul helps in this respect. Should anyone think of disobedience or secession—which hardly ever happens—the great mass would disapprove of him and oppose him. Thus, he would not be able to attempt such a thing, even if he should try very hard. (The dynasty), therefore, is safer (than ever) so far as the trouble and destruction that come from groups and tribes are concerned. The dynasty may continue in this condition, but its substance dwindles, like natural heat in a body that lacks nourishment. Eventually, (the dynasty) reaches its destined time.

As for the disintegration that comes through money, it should be known that at the beginning the dynasty has a desert attitude, as was mentioned before. It has the qualities of kindness to subjects, planned moderation in expenditure, and respect for other people's property. It avoids onerous taxation and the display of cunning or shrewdness in the collection of money and the accounting (required) from officials. Nothing at this time calls for extravagant expenditure. Therefore, the dynasty does not need much money.

Later come domination and expansion. Royal authority flourishes. This calls for luxury, which causes increased spending. The expenditure of the ruler, and of the people of the dynasty in general, grows. This (tendency) spreads to the urban population. It calls for increases in soldiers' allowances and in the salaries of the people of the dynasty. Extravagant expenditure mounts. It spreads to the subjects, because people follow the (ways) and customs of the dynasty.

The ruler, then, must impose duties on articles sold in the markets, in order to improve his revenues; he sees the luxury of the urban population testifying to their prosperity, and because he needs the money for the expenditure of his government and the salaries of his soldiers. Habits of luxury, then, further increase. The customs duties no longer pay for them. The dynasty, by this time, is flourishing in its power and its forceful hold over the subjects under its control. Its hand reaches out to seize some of the property of the subjects, either through customs duties, or through commercial transactions, or, in some cases, merely by hostile acts directed against (property holdings), on some pretext or even with none.

At this stage, the soldiers have already grown bold against the dynasty, because it has become weak and senile as far as its group feeling is concerned. (The dynasty) expects that from them, and attempts to remedy and smooth over the situation through generous allowances and much spending for (the soldiers). It cannot get around that.

At this stage, the tax collectors in the dynasty have acquired much wealth, because vast revenues are in their hands and their position has widened in importance for this reason. Suspicions of having appropriated tax money, therefore, attach to them. It becomes common for one tax collector to denounce another, because of their mutual jealousy and envy. One after another is deprived of his money by confiscation and torture. Eventually, their wealth disappears, and they are ruined. The dynasty loses the pomp and magnificence it had possessed through them.

After their prosperity is destroyed, the dynasty goes farther afield and approaches its other wealthy subjects. At this stage, feebleness has already afflicted its former might. (The dynasty) has become too weak to retain its power and forceful hold. The policy of the ruler, at this time, is to handle matters diplomatically by spending money. He considers this more advantageous than the sword, which is of little use. His need for money grows beyond what is needed for expenditure and soldiers' salaries. He never gets enough. Senility affects the dynasty more and more. The people of other regions grow bold against it.

CONSTANTINOPLE, 1453

In the century before the Visigoths breached Rome's walls, then-Emperor Constantine set up a new capitol on top of a town that had once been known as Byzantium. The eastern Roman Empire endured for 1100 years. After fending off a succession of Huns, Lombards, Avars, Slavs, Persians, Bulgars, Franks, and Venetians, the defenders of Eastern Christendom were finally dislodged from Constantine's city by the Ottoman Turks under the command of Mehmed II, whom the Byzantine historians named the Antichrist. The following account comes from a Byzantine noble, Ducas (fl. mid-15th c.), whose baptismal name is unknown.

The Romans and the emperor [Constantine XI] did not know what had happened because the entry of the Turks took place at a distance; indeed, their paramount concern was the enemy before them. The fierce Turkish warriors outnumbered the Romans twenty to one. The Romans, moreover, were not as experienced in warfare as the ordinary Turks. Their attention and concern, therefore, were focused on the Turkish ground attack. Then suddenly arrows fell from above, slaughtering many Romans. When they looked up and saw the Turks, they fled behind the walls. When the tyrant's troops witnessed the rout of the Romans, they shouted with one voice and pursued them inside, trampling upon the wretches and slaughtering them.

The emperor, despairing and hopeless, stood with sword and shield in hand and poignantly cried out, "Is there no one among the Christians who will take my head from me?" He was abandoned and alone. Then one of the Turks wounded him by striking him flush, and he, in turn, gave the Turk a blow. A second Turk delivered a mortal blow from behind and the emperor fell to the earth. They slew him as a common soldier and left him, because they did not know he was the emperor.

Only three Turks perished and all the rest made their way inside. It was the first hour of the day [six a.m.], and the sun had not yet risen. As they entered the City and spread out from the Gate of Charisios to the palace, they slew those who resisted and those who fled. Breaking into the protostrator's [the Emperor's chief horseman] home, they broke open the coffers full of treasures amassed long ago. In so doing, they aroused the noblewomen from their sleep. It was the twenty-ninth day of May, and the morning sleep of the youths and maidens was sweet indeed; they slept unafraid and carefree as they had done yesterday and the day before.

Then a great horde of mounted infidels charged down the street leading to the Great Church [Hagia Sophia]. The actions of both Turks and Romans made quite a spectacle! In the early dawn, as the Turks poured into the City and the citizens took flight, some of the fleeing Romans managed to reach their homes and rescue their children and wives. As they moved, bloodstained, across the Forum of the Bull and passed the Column of the Cross [Forum of Constantine], their wives asked, "What is to become of us?" When they heard the fearful cry, "The Turks are slaughtering Romans within the City's walls," they did not believe it at first. They cursed and reviled the ill omened messenger instead. But behind him came a second, and then a third, and all were covered with blood, and they knew that the cup of the Lord's wrath had touched their lips. Monks and nuns, therefore, and men and women, carrying their infants in their arms and abandoning their homes to anyone who wished to break in, ran to the Great Church. The thoroughfare, overflowing with people, was a sight to behold!

Why were they all seeking refuge in the Great Church? Many years before they had heard from some false prophets that the City was fated to be surrendered to the Turks who would enter with great force, and that the Romans would be cut down by them as far as the Column of Constantine the Great. Afterwards, however, an angel, descending and holding a sword, would deliver the empire and the sword to an unknown man, extremely plain and poor, standing at the Column. "Take this sword," the angel would say, "and avenge the people of the Lord." Then the Turks would take flight and the Romans would follow hard upon them, cutting them down. They would drive them from the City and from the West, and from the East as far as the borders of Persia, to a place called Monodendrion. This was the cause then of the flight into the Great Church. In one hour's time that enormous temple was filled with men and women. There was a throng too many to count, above and below, in the courtyards and everywhere. They bolted the doors and waited, hoping to be rescued by the anonymous savior.

Pillaging, slaughtering, and taking captives on the way, the Turks reached the temple before the termination of the first hour. The gates were barred, but they broke them with axes. They entered with swords flashing and, beholding the myriad populace, each Turk caught and bound his own captive. There was no one who resisted or who did not surrender himself like a sheep. Who can recount the calamity of that time and place? Who can describe the wailing and the cries of the babes, the mothers' tearful screams and the fathers' lamentations? The commonest Turk sought the most tender maiden. The lovely nun, who heretofore belonged only to the one God, was now seized and bound by another master. The rapine caused the tugging and pulling of braids of hair, the exposure of bosoms and breasts, and outstretched arms. The female slave was bound with her mistress, the master with his slave, the archimandrite [abbot] with the doorkeeper, tender youths with virgins, who had never been exposed to the sun and hardly ever seen by their own fathers, were dragged about, forcibly pushed together and flogged. The despoiler led them to a certain spot, and placing them in safekeeping, returned to take a second and even a third prize. The abductors, the avengers of God, were in a great hurry. Within one hour they had bound everyone, the male captives with cords and the women with their own veils. The infinite chains of captives who like herds of kine and flocks of sheep poured out of the temple and the temple sanctuary made an extraordinary spectacle! They wept and wailed and there was none to show them mercy.

What became of the temple treasures? What shall I say and how shall I say it? My tongue is stuck fast in my larynx. I am unable to draw breath through my sealed mouth. In that same hour the dogs hacked the holy icons to pieces, removing the ornaments. As for the chains, candelabra, holy altar coverings, and lamps, some they destroyed and the rest they seized. All the precious and sacred vessels of the holy sacristy, fashioned from gold and silver and other valuable materials, they collected in an instant, leaving the temple desolate and naked; absolutely nothing was left behind.

The frightful day on which the City fell was the Feast Day of the Holy Martyr Theodosia. All these events took place between the first hour of the day and the eighth hour [six a.m. to two p.m.]. Setting aside his suspicions and fears, the tyrant [the Turkish Sultan Mehmed II] made his entry into the City with his viziers and satraps, preceded and followed by his fire eating slaves, all of whom were archers superior to Apollo, youthful Herakleidae eager to challenge ten men. Proceeding to the Great Church, he dismounted from his horse and went inside. He marveled at the sight! When he found a Turk smashing a piece of marble pavement, he asked him why he was demolishing the floor. "For the faith," he replied. He extended his hand and struck the Turk a blow with his sword, remarking "You have enough treasure and captives. The City's buildings are mine." When the tyrant beheld the treasures which had been collected and the countless captives, he regretted his compact. The Turk was dragged by the feet and cast outside half dead. He summoned one of his vile priests who ascended the pulpit to call out his foul prayer. The son of iniquity, the forerunner of Antichrist, ascending the holy altar, offered the prayer.

The morning following the black day on which the utter destruction of our nation took place, the tyrant entered the City and went to the home of the grand duke. The latter came out to greet him and after he had made obeisance, Mehmed went inside. The grand duke's wife was sick in bed. Approaching her bed, the wolf in sheep's clothing addressed her, "Greetings, Mother. Grieve not over the events which have taken place. The Lord's will be done. I will restore to you more than you have lost. Only get well." The grand duke's sons came forward and made obeisance, and when they had expressed their gratitude, Mehmed left to tour the City. The entire City was desolate. Within, neither man nor beast nor fowl was heard to cry out or utter a sound. Only they were left who were too weak to pillage. Many were killed as one dragged away the spoils of another. He who was able seized, and he who was unable to resist, received a mortal blow and succumbed. On the second day, the thirtieth of May, the Turkish troops entered and collected whatever had been abandoned. And the City was desolate, lying dead, naked, soundless, having neither form nor beauty.

ANOTHER BALLADE*
(C. 1461)

François Villon (1431-after 1463)

And whereabouts is Callixtus the Third,
the last to die descended in that name,
who reigned four years as pope? And what occurred
to Alphonse, King of Aragon, or became
of Bourbon's gracious Duke? I ask the same
of Arthur, duke of Brittany, and again
with Charles the Seventh of France with all his fame.
But where now is the greatest—Charlemagne?

What of the Scottish King of whom I heard
that half his face was red, or so they claim,
as amethyst from forehead to his beard?
The famous King of Cyprus, what a shame!
and there's that other one, now what's his name?
But I forget now—the good King of Spain!
Where are they gone, the mighty in their fame?
But where now is the greatest—Charlemagne?

I mustn't maunder on. It's so absurd.
The world is nothing but a cheating game.
None can resist death long but is interred
and none can make provision against its claim.
But just one further question all the same:
Ladislaus, King of Bohemia? Then again
where's his grandfather gone from whom he came?
But where now is the greatest—Charlemagne?

And Guesclin's where, that Breton knight of fame?
And Alençon, the brave Duke lately slain?
The Count of the Auvergne, Dauphin by name?
But where now is the greatest—Charlemagne?

---

* Callixtus III: pope from 1455 to 1458, Alfonso de Borgia, famous for preaching a crusade against the Turks.

Alfonso V: King of Aragon and Naples, a great warrior and patron of the arts. He died in 1458.

Charles, Duke of Bourbon, died in 1456.

Arthur III, Duke of Britanny and Constable of France, died in 1458.

Charles VII: King of France from 1422 to 1461.

James II: King of Scotland, killed in 1460, besieging Roxburgh Castle.

The King of Cyprus was Jean III de Lusignan. He died in 1458.

Ladislaus, King of Bohemia, died in 1457.

Du Guesclin, constable of France under Charles V, a hero in the Hundred Years' War, died in 1380.

The Dauphin d'Auvergene may be Beraud III who died in 1426.

The Duke of Alençon "lately slain" is by a nasty joke Jean II who was not dead but deprived of his lands and titles for treason. Possibly Jean I is intended; in which case he died at the battle of Agincourt.

The whole ballade is extremely ironic since all those mentioned, except in the envoi, died between the writing of *Le Lais* in 1456 and *Le Testament* in 1461.

[DETAIL]

LAST THINGS

Detail from The Seven Deadly Sins and the Four Last Things *(date unknown),*
by Hieronymus Bosch (c. 1450-1516).

PART II

THE FALL OF NATIONS

[PROPHECY WITH DRAWINGS]

OF THE CRUELTY OF MAN

From a section called "Prophecies" in Leonardo da Vinci's (1452-1519) Notebooks. The drawings are studies for the "Battle of Anghiari" which the Florentine Republic commissioned in 1503 as a monumental mural to commemorate victory over the Milanese 63 years earlier, a project for which Leonardo studied the physiognomy of rage in man and beast.

Creatures shall be seen upon the earth who will always be fighting one with another, with very great losses and frequent deaths on either side. These shall set no bounds to their malice; by their fierce limbs a great number of the trees in the immense forests of the world shall be laid level with the ground; and when they have crammed themselves with food it shall gratify their desire to deal out death, affliction, labours, terrors and banishment to every living thing. And by reason of their boundless pride they shall wish to rise towards heaven, but the excessive weight of their limbs shall hold them down. There shall be nothing remaining on the earth or under the earth or in the waters that shall not be pursued and

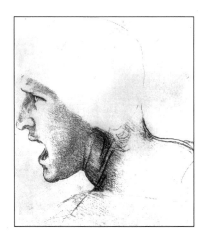

molested or destroyed, and that which is in one country taken away to another; and their own bodies shall be made the tomb and the means of transit of all the living bodies which they have slain. O Earth! what delays thee to open and hurl them headlong into the deep fissures of thy huge abysses and caverns, and no longer to display in the sight of heaven so savage and ruthless a monster?

SAILING TO JERUSALEM

Christopher Columbus (1451-1506), Admiral of the Ocean Sea, undertook his voyages with the firm conviction that the world would end in 1650. Against the indications of his nautical instruments, his study of the Bible convinced him that by sailing west he could reach the Island of Ophir in the East, on which were to be found the mines of Solomon and the garden of Eden. The mines would yield enough gold to finance a Spanish conquest of the Holy Land and Spain's subsequent shepherding of the world toward its transcendent end. In 1502, Columbus sent a succinct outline of this great plan, which he thought he had partly completed, in the form of a letter of dedication of his Book of Prophecies, *to his patrons, Ferdinand and Isabella of Spain.*

LETTER FROM THE ADMIRAL TO THE KING AND QUEEN

Most Christian and noble rulers:

The following is a statement of my proposal for the restoration of the House of God to the Holy Church Militant.

Most eminent rulers: At a very early age I began to navigate upon the seas, a calling that inclines those who pursue it to desire to understand the world's secrets. Such has been my interest for more than forty years, and I have sailed all that can be sailed in our day. I have had business and conversation with learned men among both laity and clergy, Latins and Greeks, Jews and Moslems, and many others of different religions. I prayed to the most merciful Lord concerning my desire, and he gave me the spirit and the intelligence for it. He gave me abundant skill in the mariner's arts, an adequate understanding of the stars, and of geometry and arithmetic. He gave me the mental capacity and the manual skill to draft spherical maps, and to draw the cities, rivers, mountains, islands and ports, all in their proper places.

During this time, I have searched out and studied all kinds of texts: geographies, histories, chronologies, philosophies and other subjects. With a hand that could be felt, the Lord opened my mind to the fact that it would be possible to sail from here to the Indies, and he opened my will to desire to accomplish the project. This was the fire that burned within me when I came to visit Your Highnesses. All who found out about my project denounced it with laughter and ridiculed me. All the sciences which I mentioned above were of no use to me. Quotations of learned opinions were no help. Only Your Majesties had faith and perseverance. Who can doubt that this fire was not merely mine, but also of the Holy Spirit who encouraged me with a radiance of marvelous illumination from his sacred Holy Scriptures.

The Lord purposed that there should be something clearly miraculous in this matter of the voyage to the Indies, so as to encourage me and others in the other matter of the restitution of the House of God to the Holy Church [i.e., the conquest of Jerusalem by a Christian army]. Now I lay aside all of my lifetime experience as a navigator, and my discussions with many people of many lands and cultures. And I lay aside all the sciences and books that I indicated above. I hold only to the sacred Holy Scriptures, and to the interpretations of prophecy by certain devout persons who have spoken on this subject by divine illumination.

I also believe that the Holy Spirit reveals future events not only in rational beings, but also discloses them to us in signs in the sky, in the atmosphere and in animals, whenever it pleases him, as was the case with the ox that spoke in Rome in the days of Julius Caesar.

The Holy Scriptures testify that this world must come to an end. From the creation of the world, or from Adam, until the advent of our Lord Jesus Christ there were five thousand, three hundred and forty-three years, and three hundred and eighteen days, according to the calculation by King Alfonso, which is considered to be the most exact. Following Petrus Aliacus, in the tenth heading of his *Explanation of the Agreement of Astronomy with Biblical and Historical Records*, if we add to these years an additional one thousand, five hundred and one years of waiting, this makes a total of six thousand, eight hundred, forty-five years of waiting for the completion of the age. According to this calculation, only one hundred and fifty years are lacking for the completion of the seven thousand years which would be the end of the world.

Our Savior said that before the consummation of this world, first must be fulfilled all the things that were written by the prophets.

By far the greatest portion of the prophecies of the Holy Scriptures has already been fulfilled. The Scriptures themselves testify to this, and the clear voice of the Holy Church unceasingly bears the same testimony, so that no other witness is needed. But I will speak of a particular prophecy, because it applies particularly to my experience, and it refreshes me and makes me rejoice every moment when I think of it.

Already I pointed out that for the execution of the journey to the Indies, I was not aided by intelligence, by mathematics or by maps. It was simply the fulfillment of what Isaiah had prophesied, and this is what I desire to write in this book, so that the record may remind Your Highnesses, and so that you may rejoice in the other things that I am going to tell you about our Jerusalem upon the basis of the same authority. If you have faith, you may be certain that there will be success also in that other project [the conquest of Jerusalem].

Let Your Highnesses take note of the Gospels, and of the many promises that our Savior made to us, and of the way in which experience has proved them all. Saint Peter stepped out upon the water, and to the extent that his faith remained firm, he walked upon it. Whoever finds so much faith as a grain of mustard seed will be obeyed by the mountains. Knock and it must be opened unto you. No one should be afraid to undertake any project in the name of our Savior, if it is a just cause and if he has the pure intention of his holy service. He aided St. Catherine after he had tested her. Let Your Highnesses remember how short were the funds with which you undertook the project for the Kingdom of Granada.

I said above that much of the prophecies remained to be fulfilled, and I believe that these are great events for the world. I believe that there is evidence that our Lord is hastening these things. This evidence is the fact that the Gospel must now be proclaimed to so many lands in such a short time. The Abbot Joachim [of Fiore], a Calabrian, said that the restorer of the House of Mt. Zion would come out of Spain.

[SEAL]

Columbus' Signature

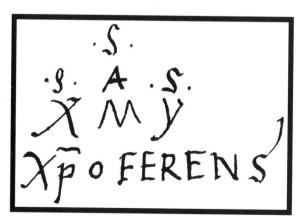

By extrapolating etymologically, Christopher Columbus thought his name signified his mission as the bearer of Christ. He wrote his signature accordingly, as a proof of portentous meaning. The Greek letters are a manuscript abbreviation for χριστόφ ("Christ") + ferens (from the Latin for "to bear").

HISPANIOLA, EARLY 1500S

According to the best current estimates, when Europeans first arrived in the New World, the aggregate population of North and South America stood at somewhere between 50 and 100 million; a century later, after decades of slaughter and disease, the figure had receded to about five to six million. Bartolomé de Las Casas (1484-1576), a Spanish adventurer, took part in the conquest of Cuba and witnessed the first large-scale massacre of the Arawak Indians on the island of Hispaniola (now divided between Haiti and the Dominican Republic). He then renounced his role in the conquests, became a priest, and addressed his Brief Account of the Destruction of the Indies *(published in 1552) to Prince Philip (soon to be Philip II) of Spain.*

The Americas were discovered in 1492, and the first Christian settlements established by the Spanish the following year. It is accordingly forty nine years now since Spaniards began arriving in numbers in this part of the world. They first settled the large and fertile island of Hispaniola [Haiti/Dominican Republic], which boasts six hundred leagues of coastline and is surrounded by a great many other large islands, all of them, as I saw for myself, with as high a native population as anywhere on earth. Of the coast of the mainland, which, at its nearest point, is a little over two hundred and fifty leagues from Hispaniola, more than ten thousand leagues had been explored by 1541, and more are being discovered every day. This coastline, too, was swarming with people and it would seem, if we are to judge by those areas so far explored, that the Almighty selected this part of the world as home to the greater part of the human race.

God made all the peoples of this area, many and varied as they are, as open and as innocent as can be imagined. At the same time, they are among the least robust of human beings: their delicate constitutions make them unable to withstand hard work or suffering and render them liable to succumb to almost any illness, no matter how mild. Even the common people are no tougher than princes or than other Europeans born with a silver spoon in their mouths and who spend their lives shielded from the rigours of the outside world. They are also among the poorest people on the face of the earth; they own next to nothing and have no urge to acquire material possessions. As a result they are neither ambitious nor greedy, and are totally uninterested in worldly power. Their diet is every bit as poor and as monotonous, in quantity and in kind, as that enjoyed by the Desert Fathers. Most of them go naked, save for a loincloth to cover their modesty; at best they may wrap themselves in a piece of cotton material a yard or two square. Most sleep on matting, although a few possess a kind of hanging net, known in the language of Hispaniola as a hammock.

It was upon these gentle lambs, imbued by the Creator with all the qualities we have mentioned, that from the very first day they clapped eyes on them the Spanish fell like ravening wolves upon the fold, or like tigers and savage lions who have not eaten meat for days. The pattern established at the outset has remained unchanged to this day, and the Spaniards still do nothing save tear the natives to shreds, murder them and inflict upon them untold misery, suffering and distress, tormenting, harrying and persecuting them mercilessly. We shall in due course describe some of the many ingenious methods of torture they have invented and refined for this purpose, but one can get some idea of the effectiveness of their methods from the figures alone. When the Spanish first journeyed there, the indigenous population of the island of Hispaniola stood at some three million; today only two hundred survive. The island of Cuba, which extends for a distance almost as great as that separating Valladolid from Rome, is now to all intents and purposes uninhabited; and two other large, beautiful and fertile islands, Puerto Rico and Jamaica, have been similarly devastated. Not a living soul remains today on any of the islands of the Bahamas, which lie to the north of Hispaniola and Cuba, even though every single one of the sixty or so islands in the group, as well as those known as the Isles of Giants and others in the area, both large and small, is more fertile and more beautiful than the Royal Gardens in Seville and the climate is as healthy as anywhere on earth. The native population, which once numbered some five hundred thousand, was wiped out by forcible expatriation to the island of Hispaniola, a policy adopted by the Spaniards in an endeavour to make up losses among the indigenous population of that island. One God-fearing individual was moved to mount an expedition to seek out those who had escaped the Spanish trawl and were still living in the Bahamas and to save their souls by converting them to Christianity, but, by the end of a search lasting three whole years, they had found only the eleven survivors I saw with my own eyes. A further thirty or so islands in the region of Puerto Rico are also now uninhabited and left to go to rack and ruin as a direct result of the same practices. All these islands, which together must run to over two thousand leagues, are now abandoned and desolate.

On the mainland, we know for sure that our fellow-countrymen have, through their cruelty and wickedness, depopulated and laid waste an area which once boasted more than ten kingdoms, each of them larger in area than the whole of the Iberian Peninsula. The whole region, once teeming with human beings, is now deserted over a distance of more than two thousand leagues: a distance, that is, greater than the journey from Seville to Jerusalem and back again.

At a conservative estimate, the despotic and diabolical behaviour of the Christians has, over the last forty years, led to the unjust and totally unwarranted deaths of more than twelve million souls, women and children among them, and there are grounds for believing my own estimate of more than fifteen million to be nearer the mark.

There are two main ways in which those who have travelled to this part of the world pretending to be Christians have uprooted these pitiful peoples and wiped them from the face of the earth. First, they have waged war on them: unjust, cruel, bloody and tyrannical war. Second, they have murdered anyone and everyone who has shown the slightest sign of resistance, or even of wishing to escape the torment to which they have subjected him. This latter policy has been instrumental in suppressing the native leaders, and, indeed, given that the Spaniards normally spare only women and children, it has led to the annihilation of all adult males, whom they habitually subject to the harshest and most iniquitous and brutal slavery that man has ever devised for his fellow-men, treating them, in fact, worse than animals. All the many and infinitely varied ways that have been devised for oppressing these peoples can be seen to flow from one or other of these two diabolical and tyrannical policies.

The reason the Christians have murdered on such a vast scale and killed anyone and everyone in their way is purely and simply greed. They have set out to line their pockets with gold and to amass private fortunes as quickly as possible so that they can then assume a status quite at odds with that into which they were born. Their insatiable greed and overweening ambition know no bounds; the land is fertile and rich, the inhabitants simple, forbearing and submissive. The Spaniards have shown not the slightest consideration for these people, treating them (and I speak from first-hand experience, having been there from the outset) not as brute animals—indeed, I would to God they had done and had shown them the consideration they afford their animals—so much as piles of dung in the middle of the road. They have had as little concern for their souls as for their bodies, all the millions that have perished having gone to their deaths with no knowledge of God and without the benefit of the Sacraments. One fact in all this is widely known and beyond dispute, for even the tyrannical murderers themselves acknowledge the truth of it: the indigenous peoples never did the Europeans any harm whatever; on the contrary, they believed them to have descended from the heavens, at least until they or their fellow-citizens had tasted, at the hands of these oppressors, a diet of robbery, murder, violence, and all other manner of trials and tribulations.

ROME (IV), 1527

European realpolitik *in the 16th century joined Pope Clement VII in military alliance with the French king, Francis I, against Charles V of Spain, whose riposte was the dispatch of an army to punish the political ambition of the papacy at Rome. Among the Spanish troops may have been some of the same men who had pillaged Mexico City six years earlier under the direction of Hernán Cortés. They held Rome hostage for nine months, until they were forced to retreat by an outbreak of plague. Luigi Guicciardini (1478-1551) served as a senior official in Clement's government.*

Meanwhile the rest of the Roman people, as well as the merchants, prelates, courtiers, and foreigners all ran back and forth in great confusion and terror looking for some refuge. Running through the streets as if they were lost, unable to leave Rome because the gates were barred, they entered the strongest places or those they considered the safest. Some took refuge in the Colonna houses, others in those of the Spanish, Flemish, and Germans who had lived for many years in Rome, and many others in the palaces of Cardinals Enckenvoirt, Aracoeli, Siena, Cesarini, and Valle.

Since it is an especially noteworthy fact, I must include here that in this calamity for themselves and for their unlucky city none of those appointed to be officers of the Church made any attempt to cut the bridges or to organize the defense of the walls of Trastevere. They did not, as they should have, resist with all their strength the attack of their cruel enemy or resolve to die manfully defending themselves with weapons in their hands. Instead, running like everyone else, they increased the panic in Rome and gave the enemy confidence of absolute victory.

When the Spanish troops realized that all the defenders had fled and that they were truly in control of the city, they began to capture houses (along with everyone and everything that was in them) and to take prisoners. The Germans, however, were obeying the articles of war and cutting to pieces anyone they came upon (an act that is very necessary in the first hours of a victory). They were quickly persuaded, however, by the Spanish captains that since the city was abandoned by its defenders, and that great riches must have been hidden in it, it would be a grave mistake not to keep alive anyone who might be able to show them where treasures were hidden or give them the names of people outside Rome who would pay their ransoms.

How many courtiers, how many genteel and cultivated men, how many refined prelates, how many devoted nuns, virgins, or chaste wives with their little children became the prey of these cruel foreigners! How many calixes, crosses, statues, and vessels of silver and gold were stolen from the altars, sacristies, and other holy places where they were stored. How many rare and venerable relics, covered with gold and silver, were despoiled by bloody, homicidal hands and hurled with impious derision to the earth. The heads of St. Peter, St. Paul, St. Andrew and many other saints; the wood of the Cross, the Thorns, the Holy Oil, and even consecrated Hosts were shamefully trodden underfoot in that fury.

In the street you saw nothing but thugs and rogues carrying great bundles of the richest vestments and ecclesiastical ornaments and huge sacks full of all kinds of vessels of gold and silver—testifying more to the riches and empty pomp of the Roman curia than to the humble poverty and true devotion of the Christian religion. Great numbers of captives of all sorts were to be seen, groaning and screaming, being swiftly led to makeshift prisons. In the streets there were many corpses. Many nobles lay there cut to pieces, covered with mud and their own blood, and many people only half dead lay miserably on the ground.

My purpose is to show what sad and unlucky ends those governments come to which rule and maintain themselves in a culture of lust, greed, and ambition, rather than in military severity, beloved poverty, and just moderation. I confess that I cannot hold back my tears when I consider what torment and suffering human beings receive from their fellow humans, and how often we are the causes of our own misery and not Fortune (even though the majority of mortals blame her). Nonetheless I will force myself to describe some part of the pitiable events occurring in Rome in the very recent past.

If anyone had been walking through the streets of Rome by day or night, he would have heard not sighs and tearful laments, but the pitiful cries and screams of hapless prisoners coming from every house and building. The grandest nobles, the richest and most refined prelates, cardinals, courtiers, merchants, and Roman citizens who fell into their hands were all treated more cruelly and with less respect in proportion to their rank; and they tortured them with greater thirst for ransom.

Many were suspended by their arms for hours at a time; others were led around by ropes tied to their testicles. Many were branded with hot irons in various parts of their bodies. Some endured extreme thirst; others were prevented from sleeping. A very cruel and effective torture was to pull out their back teeth. Some were made to eat their own ears, or nose, or testicles roasted; and others were subjected to bizarre and unheard of torments that affect me too strongly even to think of them, let alone to describe them in detail.

A priest was shamelessly and cruelly killed because he refused to administer the most holy sacrament to a mule in clerical vestments. I will not describe what happened to the noble and beautiful young matrons, to virgins and nuns, in order not to shame anyone. The majority were ransomed, and anyone can easily imagine for himself what must have happened when these women found themselves in the hands of such lustful people as the Spaniards. Rather than submit to their conquerors, many noble and pure virgins supposedly stabbed themselves or leapt from some high point into the Tiber. I, however, have never heard that anyone has been able to positively identify a woman of such virtue and chastity. This should not be surprising considering how corrupt Rome is at present, how full of abominable vices and entirely lacking in the virtues it possessed in Antiquity.

One cannot imagine therefore an unbearable form of torture that their prisoners did not experience and endure many times for the sake of cruel and insatiable greed. How patiently these torments were borne by refined and delicate prelates and effeminate courtiers, is easy to imagine, if one realizes with what difficulty in good times, they bore, not the ills of the body, but the bite of a fly. And because many of these barbarians feared that their prisoners had not revealed to them all the money and valuables that they had hidden away, they forced their prisoners, even if they were high-ranking nobles, to empty with their own hands the sewers and other disgusting places where human excrement and the like were disposed of. Anyone can imagine how much pain and suffering that must have given to those who had always been accustomed to having their houses, their clothes, their bodies, and especially their boots perfumed with sweet and alluring scents.

The immense riches of the Roman nobility, preserved in their families for many centuries, were destroyed in an hour. The incredible profits that had been accumulated and multiplied unjustly and dishonestly through years of usury, theft, simony, and other immoral means by courtiers and merchants fell in an instant into the hands of these barbarians. But why do I bother to recount the details of various fortunes or possessions that fell in such short time into the hands of these savage foreigners? Everybody knows that money, merchandise, and delicacies from all over Europe and much of the rest of the world came pouring into that city every hour to satisfy the insatiable appetites and the illicit desires of its many licentious prelates and courtiers. Because they had never feared that they might lose their possessions, the Romans were surprised, sacked, and slaughtered with incredible ease and enormous profit.

Those Germans, who had arrived only a short time before with Captain George von Frundsberg, now wore silks and brocades; huge gold chains hung across their chests and shoulders; and their arms were covered with bracelets inset with jewels of enormous value. Dressed up like mock popes and cardinals, they went for pleasure rides through Rome on beautiful hackneys and mules. Their wives and concubines, proud and richly dressed, accompanied them. The women's heads, necks, and breasts were covered with the largest pearls and the most perfect jewels pried from pontifical miters and sacred reliquaries. Their pages and servants had helmets of heavy gold and the barrels of their arquebuses were made of solid gold stripped from the altars and holy places of Rome. It would not have been possible to believe that these were the same people who had crossed the Po a few months before, after the disastrous and bitter death of Signor Giovanni, or entered the province of Romagna. Then they were exhausted, shoeless, and so poorly dressed that some of them were unable to keep even their private parts covered.

By the same token, no one would now recognize the cardinals, patriarchs, archbishops, bishops, protonotaries, generals, provincials, guardians, abbots, vicars, and all the rest of the ridiculous and infinite tribe of modern religious title-holders, who dishonor and burden the Christian religion. Now many of these men wore torn and disgraceful habits, were marked by cuts and bruises all over their bodies from the indiscriminate whippings and beatings they had received. Some had thick and greasy beards. Some had their faces branded; and some were missing teeth; others were without noses or ears. Some were castrated and so depressed and terrified that they failed to show in any way the vain and effeminate delicacy and lasciviousness that they had put on with such excessive energy for so many years in their earlier, happy days.

I will not write of the anguish and confusion that those in Castel Sant' Angelo are enduring. With the pope, there are thirteen cardinals, innumerable prelates, lords, noblewomen, merchants, couriers and soldiers, all in terror and despairing of their safety. Since they are completely surrounded and very carefully watched by their enemies, I have little knowledge of what is going on inside. We can imagine, though (since they know that they cannot escape) that they spend their time blaming Jacopo Salviati, the datary, Signor Renzo, Cardinal Armellini, and perhaps the pontiff himself, in sharp and venomous words for their obvious and multiple mistakes. No doubt it is pointless, but many blame their own past patience; and there are many among them who could not be blamed if they took cruel and fatal vengeance on these men, before the eyes of the Holy Father.

One can easily imagine the anguish and torment of the pope, constantly seeing and hearing such a scourge of punishment raised against himself and against Rome. Like the rest of those under siege, he is suffering in fear that he will soon fall into the hands of cruel enemies, obviously thirsting for his blood. And though he enjoyed great honors and sweet pleasures in the past, now he is paying for them with humiliation and pitiful distress. If he ever considered himself a wise and glorious prince, now he must acknowledge himself to be the most unfortunate and the most abject pontiff who ever lived. And since it is his fault that the Church, Rome, and Italy all find themselves in such extreme danger, we can easily imagine that he often looks toward the sky with tears in his eyes.

[PAINTING]

THE TRIUMPH OF DEATH

(1568-1569)

by Pieter Bruegel, the Elder (c. 1525-1569)

[PORTENTS]

BAD NEWS

An astrologer and physician in southern France, Michel de Nostredame (1503-1566), was reputed to have produced miraculous cures during an outbreak of plague. He adapted his skills in the arcana mundi *to the field of prophecy and wrote his* Oracles *in 1555. His augury found favor at Court, and he was invited to Paris, where he read horoscopes for the children of Catherine de Médici and Henry II of France. One of many of well-known Renaissance traders in the prophetic arts, Nostradamus' talent for obscurity and self-promotion secured him his longevity in the tradition.*

The great famine which I feel approaching, frequently shifting, then becoming universal, will be so great and so long, that one shall come to tear the root from the tree, and the child from the breast.

The great Queen, when she shall see herself vanquished, shall act in excess of masculine courage, on horse-back, she shall pass over a stream quite naked, followed by fire: to her faith she shall do outrage.

The Oriental shall come forth from his seat, to pass the Apennine mountains to see France: he shall pass through the sky, the waters and snow, and shall strike every one with his rod.

The great city shall be indeed desolated, of the inhabitants not one shall remain in it, wall, sex, temple and virgin violated, shall die by iron, fire, plague, cannon.

For a little while the temples of the colors of white and black shall be intermingled of the two: reds and yellows shall take away theirs, blood, earth, pestilence, famine, fire bewitched by water.

The well-to-do shall suddenly be cast down, the world put in trouble by the three brothers. Enemies shall seize a maritime city, famine, fire, blood, pestilence, and the double of all evils.

[SOLILOQUY]

THE DEATH OF KINGS

In his plays and sonnets, William Shakespeare (1564-1616) repeatedly returns to images of all-devouring time—that bald sexton, hasty-footed and voracious, begging alms for oblivion and feeding without remorse upon the works and days of man. None of Shakespeare's characters speaks more poignantly to the subject than Richard II, awaiting the armies of Henry Bolingbroke and his own certain doom. The play was first performed in 1595.

Of comfort no man speak:
Let's talk of graves, of worms and epitaphs;
Make dust our paper and with rainy eyes
Write sorrow on the bosom of the earth,
Let's choose executors and talk of wills:
And yet not so, for what can we bequeath
Save our deposed bodies to the ground?
Our lands, our lives and all are Bolingbroke's,
And nothing can we call our own but death
And that small model of the barren earth
Which serves as paste and cover to our bones.
For God's sake, let us sit upon the ground

And tell sad stories of the death of kings:
How some have been deposed; some slain in war;
Some haunted by the ghosts they have deposed;
Some poison'd by their wives; some sleeping kill'd;
All murder'd: for within the hollow crown
That rounds the mortal temples of a king
Keeps Death his court and there the antic sits,
Scoffing his state and grinning at his pomp,
Allowing him a breath, a little scene,
To monarchize, be fear'd and kill with looks,
Infusing him with self and vain conceit,
As if this flesh which walls about our life
Were brass impregnable, and humour'd thus
Comes at the last and with a little pin
Bores through his castle wall, and farewell king!
Cover your heads and mock not flesh and blood
With solemn reverence: throw away respect,
Tradition, form and ceremonious duty,
For you have but mistook me all this while:
I live with bread like you, feel want,
Taste grief, need friends: subjected thus,
How can you say to me, I am a king?

[SONNET]

HOLY SONNET

John Donne (1572-1631), a poet of the metaphysical school preoccupied with the mortality of the flesh, conceived of the world's end as coincident with his own.

Thou hast made me, And shall thy worke decay?
Repaire me now, for now mine end doth haste,
I runne to death, and death meets me as fast,
And all my pleasures are like yesterday,
I dare not move my dimme eyes any way,
Despaire behind, and death before doth cast
Such terrour, and my febled flesh doth waste
By sinne in it, which it t'wards hell doth weigh;
Onely thou art above, and when towards thee
By thy leave I can looke, I rise againe;
But our old subtle foe so tempteth me,
That not one houre I can my selfe, sustaine;
Thy Grace may wing me to prevent his art
And thou like Adamant draw mine iron heart.

[PORTRAIT]

Corporis hæc Animæ sit Syndon, Syndon Jesu

Amen.

Martin D. scuv. And are to be sould by R R and Ben: ffisher

A few months before his death John Donne, a poet and the dean of St. Paul's Cathedral in London, commissioned a portrait of himself as he expected to appear upon rising from the tomb at the end of time.

THE GREAT JUBILEE

Like the Roman metaphysician Lucretius in the 1st century B.C., the English physician Thomas Browne (1605-1682) placed the end of the world in the natural order of things, no more or less remarkable than the dissolution of any other set of atoms or circumstances. In the Religio Medici *(1643) Browne addresses the leading scientific and theological questions of his day, among them "that general opinion that the world grows near its end."*

Let them not therefore complain of immaturity that die about thirty; they fall but like the whole World, whose solid and well composed substance must not expect the duration and period of its constitution; when all things are completed in it, its age is accomplished; and the last and general fever may as naturally destroy it before six thousand, as me before forty. There is therefore some other hand that twines the thread of life than that of Nature; we are not only ignorant in Antipathies and occult qualities, our ends are as obscure as our beginnings, the line of our days is drawn by night, and the various effects therein by a pencil that is invisible; wherein though we confess our ignorance, I am sure we do not err if we say it is the hand of God.

Were I of Caesar's Religion, I should be of his desires, and wish rather to go off at one blow, than to be sawed in pieces by the grating torture of a disease. Men that look no farther then their outsides think health an appurtenance unto life, and quarrel with their constitutions for being sick; but I that have examined the parts of man, and know upon what tender filaments that fabrick hangs, do wonder that we are not always so; and considering the thousand doors that lead to death do thank my God that we can die but once. 'Tis not only the mischief of diseases, and villainy of poisons, that make an end of us; we vainly accuse the fury of guns, and the new inventions of death; it is in the power of every hand to destroy us, and we are beholding unto everyone we meet, he doth not kill us. There is therefore but one comfort left, that though it be in the power of the weakest arm to take away life, it is not in the strongest to deprive us of death.

[MEMENTO MORI]

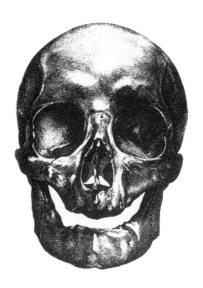

Sir Thomas Browne's skull
norma frontalis

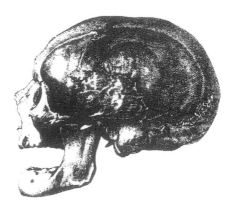

Sir Thomas Browne's skull
norma lateralis

In these moral acceptions, the way to be immortal is to die daily; nor can I think I have the true Theory of death, when I contemplate a skull, or behold a Skeleton, with those vulgar imaginations it casts upon us; I have therefore enlarged that common *Memento mori*, into a more Christian memorandum, *Memento quator novissima*, those four inevitable points of us all, Death, Judgment, Heaven, and Hell.

I believe the World grows near its end, yet is neither old nor decayed, nor shall ever perish upon the ruins of its own principles. As the work of Creation was above Nature, so is its adversary, annihilation; without which the World hath not its end, but its mutation. Now what fire should be able to consume it thus far, without the breath of God, which is the truest consuming flame, my Philosophy cannot inform me. Some believe there went not a minute to the World's creation, nor shall there go to its destruction; those six days, so punc-tually described, make not to them one moment, but rather seem to manifest the method and Idea of the great work of the intellect of God, than the manner how he proceeded in its operation. I cannot dream that there should be at the last day any such Judicial proceeding, or calling to the Bar, as indeed the Scripture seems to imply, and the literal commentators do conceive: for unspeakable mysteries in the Scriptures are often delivered in a vulgar and illus-trative way, and being written unto man, are delivered, not as they truly are, but as they may be understood.

Now to determine the day and year of this inevitable time, is not only con-vincible and statute madness, but also manifest impiety. How shall we inter-pret Elias' six thousand years, or imagine the secret communicated to a Rabbi, which God hath denied unto his Angels? It had been an excellent Quaere [question] to have posed the Devil of Delphos, and must needs have forced him to some strange amphibology [ambiguous discourse]. It hath not only mocked the predictions of sundry Astrologers in ages past, but the prophesies of many melancholy heads in these present, who neither understanding rea-sonably things past or present, pretend a knowledge of things to come: heads ordained only to manifest the incredible effects of melancholy, and to fulfill old prophecies rather than be the authors of new. *In those days there shall come Wars, and rumors of Wars*, to me seems no prophecy, but a constant truth, in all times verified since it was pronounced. That general opinion that the World grows near its end, hath possessed all ages past as nearly as ours. I am afraid that the Souls that now depart, cannot escape that lingering expostulation of the Saints under the Altar, *Quousque, Domine? How long, O Lord?* and groan in the expectation of that great Jubilee.

[CONVERSATION, OVERHEARD]

LONDON (I), 1649

An anonymous account of the beheading of Charles I at London on January 30, 1649, presumably written by a bystander.

The King being come upon the Scaffold, look'd very earnestly on the Block, spake thus (directing his Speech chiefly to Colonel *Thomlinson*)

King. I Shall be very little heard of any body here, I shall therefore speak a word unto you here: Indeed I could hold my peace very well, if I did not think that holding my peace would make some men think, that I did submit to the guilt, as well as to the punishment: but I think it is my duty to God first, and to my Countrey, for to clear my self both as an honest man, and a good King, and a good Christian. I shall begin first with my Innocency. In troth I think it not very needful for me to insist upon this, for all the world knows that I never did begin a War with the two Houses of Parliament, and I call God to witness, to whom I must shortly make an account.

Sirs, If I would have given way to an Arbitrary way, for to have all Laws changed according to the power of the Sword, I needed not to have come here, and therefore I tell you (and I pray God it be not laid to your charge) That I am the Martyr of the People.

Introth Sirs, I shall not hold you much longer, for I will onely say this to you, That intruth I could have desired some little time longer, because that I would have put this that I have said in a little more order, and a little better digested than I have done, and therefore I hope you will excuse me.

I have delivered my Conscience, I pray God that you do take those courses that are best for the good of the kingdom, and your own salvations.

Doctor Juxon. Will your Majesty (though it may be very well known your Majesties affections to Religion, yet it may be expected that you should) say somewhat for the worlds satisfaction?

King. I thank you very heartily (my Lord) for that I had almost forgotten it. Introth Sirs, My Conscience in Religion I think is very well known to all the world, and therefore I declare before you all, That I dye a Christian, according to the profession of the Church of England, as I found it left me by my Father, and this honest man I think will witness it . . . .

Then the King speaking to the Executioner, said, I shall say but very short prayers, and when I thrust out my hands—.

Then the King called to Dr. *Juxon* for his Night-cap, and having put it on, he said to the Executioner, Does my hair trouble you? who desired him to put it all under his Cap, which the King did accordingly, by the help of the Executioner and the Bishop: Then the King turning to Dr. *Juxon*, said, I have a good Cause, and a gracious God on my side.

Doctor Juxon. There is but one Stage more. This Stage is turbulent and troublesome; it is a short one: But you may consider, it will soon carry you a very great way: it will carry you from Earth to Heaven; and there you shall finde a great deal of cordial joy and comfort.

King. I go from a corruptible to an incorruptible Crown; where no disturbance can be, no disturbance in the world.

Doctor Juxon. You are exchanged from a temporal to an eternal Crown, a good exchange.

The King then said to the Executioner, is my hair well: Then the King took off his Cloak and his George, giving his George to Doctor *Juxon*, saying, Remember—. Then the King put off his Dublet, and being in his Waistcoat, put his Cloak on again, then looking upon the Block, said to the Executioner, You must set it fast.

Executioner. It is fast Sir.

King. It might have been a little higher.

Executioner. It can be no higher Sir.

King. When I put out my hands this way, then—.

After that having said two or three words as he stood to Himself with hands and eyes lift up; Immediately stooping down, laid his neck upon the Block: And then the Executioner again putting his Hair under his Cap, the King said Stay for the sign.

Executioner. Yes, I will and it please your Majesty.

And after a very little pause, the King stretching forth his hands, The Executioner at one blow severed his head from his body.

That when the Kings head was cut off, the executioner held it up, and shewed it to the Spectators.

LONDON (II), 1665

The epidemic of plague that ravaged London in 1664-1666 killed 75,000 people, about one sixth of the city's population. Daniel Defoe (1660-1731) published a fictitious account of the calamity, A Journal of the Plague Year, *in 1722, but from the historical records he borrowed the list of public decrees issued 57 years earlier by the city magistrates as a defense against the spreading of the infection.*

It remains to mention now what publick Measures were taken by the Magistrates for the general Safety, and to prevent the spreading of the Distemper, when it first broke out: I shall have frequent Occasion to speak of the Prudence of the Magistrates, their Charity, their Vigilance for the Poor, and for preserving good Order; furnishing Provisions, and the like, when the Plague was encreased, as it afterwards was. But I am now upon the Order and Regulations they published for the Government of infected Families.

I mention'd above shutting of Houses up; and it is needful to say something particularly to that; for this Part of the History of the Plague is very melancholy; *but the most grievous Story must be told.*

ORDERS *Conceived and Published by the* Lord MAYOR *and* Aldermen *of the City of* London, *concerning the Infection of the* Plague. 1665

Notice to be given of the Sickness

THE Master of every House, as soon as any one in his House complaineth, either of Botch, or Purple, or Swelling in any part of his Body, or falleth otherwise dangerously Sick, without apparent Cause of some other Disease, shall give knowledge thereof to the Examiner of Health, within two Hours after the said Sign shall appear.

Sequestration of the Sick

AS soon as any Man shall be found by this Examiner, Chirurgeon or Searcher to be sick of the Plague, he shall the same Night be sequestred in the same House, and in case he be so sequestred, then, though he afterwards die not, the House wherein he sickened, should be shut up for a Month, after the use of the due Preservatives taken by the rest.

Airing the Stuff

FOR Sequestration of the Goods and Stuff of the Infection, their Bedding, and Apparel, and Hangings of Chambers, must be well aired with Fire, and such Perfumes as are requisite within the infected House, before they be taken again to use: This to be done by the Appointment of the Examiner.

Shutting up of the House

IF any Person shall have visited any Man, known to be infected of the Plague, or entred willingly into any known infected House, being not allowed: The House wherein he inhabiteth, shall be shut up for certain Days by the Examiners Direction.

Burial of the Dead

THAT the Burial of the Dead by this Visitation, be at most convenient Hours, always either before Sun-rising, or after Sun-setting, with the Privity of the Church-wardens or Constable, and not otherwise; and that no Neighbours nor Friends be suffered to accompany the Corps to Church, or to enter the House visited, upon pain of having his House shut up, or be imprisoned.

And that no Corps dying of Infection shall be buried, or remain in any Church in time of Common-Prayer, Sermon, or Lecture. And that no Children be suffered at time of burial of any Corps in any Church, Church-yard, or Burying-place to come near the Corps, Coffin, or Grave. And that all the Graves shall be at least six Foot deep.

And further, all publick Assemblies at other Burials are to be forborn during the Continuance of this Visitation.

No infected Stuff to be uttered [marketed]

THAT no Clothes, Stuff, Bedding or Garments be suffered to be carried or conveyed out of any infected Houses, and that the Criers and Carriers abroad of Bedding or old Apparel to be sold or pawned, be utterly prohibited and restrained, and no Brokers of Bedding or old Apparel be permitted to make any outward Shew, or hang forth on their Stalls, Shopboards or Windows towards any Street, Lane, Common-way or Passage, any old Bedding or Apparel to be sold, upon pain of Imprisonment. And if any Broker or other Person shall buy any Bedding, Apparel, or other Stuff out of any infected House, within two Months after the Infection hath been there, his House shall be shut up as Infected, and so shall continue shut up twenty Days at the least.

Every visited House to be marked

THAT every House visited, be marked with a red Cross of a Foot long, in the middle of the Door, evident to be seen, and with these usual printed Words, that is to say, *Lord have Mercy upon us*, to be set close over the same Cross, there to continue until lawful opening of the same House.

Hackney-Coaches

THAT care be taken of Hackney-Coach-men, that they may not (as some of them have been observed to do) after carrying of infected Persons to the *Pest-House*, and other Places, be admitted to common use, till their Coaches be well aired, and have stood unemploy'd by the Space of five or six Days after such Service.

Care to be had of unwholsome Fish or Flesh, and of musty Corn

THAT special care be taken, that no stinking Fish, or unwholesome Flesh, or musty Corn, or other corrupt Fruits, of what Sort soever be suffered to be sold about the City, or any part of the same.

That the Brewers and Tippling-houses be looked unto, for musty and unwholsome Casks.

That no Hogs, Dogs, or Cats, or tame Pigeons, or Conies, be suffered to be kept within any part of the City, or any Swine to be, or stray in the Streets or Lanes, but that such Swine be impounded by the Beadle or any other Officer, and the Owner punished according to Act of Common-Council, and that the

Dogs be killed by the Dog-killers appointed for that purpose.

Plays

THAT all Plays, Bear-Baitings, Games, singing of Ballads, Buckler-play, or such like Causes of Assemblies of People, be utterly prohibited, and the Parties offending severely punished by every Alderman in his Ward.

Tipling-Houses

THAT disorderly Tipling in Taverns, Ale-houses, Coffe-houses, and Cellars be severely looked unto, as the common Sin of this Time, and greatest occasion of dispersing the Plague. And that no Company or Person be suffered to remain or come into any Tavern, Ale-house, or Coffe-house to drink after nine of the Clock in the Evening, according to the antient Law and Custom of this City, upon the Penalties ordained in that Behalf.

Sir *John Lawrence*   Sir *George Waterman*
Lord Mayor.   Sir *Charles Doe*. Sheriffs.

[CUNICULARII]

PROOF

In the early 1700s William Whiston (1667-1752), Sir Isaac Newton's successor as Lucasian Professor of Mathematics at Cambridge University, drew up a list of 99 "proofs" that the end of the age was at hand. Many of these were quite general. For example, "Signals" 46 and 65 portend that "Wickedness should be vastly encreas'd beyond Measure of former Ages" and that "Incontinency, Vileness, and Wickedness, shall be increased upon the Earth." Much more specific was Whiston's interpretation of the rumor that an illiterate farm woman of Surrey, named Mary Toft, had given birth to a litter of rabbits. To the torrent of pamphlets and editorials written for and against the truth of the story, Whiston added his impassioned conviction that here was fulfillment of a prophecy to be found in the apocryphal Fourth Book of Ezra, that at the end of the ages "women shall bring forth monsters." The artist, William Hogarth (1697-1764), satirized the learned Anatomists and Surgeons who agreed with Whiston.

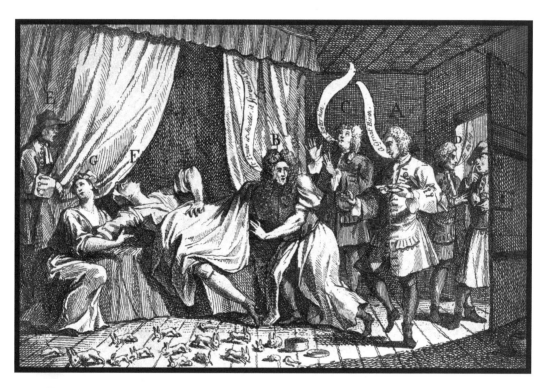

William Hogarth, Cunicularii, or the Wise Men of Godliman in Consultation

SINNERS IN THE HANDS OF AN ANGRY GOD

Minister of the Congregationalist church in Northampton, Massachusetts and the most formidable American theologian of his day, Jonathan Edwards (1703-1758) breathed intellectual fire into a movement known as the Great Awakening, a spiritual fervor that swept the colonies in the 1730s and 1740s. Edwards' sermons insist on the immediate presence of the Almighty, and the abject and tenuously provisional position of lowly humans. He thought that the tribulations described in the Book of Revelation were well under way and that the millennium would begin sometime near the year 2000.

Deuteronomy 32.35—Their foot shall slide in due time.

In this verse is threatened the vengeance of God on the wicked unbelieving Israelites, God's visible people; that notwithstanding all God's wonderful works, yet remained void of counsel and under all the cultivations of heaven, brought forth bitter and poisonous fruit.

The expression that I have chosen for my text, *their foot shall slide in due time*, seems to imply the following things relating to the punishment and destruction that these wicked Israelites were exposed to.

That they were always exposed to destruction; as one that stands or walks in slippery places is always exposed to fall. The same is expressed, Psalm 73.18: "Surely thou didst set them in slippery places; thou castedst them down into destruction."

Another thing implied is, that they are liable to fall of themselves, without being thrown down by the hand of another; as he that stands or walks on slippery ground needs nothing but his own weight to throw him down.

That the reason why they are not fallen already, and do not fall now, is only that God's appointed time is not come. For it is said that when that due time, or appointed time comes, *their feet shall slide*. Then they shall be left to fall, as they are inclined by their own weight. God will not hold them up in these slippery places any longer.

The observation from the words that I would now insist upon is this.

There is nothing that keeps wicked men at any one moment out of hell, but the mere pleasure of God.

By the mere pleasure of God, I mean his sovereign pleasure, his arbitrary will, restrained by no obligation, hindered by no manner of difficulty.

There is no want of power in God to cast wicked men into hell at any moment. Men's hands cannot be strong when God rises up: the strongest have no power to resist him, nor can any deliver out of his hands.

He is not only able to cast wicked men into hell, but he can most easily do it. Sometimes an earthly prince meets with a great deal of difficulty to subdue a rebel, that has found means to fortify himself, and has made himself strong by the number of his followers. But it is not so with God. There is no fortress that is any defence against the power of God. Though hand join in hand, and vast multitudes of God's enemies combine and associate themselves, they are easily broken in pieces: they are as great heaps of light chaff before the whirlwind; or large quantities of dry stubble before devouring flames. We find it easy to tread on and crush a worm that we see crawling on the earth; so it is easy for us to cut or singe a slender thread that any thing hangs by; thus easy is it for God, when he pleases, to cast his enemies down to hell.

The reason why they do not go down to hell at each moment, is not because God, in whose power they are, is not then very angry with them; as angry, as he is with many of those miserable creatures that he is now tormenting in hell, and do there feel and bear the fierceness of his wrath. Yea, God is a great deal more angry with great numbers that are now on earth; yea, doubtless, with many that are now in this congregation, that, it may be, are at ease and quiet, than he is with many of those that are now in the flames of hell.

So that it is not because God is unmindful of their wickedness, and does not resent it, that he does not let loose his hand and cut them off. God is not altogether such a one as themselves, though they may imagine him to be so. The wrath of God burns against them; their damnation does not slumber; the pit is prepared; the fire is made ready; the furnace is now hot; ready to receive them; the flames do now rage and glow.

It is no security to wicked men for one moment, that there are no visible means of death at hand. It is no security to a natural man, that he is now in health, and that he does not see which way he should now immediately go out of the world by any accident, and that there is no visible danger in any respect in his circumstances. The manifold and continual experience of the world in all ages, shows that this is no evidence that a man is not on the very brink of eternity, and that the next step will not be into another world. The unseen, unthought of ways and means of persons' going suddenly out of the world are innumerable and inconceivable. Unconverted men walk over the pit of hell on a rotten covering, and there are innumerable places in this covering so weak that they will not bear their weight, and these places are not seen. The arrows of death fly unseen at noonday; the sharpest sight cannot discern them. God has so many different, unsearchable ways of taking wicked men out of the world and sending them to hell, that there is nothing to make it appear, that God had need to be at the expense of a miracle, or go out of the ordinary course of his providence, to destroy any wicked man, at any moment.

This that you have heard is the case of every one of you that are out of Christ. That world of misery, that lake of burning brimstone, is extended abroad under you. There is the dreadful pit of the glowing flames of the wrath of God; there is hell's wide gaping mouth open; and you have nothing to stand upon, nor any thing to take hold of. There is nothing between you and hell but the air; it is only the power and mere pleasure of God that holds you up.

You probably are not sensible of this; you find you are kept out of hell, but do not see the hand of God in it; but look at other things, as the good state of your bodily constitution, your care of your own life, and the means you use for your own preservation. But indeed these things are nothing; if God should withdraw his hand, they would avail no more to keep you from falling, than the thin air to hold up a person that is suspended in it.

Your wickedness makes you as it were heavy as lead, and to tend downwards with great weight and pressure towards hell; and if God should let you go, you would immediately sink and swiftly descend and plunge into the bottomless gulf, and your healthy constitution, and your own care and prudence, and best contrivance, and all your righteousness, would have no more influence to uphold you and keep you out of hell, than a spider's web would have to stop a falling rock.

The bow of God's wrath is bent, and the arrow made ready on the string, and justice bends the arrow at your heart, and strains the bow, and it is nothing but the mere pleasure of God, and that of an angry God, without any promise or obligation at all, that keeps the arrow one moment from being made drunk with your blood.

Thus are all you that never passed under a great change of heart, by the mighty power of the Spirit of God upon your souls; all that were never born again, and made new creatures, and raised from being dead in sin, to a state of new, and before altogether unexperienced light and life, (however you may have reformed your life in many things, and may have had religious affections, and may keep up a form of religion in your families and closets, and in the houses of God, and may be strict in it,) you are thus in the hands of an angry God; it is nothing but his mere pleasure that keeps you from being this moment swallowed up in everlasting destruction.

How dreadful is the state of those that are daily and hourly in danger of this great wrath and infinite misery! But this is the dismal case of every soul in this congregation that has not been born again, however moral and strict, sober and religious, they may otherwise be. Oh that you would consider it, whether you be young or old! There is reason to think, that there are many in this congregation now hearing this discourse, that will actually be the subjects of this very misery to all eternity. We know not who they are, or in what seats they sit, or what thoughts they now have. It may be they are now at ease, and hear all these things without much disturbance, and are now flattering themselves that they are not the persons; promising themselves that they shall escape. If we knew that there was one person, and but one, in the whole congregation, that was to be the subject of this misery, what an awful thing it would be to think of! If we knew who it was, what an awful sight would it be to see such a person! How might all the rest of the congregation lift up a lamentable and bitter cry over him! But alas! Instead of one, how many is it likely will remember this discourse in hell! And it would be a wonder, if some that are now present should not be in hell in a very short time, before this year is out. And it would be no wonder if some persons, that now sit here in some seats of this meeting-house in health, and quiet and secure, should be there before to-morrow morning.

LISBON, 1755

On November 1, 1755, at 9:40 a.m., one of the largest earthquakes ever recorded shook the city of Lisbon into a heap of rubble. Sixty thousand people perished in the first shocks of the earthquake and the subsequent tidal wave and fire. Tens of thousand of these died on their knees, celebrating mass for All Saint's Day, when their churches collapsed on top of them. Two unidentified correspondents of the Gentleman's Magazine *sent accounts to their readers in London.*

[I]

Lisbon harbour, Nov. 19, 1755

On Saturday the 1st instant [this month], about half an hour past 9 o'clock, I was retired to my room after breakfast, when I perceived the house begin to shake, but did not apprehend the cause, but as I saw the neighbours about me all running down stairs, I also made the best of my way, and by the time I had crossed the street, and got under the piazzas of some low houses, it was darker than the darkest night I ever saw, and continued so for about a minute, occasioned by the clouds of dust from the falling of houses on all sides. After it cleared up, I ran into a large square adjoining, the palace to the west, the street I lived in to the north, the river to the south, and the custom-house and warehouses to the east. But this dismal earthquake had such an influence upon the sea and river, that the water rose, in about ten minutes, several yards perpendicular; in that time I ran up into my room, got my hat and wig, and cloak, locked up my doors, and returned; but being alarmed with a cry that the sea was coming in, all people crowded forward to run to the hills, I among the rest, with Mr. Wood and family.

We went near two miles through the streets, climbing over ruins of churches, houses, & c. stepping over hundreds of dead and dying people, killed by the falling of buildings; carriages, chaises and mules, lying all crushed to pieces; and that day being a great festival in their church, and just at the time of celebrating their first mass, thousands were assembled in the churches, the major part of whom were killed, for the great buildings, particularly those built on any eminence, suffered the most damage, very few of the churches or convents having escaped. Before we got quite clear of the buildings another shock came, just as I was passing over the ruins of a great church, but I happily got clear before any more tumbled down. We staid near two hours in an open field; but a dismal scene it was, the people howling and crying, and the sacrament going about to dying persons; so I advised, as the best, to return to the square, near our own house, and there wait the event, which we did immediately; but by the time we got there, the city was in flames in several distant parts at the same time.

This compleated the destruction of the city, for in the terror all persons were, no attempt was made to stop it, and the wind was very high, so that it was communicated from one street to another by the flakes of fire driven by the winds: It raged with great violence for eight days, and this in the principal and most thronged parts of the city. The people being fled into the fields half naked, the fire consumed all sorts of merchandize, household goods, and wearing apparel, so that hardly any thing is left to cover people's nakedness, and they live in tents in the fields. If the fire had not happened, people would have recovered their effects out of the ruins, but this has made such a scene of desolation and misery, as words cannot describe. The king's palaces in the city are totally destroyed. The tobacco and other warehouses, with the cargoes of three Brazil fleets, shared the same fate; in short, there are few goods left in the whole city.

I believe few outstanding debts will be recovered, for those who have lost all cannot pay; and it is much to be feared others who saved any effects will appear as poor as they can, to evade parting with any thing. All law-suits are ended, for the records and papers are destroyed; would to God that was the only loss, it would rather be an happiness to the kingdom than otherwise.

After we returned to the square, we got our books and every thing valuable out of the house; but when the fire increased and surrounded us, some of our people left us, and got aboard ship, and left us with every thing in the square. When the fire reached the houses on the north, the wind blew upon us large showers of fire like hail, and it became so hot and full of smoke, that we were almost blind.

I then dragged what I could down to the water side, with the assistance of one man, in order to get a boat and carry them off. At last I procured one by bidding a high price, but could only get on board a portmanteau, with books, papers, and a few other things, leaving all the rest to providence; we got on board a Portuguese vessel. The shocks continued daily till Sunday last; about three o'clock in the afternoon we had one which made the ship tremble, but have not perceived any since. The fire lasted as long, smothered and breaking out at times; I believe it is now quite extinguished. It is computed upwards of 50,000 souls perished in Lisbon.

[II]

Lisbon, Nov. 19

What chiefly contributed to the destruction of the city was the narrowness of the streets. It is not to be express'd by human tongue how dreadful and how awful it was to enter the city after the fire was abated, and looking upwards one was struck with terror in beholding frightful pyramids of ruined fronts, some inclining one way, some another; then, on the contrary, one was struck with horror in beholding dead bodies by six or seven in a heap, crush'd to death, half buried and half burnt; and if one went through the broad places or squares, nothing to be met with but people bewailing their misfortunes, wringing their hands, and crying the world is at an end. If you go out of the city, you behold nothing but barracks or tents made with canvass or ship's sails, where the poor inhabitants lye.

The king the 4th day gave orders for soldiers to be posted at all the passable avenues of the city, to hinder persons robbing the deserted houses, and orders were given to suffer masters of houses to save what they could; and in going out every one was examined and strictly searched: Horse and dragoons were posted on the roads to stop any body who seemed inclined to run away into the neighbouring countries, particularly labouring men and artificers. Thieves were apprehended, who being found with goods on them, and no body appearing to own them, were condemned and hung the next day, for which purpose gallows were erected in the most conspicuous parts of the city.

[SATIRE]

DR. PANGLOSS VISITS LISBON

The Lisbon earthquake of 1755 inspired heated debate among Enlightenment philosophers. Rousseau and his followers held that "everything happens for the best," that if we only knew the underlying causes of events, no matter how terrible they might appear at the time, eventually they would reveal themselves to have a salutary effect in the grand scheme of a cosmos based on Reason. Rousseau wrote a letter to Voltaire (1694-1778) explaining the earthquake along these philosophical lines. Voltaire answered politely, and then, a few years later, wrote Candide, *a tract mocking Rousseau's naive theodicy in the characters of Dr. Pangloss and his student Candide.*

When they [Candide and Pangloss] had recovered a little, they walked toward Lisbon. They still had some money left, with which they hoped to save themselves from starvation, after having escaped from the storm.

They had scarcely set foot in the city, mourning the death of their benefactor, when they felt the earth tremble beneath them. The sea boiled up in the harbor and smashed the vessels lying at anchor. Whirlwinds of flame and ashes covered the streets and squares, houses collapsed, roofs were thrown onto foundations and the foundations crumbled; thirty thousand inhabitants of all ages and both sexes were crushed beneath the ruins.

The sailor whistled, swore and said, "I'll get something out of this."

"What can be the sufficient reason for this phenomenon?" said Pangloss.

"This is the end of the world!" cried Candide.

The sailor immediately rushed into the midst of the wreckage, braved death to find money, found some, took it with him, got drunk and, after sobering up a little, bought the favors of the first willing girl he met in the ruins of the destroyed houses, amid the dead and dying. But Pangloss pulled him by the sleeve and said to him, "You're behaving badly, my friend: you're not respecting universal reason, you've chosen a bad time for this."

"By the blood of Christ! I'm a sailor and I was born in Batavia: I've walked on the crucifix four times during four stays in Japan—you've come to the right man with your universal reason!"

Candide had been wounded by several splinters of stone. He was lying in the street, covered with rubble. He said to Pangloss, "Alas! Get me some wine and oil: I'm dying."

"This earthquake is nothing new," replied Pangloss. "The town of Lima in America felt the same shock last year. Same causes, same effects; there is surely a vein of sulphur running underground from Lima to Lisbon."

"Nothing is more likely," said Candide, "but, in the name of God, bring me some oil and wine!"

"What do you mean, likely?" retorted the philosopher. "I maintain that the fact is demonstrated."

Candide lost consciousness, and Pangloss brought him a little water from a nearby fountain.

The next day, having found a little food as they slipped through the ruins, they recovered some of their strength. Then they worked like the others to help those inhabitants who had escaped death. Some of the citizens they assisted gave them as good a dinner as was possible in such a disaster. The meal was sad, it is true. The hosts wet their bread with their tears, but Pangloss comforted them by assuring them that things could not have been otherwise: "For," he said, "all is for the best. For if there's a volcano at Lisbon, it couldn't be anywhere else. For it's impossible for things not to be where they are. For all is well."

A little man in black, an officer of the Inquisition, who was sitting beside him, spoke up politely and said, "Apparently you don't believe in original sin, sir; *for* if all is for the best, there can be no fall or punishment."

"I humbly beg Your Excellency's pardon," replied Pangloss still more politely, "for the fall of man, and his curse, were necessary components of the best of all possible worlds."

"Then you don't believe in free will, sir?" said the officer.

"Excuse me, Your Excellency," said Pangloss, "but freedom can subsist with absolute necessity, for it was necessary that we be free; for, after all, a determined will—"

Pangloss was in the middle of his sentence when the officer nodded to his armed attendant, who was pouring him out a glass of port, or Oporto wine.

After the earthquake had destroyed three-quarters of Lisbon, the wise men of the country could think of no more effective way of avoiding total ruin than giving the populace a fine auto-da-fé. It was decided by the University of Coimbra that the sight of several people being slowly burned with great ceremony was an infallible means of preventing the earth from quaking.

They had therefore arrested a Biscayan convicted of marrying the godmother of his godchild, and two Portuguese who had taken the pork from the outside of their chicken before eating it; and, after dinner, Dr. Pangloss and his disciple Candide were bound and taken away, one for having spoken, the other for having listened with an air of approval. They were separated and each was placed in an extremely cool room where no one was ever bothered by the sun. A week later they were both dressed in sanbenitos and paper miters. Candide's miter and sanbenito bore painted flames, pointed downward, and devils without tails or claws; but Pangloss's devils had claws and tails, and his flames were upright. Thus attired, they walked in a procession and heard a deeply moving sermon, followed by beautiful polyphonic music. Candide was flogged in time with the singing, the Biscayan and the two men who had refused to eat pork were burned, and Pangloss was hanged, although this was not customary. That same day the earth shook again, with a terrible uproar.

Terrified, bewildered, frantic, covered with blood, quivering all over, Candide said to himself, "If this is the best of all possible worlds, what are the others like? I wouldn't complain if it were just that I'd been flogged: the Bulgars flogged me too. But my dear Pangloss, the greatest of philosophers—did I have to see you hanged, without knowing why? . . . "

ESSAKA, 1755

Between 1500 and the 1860s nine-and-a-half million Africans were forcibly transported across the Atlantic to work as slaves in the New World. About 40 percent of these went to Brazil, another 40 percent to the Caribbean, and the remainder divided between Spain's American possessions and the United States. Olaudah Equiano (c. 1745-1797), an Igbo prince from Benin, was one of those sent to the Caribbean. He traveled widely with his owner, received an education, and was freed. He settled in England and became a popular lecturer for the abolitionist cause. His autobiography, The Interesting Narrative of the Life of Olaudah Equiano, or Gustavus Vassa, the African *(1789), was enormously popular in England and the United States, running through nine editions in five years.*

That part of Africa, known by the name of Guinea, to which the trade of slaves is carried on, extends along the coast above 3,400 miles, from Senegal to Angola, and includes a variety of kingdoms. Of these the most considerable is the kingdom of Benin, both as to the extent and wealth, the richness and culture of the soil, the power of its king, and the number and warlike disposition of its inhabitants. It is situated nearly under the line, and extends along the coast about 170 miles, but runs back into the interior of Africa to a distance hitherto, I believe, unexplored by any traveller; and seems only terminated at length by the empire of Abyssinia [Ethiopia], near 1,500 miles from its beginning. This kingdom is divided into many provinces or districts; in one of the most remote and fertile of which, named Essaka, situated in a charming fruitful vale, I was born, in the year 1745. The distance of this province from the capital of Benin and the sea coast must be very considerable: for I had never heard of white men or Europeans, nor of the sea; and our subjection to the king of Benin was little more than nominal. Every transaction of the government, as far as my slender observation extended, was conducted by the chiefs or elders of the place. The manners and government of a people who have little commerce with other countries, are generally very simple; and the history of what passes in one family or village, may serve as a specimen of the whole nation.

One day, when all our people were gone out to their work as usual, and only I and my sister were left to mind the house, two men and a woman got over our walls, and in a moment seized us both; and without giving us time to cry out, or to make any resistance, they stopped our mouths and ran off with us into the nearest wood. Here they tied our hands, and continued to carry us as far as they could, till night came on, when we reached a small house, where the robbers halted for refreshment and spent the night. We were then unbound, but were unable to take any food; and being quite overpowered by fatigue and grief, our only relief was some sleep, which allayed our misfortune for a short time.

All the nations and people I had hitherto passed through resembled our own in their manners, customs, and language: but I came at length to a country, the inhabitants of which differed from us in all these particulars. I was very much struck with this difference, especially when I came among a people who did not circumcise, and who ate without washing their hands. They cooked their provisions also in iron pots, and had European cutlasses and cross bows, which were unknown to us; and fought with their fists among themselves. Their women were not so modest as ours, for they ate, drank, and slept with their men. But, above all, I was amazed to see no sacrifices or offerings among them. In some of those places the people ornamented themselves with scars, and likewise filed their teeth very sharp. They sometimes wanted to ornament me in the same manner, but I would not suffer them; hoping that I might sometime be among a people who did not thus disfigure themselves, as I thought they did. At last I came to the banks of a large river, covered with canoes, in which the people appeared to live, with their household utensils, and provisions of all kinds. I was beyond measure astonished at this, as I had never before seen any water larger than a pond or a rivulet: and my surprise was mingled with no small fear when I was put into one of these canoes, and we began to paddle and move along the river. We continued going on thus till night; and when we came to land, and made fires on the banks, each family by themselves, some dragged their canoes on shore, others cooked in theirs, and laid in them all night. Thus I continued to travel, both by land and by water, through different countries and various nations, till at the end of six or seven months after I had been kidnapped, I arrived at the sea coast.

The first object that saluted my eyes when I arrived on the coast was the sea, and a slave ship, which was then riding at anchor, and waiting for its cargo. These filled me with astonishment, that was soon converted into terror, which I am yet at a loss to describe, and much more the then feelings of my mind when I was carried on board. I was immediately handled and tossed up to see if I was sound, by some of the crew; and I was now persuaded that I had got into a world of bad spirits, and that they were going to kill me. Their complexions too, differing so much from ours, their long hair, and the language they spoke which was very different from any I had ever heard, united to confirm me in this belief. Indeed such were the horrors of my views and fears at the moment, that if ten thousand worlds had been my own, I would have freely parted with them all to have exchanged my condition with the meanest slave in my own country. When I looked round the ship too, and saw a large furnace of copper boiling and a multitude of black people, of every description, chained together, every one of their countenances expressing dejection and sorrow, I no longer doubted of my fate; and, quite overpowered with horror and anguish, I fell motionless on the deck, and fainted. When I recovered a little, I found some black people about me, who I believed were some of those who brought me on board, and had been receiving their pay: they talked to me in order to cheer me, but all in vain. I asked them if we were not to be eaten by those white men with horrible looks, red faces, and long hair.

Soon after this the blacks who brought me on board went off, and left me abandoned to despair. I now saw myself deprived of all chance of returning to my native country, or even the least glimpse of gaining the shore, which I now considered as friendly; and I even wished for my former slavery, in preference to my present situation, which was filled with horrors of every kind, still heightened by my ignorance of what I was to undergo. I was not long suffered to indulge my grief. I was soon put down under the decks, and there I received such a salutation in my nostrils as I had never experienced in my life: so that, with the loathsomeness of the stench, and with my crying together, I became so sick and low that I was not able to eat, nor had I the least desire to taste any thing. I now wished for the last friend, death, to relieve me; but soon, to my grief, two of the white men offered me eatables; and, on my refusing to eat, one of them held me fast by the hands, and laid me across, I think, the windlass, and tied my feet, while the other flogged me severely. I had never experienced any thing of this kind before, and although, not being used to the water, I naturally feared that element the first time I saw it, yet nevertheless, could I have got over the nettings, I would have jumped over the side, but I could not; and besides the crew used to watch us very closely, who were not chained down to the decks, lest we should leap into the water. I have seen some of these poor African prisoners most severely cut for attempting to do so, and hourly whipped for not eating. This indeed was often the case with myself. In a little time after, amongst the poor chained men, I found some of my own nation, which in a small degree gave ease to my mind. I inquired of these what was to be done with us. They gave me to understand we were to be carried to these white people's country to work for them. I was then a little revived, and thought if it were no worse than working, my situation was not so desperate. But still I feared I should be put to death, the white people looked and acted, as I thought, in so savage a manner; for I had never seen among any people such instances of brutal cruelty: and this is not only shewn towards us blacks, but also to some of the whites themselves. One white man in particular I saw, when we were permitted to be on deck, flogged so unmercifully with a large rope near the foremast, that he died in consequence of it; and they tossed him over the side as they would have done a brute. This made me fear these people the more; and I expected nothing less than to be treated in the same manner. I could not help expressing my fearful apprehensions to some of my countrymen; I asked them if these people had no country, but lived in this hollow place, the ship. They told me they did not, but came from a distant one. "Then," said I, "how comes it, that in all our country we never heard of them?" They told me, because they lived so very far off. I then asked, where their women were: had they any like themselves. I was told they had. "And why," said I, "do we not see them?" They answered, because they were left behind. I asked how the vessel could go. They told me they could not tell; but that there was cloth put upon the masts by the help of the ropes I saw, and then the vessel went on; and the white men had some spell or magic they put in the water, when they liked, in order to stop the vessel. I was exceedingly amazed at this account, and really thought they were spirits. I therefore wished much to be from amongst them, for I expected they would sacrifice me; but my wishes were in vain, for we were so quartered that it was impossible for any of us to make our escape.

While we stayed on the coast I was mostly on deck. At last, when the ship, in which we were, had got in all her cargo, they made ready with many fearful noises, and we were all put under deck, so that we could not see how they managed the vessel.

But this disappointment was the least of my grief. The stench of the hold, while we were on the coast, was so intolerably loathsome, that it was dangerous to remain there for any time, and some of us had been permitted to stay on the deck for the fresh air; but now that the whole ship's cargo were confined together, it became absolutely pestilential. The closeness of the place, and the heat of the climate, added to the number in the ship, being so crowded that each had scarcely room to turn himself, almost suffocated us. This produced copious perspirations, so that the air soon became unfit for respiration, from a variety of loathsome smells, and brought on a sickness among the slaves, of which many died, thus falling victims to the improvident avarice, as I may call it, of their purchasers. This deplorable situation was again aggravated by the galling of the chains, now become insupportable; and the filth of necessary tubs, into which the children often fell, and were almost suffocated. The shrieks of the women, and the groans of the dying, rendered it a scene of horror almost inconceivable. Happily, perhaps, for myself, I was soon reduced so low here that it was thought necessary to keep me almost continually on deck; and from my extreme youth, I was not put in fetters. In this situation I expected every hour to share the fate of my companions, some of whom were almost daily brought upon deck at the point of death, and I began to hope that death would soon put an end to my miseries. Often did I think many of the inhabitants of the deep much more happy than myself; I envied them the freedom they enjoyed, and as often wished I could change my condition for theirs.

YORKTOWN, 1781

*When the British general Lord Charles Cornwallis (1738-1805) surren-
dered his sword and his army to George Washington at Yorktown,
Virginia, in October, 1781, the American band played "The World Turned
Upside Down," a jaunty and popular tune of the time heard on that occasion as a not-so-oblique commentary on the reversal of colonial fortune.
Those American Tories who had taken the side of the British, roughly a
third of the citizenry, forfeited their property and left the country as exiles.
Cornwallis' letter to Sir Henry Clinton (the British officer still in command
in New York City), and the exchange of letters with Washington (arranging the terms of surrender), announce an end of a world in the language of
18th-century civility.*

Sir,—I have the mortification to inform your excellency that I have been forced
to give up the posts of York and Gloucester, and to surrender the troops under
my command, by capitulation on the 19th instant [this month], as prisoners of
war to the combined forces of America and France.

I never saw this post in a very favorable light; but when I found I was to be
attacked in it, in so unprepared a state, by so powerful an army and artillery,
nothing but the hopes of relief would have induced me to attempt its defense;
for I would either have endeavored to escape to New York by rapid marches
from the Gloucester side, immediately on the arrival of General Washington's
troops at Williamsburgh, or, I would, notwithstanding the disparity of numbers, have attacked them in the open field, where it might have been just possible that fortune would have favored the gallantry of the handful of troops
under my command. But, being assured by your excellency's letters that every
possible means would be tried by the navy and army to relieve us, I could not
think myself at liberty to venture upon either of those desperate attempts; therefore, after remaining for two days in a strong position in front of this place, in
hopes of being attacked, upon observing that the enemy were taking measure
which could not fail of turning my left flank in a short time, and receiving on

the second evening your letter of the 24th of September, that the relief would fail about the 5th of October, I withdrew within the works on the night of the 29th of September, hoping by the labor and firmness of the soldiers to protect the defence until you could arrive. Everything was to be expected from the spirit of the troops; but every disadvantage attended their labor, as the work was to be continued under the enemy's fire.

Our works in the mean time were going to ruin; and not having been able to strengthen them by abattis, nor in any other manner than by a light fraizing, which the enemy's artillery were demolishing wherever they fired. Our numbers had been diminished by the enemy's fire, but particularly by sickness; and the strength and spirit of those in the works were much exhausted by the fatigue of constant watching and unremitting duty. Under all these circumstances, I thought it would have been wanton and inhuman to the last degree to sacrifice the lives of this small body of gallant soldiers, who had ever behaved with so much fidelity and courage, by exposing them to an assault which, from the numbers and precautions of the enemy, could not fail to succeed. I therefore proposed to capitulate, and I have the honor to enclose to your excellency the copy of the correspondence between General Washington and me on that subject, and the terms of the capitulation agreed upon. I sincerely lament that better could not be obtained; but I have neglected nothing in my power to alleviate the misfortune and distress of both officers and soldiers. The men are well clothed and provided with necessaries, and I trust will be regularly supplied by the means of the officers that are permitted to remain with them. The treatment in general that we have received from the enemy since our surrender has been perfectly good and proper; but the kindness and attention that has been showed to us by the French officers in particular, their delicate sensibility of our situation, their generous and pressing offer of money, both public and private, to any amount, has really gone beyond what I can possibly describe, and will, I hope, make an impression on the breast of every officer, whenever the fortune of war should put any of them into our power.

I transmit returns of our killed and wounded; the loss of seamen and townspeople was likewise considerable. I trust your excellency will please to hasten the return of the *Bonetta*, after landing her passengers, in compliance with the article of capitulation.

Lieutenant-Colonel Abercrombie will have the honor to explain this despatch, and is well qualified to explain to your excellency every particular relating to our past and present situation.

I have the honor to be, &c.

CORNWALLIS.

[CORRESPONDENCE]

Earl Cornwallis's letter to General Washington, dated York, in Virginia, October 17th, 1781.

Sir,—I propose a cessation of hostilities for twenty-four hours, and that two officers may be appointed by each side, to meet at Mr. Moore's house, to settle terms for the surrender of the posts of York and Glocester.

I have the honor to be, &c.

CORNWALLIS.

General Washington's letter to Earl Cornwallis, dated Camp Before York, 17th October, 1781.

My Lord,—I have the honor of receiving your lordship's letter of this date.

An ardent desire to save the effusion of human blood will readily incline me to listen to such terms for the surrender of your posts and garrisons at York and

Gloucester as are admissible.

I wish, previous to the meeting of the commissioners, that your lordship's proposals, in writing, may be sent to the American lines; for which purpose a suspension of hostilities during two hours from the delivery of this letter will be granted.

I have the honor to be, &c.

G. WASHINGTON.

Earl Cornwallis's letter to General Washington, dated York, in Virginia, 17th Day of October, 1781, Half-past 4 p.m.

Sir,—I have this moment been honored with your Excellency's letter, dated this day.

The time limited for sending my answer will not admit of entering into the detail of articles; but the basis of my proposals will be, that the garrisons of York and Gloucester shall be prisoners of war, with the customary honors; and for the convenience of the individuals which I have the honor to command, that the British shall be sent to Britain and the Germans to Germany, under engagement not to serve against France, America, or their allies, until released or regularly exchanged: That all arms and public stores shall be delivered up to you; but that the usual indulgence of side-arms to officers, and of retaining private property, shall be granted to officers and soldiers: And that the interest of several individuals, in civil capacities and connected with us, shall be attended to.

If your excellency thinks that a continuance of the suspension of hostilities will be necessary to transmit your answer, I shall have no objection to the hour that you may propose.

I have the honor to be, &c.

CORNWALLIS.

General Washington's letter to Earl Cornwallis, dated Camp Before York, 18th October, 1781.

My Lord,—To avoid unnecessary discussions and delays, I shall at once, in answer to your lordship's letter of yesterday, declare the general basis upon which a definitive treaty of capitulation may take place.

The garrisons of York and Gloucester, including the seamen as you propose, shall be received prisoners of war. The condition annexed, of sending the British and German troops to the parts of Europe to which they respectively belong is inadmissible: Instead of this, they will be marched to such parts of the country as can most conveniently provide for their subsistence; and the benevolent treatment of the prisoners, which is invariably observed by the Americans, will be extended to them. The same honors will be granted to the surrendering army as were granted to the garrison of Charlestown.

The shipping and boats in the two harbors, with all their guns, stores, tackling, furniture, and apparel, shall be delivered in their present state to an officer of the navy appointed to take possession of them.

The artillery arms, accoutrements, military chest, and public stores of every denomination shall be delivered, unimpaired, to the heads of the departments to which they respectively belong.

The officers shall be indulged in retaining their side-arms; and the officers and soldiers may preserve their baggage and effects, with this reserve, that property taken in the country will be reclaimed.

Your lordship will be pleased to signify your determination, either to accept or reject the proposals now offered, in the course of two hours from the delivery of this letter, that commissioners may be appointed to digest the articles of capitulation, or a renewal of hostilities may take place.

I have the honor to be, &c.

G. WASHINGTON.

Earl Cornwallis's letter to General Washington, dated York, in Virginia, 18th October, 1781.

Sir,—I agree to open a treaty of capitulation upon the basis of the garrisons of York and Gloucester, including seamen, being prisoners of war, without annexing the condition of their being sent to Europe; but I expect to receive a compensation in the articles of capitulation for the surrender of Gloucester in its present state of defence.

I shall in particular desire that the sloop of war *Bonetta* may be left entirely at my disposal from the hour that the capitulation is signed, to receive an aide-de-camp to carry my despatches to Sir Henry Clinton. Such soldiers as I may think proper to send as passengers in her, to be manned with fifty of her own crew, and to be permitted to sail, without examination, when my despatches are ready; engaging, on my part, that the ship shall be brought back and delivered to you if she escapes the dangers of the sea; that the crew and soldiers shall be accounted for in future exchanges; that she shall carry off no officer without your consent, nor public property of any kind; and I shall likewise desire, that the traders and inhabitants may preserve their property, and that no person may be punished or molested for having joined the British troops.

If you choose to proceed to negotiations on these grounds, I shall appoint two field officers of my army to meet two officers from you, at any time or place that you may think proper, to digest the articles of capitulation.

I have the honor to be, &c.

CORNWALLIS.

Paris (I), 1793

The French King Louis XVI having been executed in January 1793, the more radical forces of the French Revolution seized the government by mid-summer. Robespierre, Carnot and their followers set up the Committee of Public Safety and took over the Committee on General Security, the two institutions through which they administered the Reign of Terror. On September 17 the Jacobins issued the Law of Suspects, and shortly thereafter the French Queen, Marie Antoinette (1755-1793), and 17,000 other leading figures associated with the French monarchy, died on the guillotine. Seven hours and 45 minutes before her execution, the Queen wrote to her husband's sister.

October 16th, [1793] at half-past four in the morning.

It is to you, my sister, that I am writing for the last time. I have just been sentenced to death, but not one that is shameful, for it is only shameful for criminals, and I am going to rejoin your brother. Innocent like him, I hope I shall exhibit the same firmness that he did in his last moments. I am calm, as well I may be with a clear conscience, though it upsets me deeply to have to leave my children. You know I lived only for them and for you, my good and loving sister. In the kindness of your heart you sacrificed everything to be with us, and now I leave you in a terrible situation. It was only during the trial that I learned my daughter had been separated from you. Alas! Poor child. I dare not write to her, since she would not receive the letter. I do not know whether this will reach you. Even so, I send them both my blessing through you, and hope that one day when they are older, they will be reunited with you in your tender care.

If only they will go on thinking in the way I tried to teach them, which is that right principles and devotion to duty are the basis of life, and that mutual love and confidence will bring its own happiness. I hope my daughter is now old enough to realize it is her duty to help her brother to grow up, and give him advice as an elder sister; and that he in his turn will try to help her and show affection; that whatever situation they find themselves in, they will look to us as an example, and only find happiness in being together. How much consolation we have gained from our mutual affection in our troubles. Again, in happier times, to share one's enjoyment with a friend is to double it, and where can one find a more loving or intimate friend than in one's own family? I hope that my son will never forget his father's last words which I now repeat: He must never try to avenge our death!

I have to mention something that is extremely painful to me, because I know how much the boy must have hurt you. Forgive him, my dear sister: remember how young he is, and how easy it is to put words into his mouth and make him say what is wanted. I hope that one day he will realize the value of your kindness towards them both.

All that is left is for me to tell you my last thoughts. I should have liked to have written them before the start of the trial, but quite apart from the fact I was not allowed to write, things have happened so quickly I should not have had time.

I die in the Catholic, Apostolic and Roman religion, that of my father in which I was brought up, and which I have always professed. Having no hope of spiritual consolation, and I do not even know if there are still priests of this religion here, and feeling that even if there were they would run great risks in coming to me, I sincerely ask God's pardon for all transgressions that I may have committed since my birth. I hope that He will at last hear my prayers, as well as my wish for a long time now that in His mercy and goodness He will receive my soul.

I ask all those known to me, especially you, my sister, to forgive me any unhappiness which I may have caused them. I forgive my enemies the wrong they have done me. I say farewell now to my aunts, brothers and sisters. I used to have friends. Among my greatest regrets in dying is the thought of being separated for ever from them, and of their unhappiness. Let them know, at least, that I thought of them till the end.

Goodbye, my good and loving sister. I hope this letter will reach you. Think of me always. I send you my deepest love, and also to my poor, dear children. It is unbearable to leave them for ever. Goodbye. Goodbye. I must now attend to my spiritual duties. Since I am not free perhaps they will bring me a nonjuring priest. If that is so, I shall have nothing to do with him and treat him like a complete stranger.

[MENU]

Marie Antoinette's Last Supper

Vermicelli

Soup

[CHRONOMETRY]

Legislating the End of Time

The revolutionary government of France declared that time ended on September 22, 1792, nine hours 18 minutes and 30 seconds after midnight—the autumnal equinox and the day after the republic was founded. Article I, section 2, of the "Decree on the Era," issued November 24, 1793 (4 Frimaire, year 2), states flatly that "The common era is abolished." The French government reasoned that the old means of keeping time were corrupted by the past and it was "necessary to engrave with a new and pure chisel the history of reborn France." Article I, section 11, declared that the day now consisted of ten hours. Each hour contained 100 decimal minutes. With the ticking of every decimal second (100 each minute) the good citizen would be reminded of the revolution. The decree instructs professors, teachers, fathers, and mothers to instill this system of timekeeping in the young. The clock-face below is included as a foldout diagram in the decree, along with detailed instructions that good citizens should use to recalibrate their senses of time.

[GRAPHIC]

Convention nationale [France, 1792-95], "Calendrier de la République française, précédé du décret su l'ère . . . ," du 4 frimaire An 2, (Paris, Year 2, [1793])

PARIS (II), 1794

Friend of liberty and of the sans culotte mob, Maximilien-François-Marie-Isidore de Robespierre (1758-1794) began his political career in 1789 at the age of 30. Five years later, trapped in the same mechanism of Revolution that he had turned into a Reign of Terror, he made his last speech to the National Convention on 8 Thermidor (July 26, 1794), two days before he died on the guillotine.

Citizens, let others paint flattering pictures, I am about to utter useful truths. What is the foundation of this odious system of terror and calumny against me? Am I dreaded by patriots? I, who have destroyed the factions leagued against them. Am I dreaded by the National Convention? What am I without it ? Who, like me, has defended the Convention at the peril of his life ? Who devoted himself for its preservation, when execrable factions conspired its ruin? Who devoted himself to its glory when the vile hirelings of tyranny preached atheism in its name, when so many others witnessed in silence the crimes of their accomplices, and seemed only awaiting the signal of bloodshed, to destroy the people's representatives? Let others note the absurdity of the charges brought against us, I see only their atrocity. You will render an account to public opinion—monsters that you are—for your frightful perseverance in prosecuting the people's friends. You, who endeavour to rob me of the esteem of the National Convention; that esteem which is the most glorious reward that man could reap from his labours, and which I have neither usurped nor surprised, but which I have been forced to conquer. To a sensitive mind there is no punishment equal to that of being regarded as an object of detestation by those whom he reveres and loves. To make him appear so is the greatest of crimes.

They call me tyrant. If I were a tyrant they would grovel at my feet. I should cover them with gold, I should permit them to accomplish every crime, and they would be grateful. If I were a tyrant, the kings whom we have vanquished, far from denouncing me (what tender interest they take in our liberty!) would proffer me their guilty aid. What tyrant protects me? To what faction do I belong?

To yourselves! You—the people!—principles! That is the faction to which I belong, and against which all the guilty are in league. What am I whom they accuse? The slave of liberty, the living martyr of the Republic, the victim no less than the enemy of crime. Were it not for my conscience, I should be the most miserable of men.

In accusing me of aspiring to the dictatorship, they accuse me also of all their iniquities and of all the severities which the safety of the country rendered necessary. To the nobles they said, it is Robespierre alone who proscribes you. To the patriots they said, he wishes to save the nobles. To the priests they said, it is he alone who persecutes you; were it not for him, you would be at peace and triumphant. To the fanatics they said, it is he who destroys religion. To persecuted patriots they said, it is he alone who orders this or who will not prevent it. To others they said, your fate depends upon him alone. They took particular pains to show that the revolutionary tribunal was a tribunal of blood created by me alone, and which I ruled absolutely that I might crush both the well disposed and the guilty; for they wished to raise up against me enemies of all kinds. This cry filled the prisons.

But at all times my influence has been limited to pleading the cause of the country before its representatives, and to appeal to the tribunal of public opinion. I have combated the factions that menaced you, I have endeavoured to uproot their system of corruption and of disorder, which I look upon as the sole obstacle to the establishment of the Republic. It has appeared to me that the Republic could only be established upon the eternal basis of morality.

Wherefore do those who recently said that we were walking upon volcanoes believe that we today walk upon roses? Those who tell you that the establishment of the Republic is so facile an enterprise deceive you. Your victories are spoken of with an academic frivolity which would make one believe that they had cost our heroes neither blood nor toil. We shall not subdue Europe by rhetorical phrases, nor even by warlike exploits, but by the wisdom of our laws, by the majesty of our deliberations, and by the greatness of our characters. Liberty has no other guarantee than the strict observance of those principles of universal morality which you have proclaimed. What matters it to us to have vanquished kings, if we ourselves are vanquished by the vices which produce tyranny.

People, remember that if in the Republic justice reigns not with absolute power, and if the name does not signify love of equality and patriotism, liberty is only an empty name! People, thou who art feared, who art flattered, and who art despised; thou, a recognized sovereign, always treated as a slave, remember that where justice reigns not, the passions of magistrates rule, and the people has changed its fetters but not its destiny.

Thus the villains impose on us the necessity of betraying the people or of being styled dictator. Shall we subscribe to this necessity? No, let us defend the people even at the risk of being esteemed by them. Let our enemies reach the scaffold by the path of crime; we will seek it by the path of virtue!

"A Tremendous, Unformed Spectre"

Appalled by the anarchy loosed on the world by the French Revolution, Edmund Burke (1729-1797), the Irish writer and statesman distinguished by his long career in the British Parliament, voiced his objections to the Jacobin government in France in a language that could as easily have described the Beast of the Apocalypse. He set forth his opinion, in a series of letters addressed to "a former member of Parliament," in the last year of his life.

My Dear Sir,—

Deprived of the old government, deprived in a manner of all government, France, fallen as a monarchy, to common speculators might have appeared more likely to be an object of pity or insult, according to the disposition of the circumjacent powers, than to be the scourge and terror of them all: but out of the tomb of the murdered monarchy in France has arisen a vast, tremendous, unformed spectre, in a far more terrific guise than any which ever yet have overpowered the imagination and subdued the fortitude of man. Going straight forward to its end, unappalled by peril, unchecked by remorse, despising all common maxims and all common means, that hideous phantom overpowered those who could not believe it was possible she could at all exist. Those who bow to the enemy abroad will not be of power to subdue it at home. It is impossible not to observe, that, in proportion as we approximate to the poisonous jaws of anarchy, the fascination grows irresistible. In proportion as we are attracted towards the focus of illegality, irreligion, and desperate enterprise, all the venomous and blighting insects of the state are awakened into life. The promise of the year is blasted and shriveled and burned up before them. Our most salutary and most beautiful institutions yield nothing but dust and smut; the harvest of our law is no more than stubble. It is in the nature of these eruptive diseases in the state to sink in by fits and reappear. But the fuel of the malady remains, and in my opinion is not in the smallest degree mitigated in its malignity, though it waits the favorable moment of a freer communication with the source of regicide to exert and to increase its force.

Is it that the people are changed, that the commonwealth cannot be protected by its laws? I hardly think it. On the contrary, I conceive that these things happen because men are not changed, but remain always what they always were; they remain what the bulk of us ever must be, when abandoned to our vulgar propensities, without guide, leader, or control: that is, made to be full of a blind elevation in prosperity; to despise untried dangers; to be overpowered with unexpected reverses; to find no clew in a labyrinth of difficulties; to get out of a present inconvenience with any risk of future ruin; to follow and to bow to fortune; to admire successfull, though wicked enterprise, and to imitate what we admire; to contemn the government which announces danger from sacrilege and regicide whilst they are only in their infancy and their struggle, but which finds nothing that can alarm in their adult state, and in the power and triumph of those destructive principles. In a mass we cannot be left to ourselves. We must have leaders. If none will undertake to lead us right, we shall find guides who will contrive to conduct us to shame and ruin.

We are in a war of a *peculiar* nature. It is not with an ordinary community, which is hostile or friendly as passion or as interest may veer about,— not with a state which makes war through wantonness, and abandons it through lassitude. We are at war with a system which by its essence is inimical to all other governments, and which makes peace or war as peace and war may best contribute to their subversion. It is with an armed doctrine that we are at war. It has, by its essence, a faction of opinion and of interest and of enthusiasm in every country. To us it is a colossus which bestrides our Channel. It has one foot on a foreign shore, the other upon the British soil. Thus advantaged, if it can at all exist, it must finally prevail. Nothing can so completely ruin any of the old governments, ours in particular, as the acknowledgment, directly or by implication, of any kind of superiority in this new power. A government of the nature of that set up at our very door has never been hitherto seen or even imagined in Europe. What our relation to it will be cannot be judged by other relations. Instead of the religion and the law by which they were in a great politic communion with the Christian world, they have constructed their republic on three bases, all fundamentally opposite to those on which the communities of Europe are built. Its foundation is laid in Regicide, in Jacobinism, and in Atheism; and it has joined to those principles a body of systematic manners which secures their operation.

I call a commonwealth *Regicide* which lays it down as a fixed law of Nature and a fundamental right of man, that all government, not being a democracy, is an usurpation,—that all kings, as such, are usurpers, and, for being kings, may and ought to be put to death, with their wives, families, and adherents. The commonwealth which acts uniformly upon those principles, and which, after abolishing every festival of religion, chooses the most flagrant act of a murderous regicide treason for a feast of eternal commemoration, and which forces all her people to observe it,— this I call *Regicide by Establishment.*

Jacobinism is the revolt of the enterprising talents of a country against its property. When private men form themselves into associations for the purpose of destroying the preexisting laws and institutions of their country,—when they secure to themselves an army by dividing amongst the people of no property the estates of the ancient and lawful proprietors,—when a state recognizes those acts,—when it does not make confiscations for crimes, but makes crimes for confiscations,—when it has its principal strength and all its resources in such a violation of property,—when it stands chiefly upon such a violation, massacring by judgments, or otherwise, those who make any struggle for their old legal government, and their legal, hereditary, or acquired possessions,—I call this Jacobinism by Establishment.

I call it *Atheism by Establishment*, when any state, as such, shall not acknowledge the existence of God as a moral governor of the world,—when it shall offer to Him no religious or moral worship,—when it shall abolish the Christian religion by a regular decree,—when it shall persecute, with a cold, unrelenting, steady cruelty, by every mode of confiscation, imprisonment, exile, and death, all its ministers,—when it shall generally shut up or pull down churches,—when the few buildings which remain of this kind shall be opened only for the purpose of making a profane apotheosis of monsters whose vices and crimes have no parallel amongst men, and whom all other men consider as objects of general detestation and the severest animadversion of law. When, in the place of that religion of social benevolence and of individual self-denial, in mockery of all religion, they institute impious, blasphemous, indecent theatric rites, in honor of their vitiated, perverted reason, and erect altars to the personification of their own corrupted and bloody republic,—when schools and seminaries are founded at public expense to poison mankind, from generation to generation, with the horrible maxims of this impiety,—when, wearied out with incessant martyrdom, and the cries of a people hungering and thirsting for religion, they permit it only as a tolerated evil,—I call this *Atheism by Establishment*.

MALTHUSIANISM

In 1798 the British economist Thomas Robert Malthus (1766-1834) consulted his data and statistical regressions and concluded that most human beings wage a futile battle against starvation. His theory of overpopulation added the weight of the emerging sciences to the tradition of apocalyptic prophecy.

I have mentioned some cases where population may permanently increase without a proportional increase in the means of subsistence. But it is evident that the variation in different states, between the food and the numbers supported by it, is restricted to a limit beyond which it cannot pass. In every country, the population of which is not absolutely decreasing, the food must be necessarily sufficient to support, and to continue, the race of labourers.

Other circumstances being the same, it may be affirmed that countries are populous according to the quantity of human food which they produce, and happy according to the liberality with which that food is divided, or the quantity which a day's labour will purchase. Corn countries are more populous than pasture countries, and rice countries more populous than corn countries. The lands in England are not suited to rice, but they would all bear potatoes; and Dr. Adam Smith observes that if potatoes were to become the favourite vegetable food of the common people, and if the same quantity of land was employed in their culture as is now employed in the culture of corn, the country would be able to support a much greater population, and would consequently in a very short time have it.

The happiness of a country does not depend, absolutely, upon its poverty or its riches, upon its youth or its age, upon its being thinly or fully inhabited, but upon the rapidity with which it is increasing, upon the degree in which the yearly increase of food approaches to the yearly increase of an unrestricted population. This approximation is always the nearest in new colonies, where the knowledge and industry of an old state operate on the fertile unappropriated land of a new one. In other cases, the youth or the age of a state is not in this respect of very great importance. It is probable that the food of Great Britain is divided in as great plenty to the inhabitants, at the present period, as it was two thousand, three thousand, or four thousand years ago. And there is reason to believe that the poor and thinly inhabited tracts of the Scotch Highlands are as much distressed by an overcharged population as the rich and populous province of Flanders.

Were a country never to be overrun by a people more advanced in arts, but left to its own natural progress in civilization; from the time that its produce might be considered as an unit, to the time that it might be considered as a million, during the lapse of many hundred years, there would not be a single period when the mass of the people could be said to be free from distress, either directly or indirectly, for want of food. In every state in Europe, since we have first had accounts of it, millions and millions of human existences have been repressed from this simple cause; though perhaps in some of these states an absolute famine has never been known.

Famine seems to be the last, the most dreadful resource of nature. The power of population is so superior to the power in the earth to produce subsistence for man, that premature death must in some shape or other visit the human race. The vices of mankind are active and able ministers of depopulation. They are the precursors in the great army of destruction; and often finish the dreadful work themselves. But should they fail in this war of extermination, sickly seasons, epidemics, pestilence, and plague, advance in terrific array, and sweep off their thousands and ten thousands. Should success be still incomplete, gigantic inevitable famine stalks in the rear, and with one mighty blow levels the population with the food of the world.

[ETCHING]

THE RAVAGES OF WAR

(1810-1814)

by Francisco de Goya (1746-1828)

THE LAST MAN

By the end of the 18th century scientists had come to agree that the odd designs encased in ancient rock formations were the meager remains of myriad forms of prehistoric animals. Mary Shelley (1797-1851) seized on the implication for the human species in her novel, The Last Man, *published in 1826. She projects her story into the 21st century and a final epidemic of plague, and she leaves her hero, Lionel Verney, in the year 2100, the sole survivor of the human race, wandering among the ruins of Rome.*

Have any of you, my readers, observed the ruins of an anthill immediately after its destruction? At first it appears entirely deserted of its former inhabitants; in a little time you see an ant struggling through the upturned mould; they reappear by twos and threes, running hither and thither in search of their lost companions. Such were we upon earth, wondering aghast at the effects of pestilence. Our empty habitations remained, but the dwellers were gathered to the shades of the tomb.

As the rules of order and pressure of laws were lost, some began with hesitation and wonder to transgress the accustomed uses of society. Palaces were deserted, and the poor man dared at length, unreproved, intrude into the splendid apartments, whose very furniture and decorations were an unknown world to him. It was found, that, though at first the stop put to all circulation of property, had reduced those before supported by the factitious wants of society to sudden and hideous poverty, yet when the boundaries of private possession were thrown down, the products of human labour at present existing were more, far more, than the thinned generation could possibly consume. To some among the poor this was matter of exultation. We were all equal now; magnificent dwellings, luxurious carpets, and beds of down, were afforded to all. Carriages and horses, gardens, pictures, statues, and princely libraries, there were enough of these even to superfluity; and there was nothing to prevent each from assuming possession of his share. We were all equal now; but near at hand was an equality still more levelling, a state where beauty and strength, and wisdom, would be as vain as riches and birth. The grave yawned beneath us all, and its prospect prevented any of us from enjoying the ease and plenty which in so awful a manner was presented to us.

Where could we turn, and not find a desolation pregnant with the dire lesson of example? The fields had been left uncultivated, weeds and gaudy flowers sprung up,—or where a few wheat-fields shewed signs of the living hopes of the husbandman, the work had been left halfway, the ploughman had died beside the plough; the horses had deserted the furrow, and no seedsman had approached the dead; the cattle unattended wandered over the fields and through the lanes; the tame inhabitants of the poultry yard, baulked of their daily food, had become wild—young lambs were dropt in flower-gardens, and the cow stalled in the hall of pleasure. Sickly and few, the country people neither went out to sow nor reap; but sauntered about the meadows, or lay under the hedges, when the inclement sky did not drive them to take shelter under the nearest roof. Many of those who remained, secluded themselves; some had laid up stores which should prevent the necessity of leaving their homes;—some deserted wife and child, and imagined that they secured their safety in utter solitude. Such had been Ryland's plan, and he was discovered dead and half-devoured by insects, in a house many miles from any other, with piles of food laid up in useless superfluity.

London did not contain above a thousand inhabitants; and this number was continually diminishing. Most of them were country people, come up for the sake of change; the Londoners had sought the country. The busy eastern part of the town was silent, or at most you saw only where, half from cupidity, half from curiosity, the warehouses had been more ransacked than pillaged: bales of rich India goods, shawls of price, jewels, and spices, unpacked, strewed the floors. In some places the possessor had to the last kept watch on his store, and died before the barred gates. The massy portals of the churches swung creaking on their hinges; and some few lay dead on the pavement. The wretched female, loveless victim of vulgar brutality, had wandered to the toilet of high-born beauty, and, arraying herself in the garb of splendour, had died before the mirror which reflected to herself alone her altered appearance. Women whose delicate feet had seldom touched the earth in their luxury, had fled in fright and horror from their homes, till, losing themselves in the squalid streets of the metropolis, they had died on the threshold of poverty.

The hunger of Death was now stung more sharply by the diminution of his food: or was it that before, the survivors being many, the dead were less eagerly counted? Now each life was a gem, each human breathing form of far, O! far more worth than subtlest imagery of sculptured stone; and the daily, nay, hourly decrease visible in our numbers, visited the heart with sickening misery. This summer extinguished our hopes, the vessel of society was wrecked, and the shattered raft, which carried the few survivors over the sea of misery, was riven and tempest tost. Man existed by twos and threes; man, the individual who might sleep, and wake, and perform the animal functions; but man, in himself weak, yet more powerful in congregated numbers than wind or ocean; man, the queller of the elements, the lord of created nature, the peer of demi-gods, existed no longer.

Farewell to the patriotic scene, to the love of liberty and well earned meed of virtuous aspiration!—farewell to crowded senate, vocal with the councils of the wise, whose laws were keener than the sword blade tempered at Damascus!—farewell to kingly pomp and warlike pageantry; the crowns are in the dust, and the wearers are in their graves!—farewell to the desire of rule, and the hope of victory; to high vaulting ambition, to the appetite for praise, and the craving for the suffrage of their fellows! The nations are no longer! No senate sits in council for the dead; no scion of a time honoured dynasty pants to rule over the inhabitants of a charnel house; the general's hand is cold, and the soldier has his untimely grave dug in his native fields, unhonoured, though in youth. The market-place is empty, the candidate for popular favour finds none whom he can represent. To chambers of painted state farewell!—To midnight revelry, and the panting emulation of beauty, to costly dress and birth-day shew, to title and the gilded coronet, farewell!

Farewell to the giant powers of man,—to knowledge that could pilot the deep-drawing bark through the opposing waters of shoreless ocean,—to science that directed the silken balloon through the pathless air,—to the power that could put a barrier to mighty waters, and set in motion wheels, and beams, and vast machinery, that could divide rocks of granite or marble, and make the mountains plain!

[POEM]

OZYMANDIAS

(1818)

Percy Bysshe Shelley (1792-1822)

I met a traveler from an antique land
Who said: Two vast and trunkless legs of stone
Stand in the desert . . . Near them, on the sand,
Half sunk, a shattered visage lies, whose frown,
And wrinkled lip, and sneer of cold command,
Tell that its sculptor well those passions read
Which yet survive, stamped on these lifeless things,
The hand that mocked them, and the heart that fed:
And on the pedestal these words appear:
"My name is Ozymandias, king of kings:
Look on my works, ye Mighty, and despair!"
Nothing beside remains. Round the decay
Of that colossal wreck, boundless and bare
The lone and level sands stretch far away.

[TREATY]

NEW ECHOTA, 1835

The Treaty of New Echota, named for a town in the Cherokee nation in Georgia, was drawn up in 1835 for the purpose of evicting the Cherokees from their ancestral land. It was endorsed by 350 of the 17,000-member tribe. The Cherokee leadership argued against the encroachment upon their lands in U.S. Supreme Court. They won. The treaty was nevertheless put into force when President Andrew Jackson defied the Court, and sent seven thousand soldiers to herd the Cherokee to Oklahoma at gunpoint.

Article 1

The Cherokee nation hereby cede relinquish and convey to the United States all the lands owned claimed or possessed by them east of the Mississippi river, and hereby release all their claims upon the United States for spoliations of every kind for and in consideration of the sum of five millions of dollars to be expended paid and invested in the manner stipulated and agreed upon in the following articles. But as a question has arisen between the commissioners and the Cherokees whether the Senate in their resolution by which they advised "that a sum not exceeding five millions of dollars be paid to the Cherokee Indians for all their lands and possessions east of the Mississippi river" have included and made any allowance or consideration for claims for spoliations it is therefore agreed on the part of the United States that this question shall be again submitted to the Senate for their consideration and decision and if no allowance was made for spoliations that then an additional sum of three hundred thousand dollars be allowed for the same.

Article 8

The United States also agree and stipulate to remove the Cherokees to their new homes and to subsist them one year after their arrival there and that a sufficient number of steamboats and baggage-wagons shall be furnished to remove them comfortably, and so as not to endanger their health, and that a physician well supplied with medicines shall accompany each detachment of emigrants removed by the Government. Such persons and families as in the opinion of the emigrating agent are capable of subsisting and removing themselves shall be permitted to do so; and they shall be allowed in full for all claims for twenty dollars for each member of their family; and in lieu of their one year's rations they shall be paid the sum of thirty-three dollars and thirty-three cents if they prefer it.

ON THE TRAIL OF TEARS, 1838

During the latter half of the 18th century the Cherokee Nation in Georgia lived at peace with the other residents of the state, maintaining both a free press and a system of representative government. But in 1838 the discovery of gold on their ancestral lands set in motion a series of events that resulted in their forced march to Oklahoma along what became known as "The Trail of Tears." Of the 15,000 men, women, and children who walked the 800 miles from Georgia, under armed escort and at the order of President Andrew Jackson, 4000 died of sickness, exposure, and starvation. Evan Jones (1788-1873), a Baptist missionary who emigrated from Wales to Philadelphia as a boy and then lived with the Cherokees for many years, accompanied them on their way west.

May 21

Our minds have, of late, been in a state of intense anxiety and agitation. The

24th of May is rapidly approaching. The major-general has arrived, and issued his summons, declaring that every man, woman and child of the Cherokees must be on their way to the west before another moon shall pass. The troops, by thousands, are assembling around the devoted victims. The Cherokees, in the mean time, apprized of all that is doing, wait the result of these terrific preparations; with feelings not to be described. Wednesday, the 16th inst. [the current month], was appointed as a day of solemn prayer.

May 31

We have cause for thankfulness that some few glimmerings of hope have at length penetrated the gloom. The delegation at Washington have at last come to an understanding with the Secretary of War on the basis of a new arrangement; the Indians to cede the country east, to remove within two years to the west, to be protected during their stay, and escorted to their place of destination; to remove themselves, and have a title in fee to the country west of Arkansas; to receive a gross sum to cover all demands. May the Lord direct all for the advancement of his own glory!

June 16

The Cherokees are nearly all prisoners. They have been dragged from their houses, and encamped at the forts and military posts, all over the nation. In Georgia, especially, multitudes were allowed no time to take any thing with them, except the clothes they had on. Well-furnished houses were left a prey to plunderers, who, like hungry wolves, follow in the train of the captors. These wretches rifle the houses, and strip the helpless, unoffending owners of all they have on earth. Females, who have been habituated to comforts and comparative affluence, are driven on foot before the bayonets of brutal men. Their feelings are mortified by vulgar and profane vociferations. It is a painful sight. The property of many has been taken, and sold before their eyes for almost nothing—the sellers and buyers, in many cases, being combined to cheat the poor Indians. These things are done at the instant of arrest and consternation; the soldiers standing by, with their arms in hand, impatient to go on with their work, could give little time to transact business. The poor captive, in a state of distressing agitation, his weeping wife almost frantic with terror, surrounded by a group of crying, terrified children, without a friend to speak a consoling word, is in a poor condition to make a good disposition of his property and is in most cases stripped of the whole, at one blow. Many of the Cherokees, who, a few days ago, were in comfortable circumstances, are now victims of abject poverty. Some, who have been allowed to return home, under passport, to inquire after their property, have found their cattle, horses, swine, farming-tools, and house-furniture all gone. And this is not a description of extreme cases. It is altogether a faint representation of the work which has been perpetrated on the unoffending, unarmed and unresisting Cherokees.

December 30

We have now been on our road to Arkansas seventy-five days, and have travelled five hundred and twenty-nine miles. We are still nearly three hundred miles short of our destination. We have been greatly favored by the kind providence of our heavenly Father. We have as yet met with no serious accident, and have been detained only two days by bad weather. It has, however, been exceedingly cold for some time past, which renders the condition of those who are but thinly clad, very uncomfortable. I am afraid that, with all the care that can be exercised with the various detachments, there will be an immense amount of suffering, and loss of life attending the removal. Great numbers of the old, the young, and the infirm, will inevitably be sacrificed. And the fact that the removal is effected by coercion, makes it the more galling to the feelings of the survivors.

SCHULL, CAHERAGH, DUNGARVAN, LONDONDERRY, 1846-47

The Irish famine of 1846, induced by a catastrophic failure of the potato crop, raised the cost of guns and ammunition as well as the price of escape. The saying "A million dead, a million fled" is a fair approximation of the losses. Contemporary newspapers from County Cork related tales of shock and horror [I and II]. Alexander Somerville (1811-1885), a Scottish journalist, took a tour of Ireland during the famine and sent back eyewitness reports to his readers at the Manchester Examiner *[III]. In a letter, J. J. Cooke, shipper, delivers the bad news to one Reverend Gage [IV].*

[I]

Schull, County Cork

The famine grew more horrible towards the end of December 1846, many were buried with neither inquest nor coffin. An inquest was held by Dr. Sweetman on three bodies. The first was that of the father of two very young children whose mother had already died of starvation. His death became known only when the two children toddled into the village of Schull. They were crying of hunger and complaining that their father would not speak to them for four days; they told how he was "as cold as a flag". The other bodies on which an inquest was held were those of a mother and child who had both died of starvation. The remains had been gnawed by rats.

[II]

Caheragh, County Cork

The following is a statement of what I *saw* yesterday evening on the lands of

Toureen. In a cabbage garden I saw (as I was informed) the bodies of Kate Barry and her two children very lightly covered with earth, the hands and legs of her large body entirely exposed, the flesh completely eaten off by the dogs, the skin and hair of the head lying within a couple of yards of the skull, which, when I first threw my eyes on it, I thought to be part of a horse's tail. Within about thirty yards of the above-mentioned garden, at the opposite side of the road, are two most wretched-looking old houses, with two dead bodies in each, Norry Regan, Tom Barry, Nelly Barry (a little girl), and Charles McCarthy (a little boy), all dead about a fortnight, and not yet interred; Tim Donovan, Darrig, on the same farm, died on Saturday, his wife and sister the only people I saw about the cabin, said they had no means to bury him. You will think this very horrifying; but were you to witness the state of the dead and dying here at Toureen, it would be too much for flesh and blood to behold. May the Lord avert, by his gracious interposition, the merited tokens of his displeasure.

I need make no comment on this, but ask, *are we living in a portion of the United Kingdom?*

[III]

Dungarvan, County Waterford

Coming over the hills, the other day, to this place, I was accosted by a man who carried a gun in his hand, and asked if I was Captain Somebody, whom he named, of the constabulary. What he would have said if I had been the captain I do not know. He proceeded to tell me that he was a farmer and a tailor; that he had twelve boys (men) at work for him; that he contracted to make greatcoats for the constabulary, and paid the boys 7s. 6d. per week; that he had as many potatoes as would plant three acres of ground; that he had three hundred barrels of oats, sixty barrels being thrashed and lying in the barn; that the barn had been twice attacked in the night; and that he had been to Clonmel to buy a gun and a pistol, and percussion caps, for himself and the boys to defend the oats and the seed potatoes.

On mentioning what this man told me to some gentlemen who are neither to be despised for their want of sagacity nor suspected of the want of liberality, they said that the man might be telling the truth, but it was just possible that he had been buying arms, like many others, and contrived an excuse for being seen with them in his possession on the highway. For myself, I saw no reason to doubt the man's story; most of the farmers have corn in their possession, and all who have it feel uneasy about it. They are purchasing arms and ammunition to defend it, and are doing this the more anxiously and generally that they see the common people, the very poorest, procuring arms everywhere.

[IV]

Londonderry April 19 1847

Rev. Mr Gage

In reply to your letter of the 16th inst [this month]: Mrs Gage in her letter of the 13th March states that there will be eighty persons or thereabouts emigrating. This is the only information we had as to the number. Now, in your list there is above 100. If we could take them all in our ship, we would do so with pleasure; but the number going and anxious to get away this spring is so great that, unless we would act unfairly towards our other friends and shut them out altogether, we could not take all yours.

We never engaged to take any fixed number; we never engaged to take them all in one ship—in fact, we never came to a point of a bargain in the matter, only as to the price which was fixed. However, as our plan is not satisfactory to the people, we cannot of course hold them to a bargain and therefore, if they choose not to accept of our offer, we will cancel the agreement. Please let us know whether we will have them or not on the terms stated.

Yours respectfully
J. J. Cooke.

On Extinction

Charles Darwin (1809-1882) published On the Origin of Species in 1859. Others before him had accepted the possibility of extinction, but always as an aberration in the order of things. Darwin endowed the possibility with the status of a natural law.

The old notion of all the inhabitants of the earth having been swept away at successive periods by catastrophes, is very generally given up, even by those geologists as Elie de Beaumont, Murchison, Barrande, etc., whose general views would naturally lead them to this conclusion. On the contrary, we have every reason to believe, from the study of the tertiary formations, that species and groups of species gradually disappear, one after another, first from one spot, then from another, and finally from the world. Both single species and whole groups of species last for very unequal periods; some groups, as we have seen, having endured from the earliest known dawn of life to the present day; some having disappeared before the close of the palæozoic period. No fixed law seems to determine the length of time during which any single species or any single genus endures. There is reason to believe that the complete extinction of the species of a group is generally a slower process than their production: if the appearance and disappearance of a group of species be represented, as before, by a vertical line of varying thickness, the line is found to taper more gradually at its upper end, which marks the progress of extermination, than at its lower end, which marks the first appearance and increase in numbers of the species. In some cases, however, the extermination of whole groups of beings, as of ammonites towards the close of the secondary period, has been wonderfully sudden.

The whole subject of the extinction of species has been involved in the most gratuitous mystery. Some authors have even supposed that as the individual has a definite length of life, so have species a definite duration. No one I think can have marvelled more at the extinction of species, than I have done. When I found in La Plata the tooth of a horse embedded with the remains of

Mastodon, Megatherium, Toxodon, and other extinct monsters, which all co-existed with still living shells at a very late geological period, I was filled with astonishment; for seeing that the horse, since its introduction by the Spaniards into South America, has run wild over the whole country and has increased in numbers at an unparalleled rate, I asked myself what could so recently have exterminated the former horse under conditions of life apparently so favourable. But how utterly groundless was my astonishment! Professor Owen soon perceived that the tooth, though so like that of the existing horse, belonged to an extinct species. Had this horse been still living, but in some degree rare, no naturalist would have felt the least surprise at its rarity; for rarity is the attribute of a vast number of species of all classes, in all countries. If we ask ourselves why this or that species is rare, we answer that something is unfavourable in its conditions of life; but what that something is, we can hardly ever tell.

It is most difficult always to remember that the increase of every living being is constantly being checked by unperceived injurious agencies; and that these same unperceived agencies are amply sufficient to cause rarity, and finally extinction. We see in many cases in the more recent tertiary formations, that rarity precedes extinction; and we know that this has been the progress of events with those animals which have been exterminated, either locally or wholly, through man's agency.

The theory of natural selection is grounded on the belief that each new variety, and ultimately each new species, is produced and maintained by having some advantage over those with which it comes into competition; and the consequent extinction of less-favoured forms almost inevitably follows. It is the same with our domestic productions: when a new and slightly improved variety has been raised, it at first supplants the less improved varieties in the same neighbourhood; when much improved it is transported far and near, like our short-horn cattle, and takes the place of other breeds in other countries. Thus the appearance of new forms and the disappearance of old forms, both natural and artificial, are bound together. In certain flourishing groups, the number of new specific forms which have been produced within a given time is probably greater than that of the old specific forms which have been exterminated;

but we know that the number of species has not gone on indefinitely increasing, at least during the later geological periods, so that looking to later times we may believe that the production of new forms has caused the extinction of about the same number of old forms.

The competition will generally be most severe, as formerly explained and illustrated by examples, between the forms which are most like each other in all respects. Hence the improved and modified descendants of a species will generally cause the extermination of the parent-species; and if many new forms have been developed from any one species, the nearest allies of that species, *i.e.*, the species of the same genus, will be the most liable to extermination. Thus, as I believe, a number of new species descended from one species, that is a new genus, comes to supplant an old genus, belonging to the same family. But it must often have happened that a new species belonging to some one group will have seized on the place occupied by a species belonging to a distinct group, and thus caused its extermination; and if many allied forms be developed from the successful intruder, many will have to yield their places; and it will generally be allied forms, which will suffer from some inherited inferiority in common.

Thus, as it seems to me, the manner in which single species and whole groups of species become extinct, accords well with the theory of natural selection. We need not marvel at extinction; if we must marvel, let it be at our presumption in imagining for a moment that we understand the many complex contingencies, on which the existence of each species depends. If we forget for an instant, that each species tends to increase inordinately, and that some check is always in action, yet seldom perceived by us, the whole economy of nature will be utterly obscured. Whenever we can precisely say why this species is more abundant in individuals than that; why this species and not another can be naturalised in a given country; then, and not till then, we may justly feel surprised why we cannot account for the extinction of this particular species or group of species.

RICHMOND, 1865

Once it was certain that the South had lost the Civil War, Jefferson Davis (1808-1889), the President of the Confederacy, abandoned Richmond in the hope of escaping to Europe. He meant to take ship in Florida, but on the road south he and his wife were captured by Union cavalry at Irwinville, Georgia. His personal secretary, Burton N. Harrison (1838-1904), wrote an account of the interrupted journey that was subsequently published in the Century Magazine *of New York in 1883.*

In anticipation of the capture of Richmond, the President had decided to remove his family to a place of probable security. He desired, however, to keep them as near as might be to the position General Lee intended to occupy when obliged to withdraw from the lines around Richmond and Petersburg, and I was requested to accompany Mrs. Davis and the children on their journey to Charlotte, North Carolina.

Under the President's directions, we set to work at once to arrange for a railway train to convey the more important officers of the Government and such others as could be got aboard, with our luggage and as much material as it was desired to carry along, including the boxes of papers that had belonged to the executive office in Richmond. With the coöperation of the officers of the Quartermaster's Department, the train was, with difficulty, got ready; and the guards I placed upon it excluded all persons and material not specially authorized by me to go aboard. Of course, a multitude was anxious to embark, and the guards were kept busy in repelling them.

We halted for several days at Greensboro' for consultation with General Joseph E. Johnston, whose army was then confronting Sherman. The people in that part of North Carolina had not been zealous supporters of the Confederate Government; and, so long as we remained in the State, we observed their indifference to what should become of us. It was rarely that anybody asked one of us to his house; and but few of them had the grace even to explain their fear that, if they entertained us, their houses would be burned by the enemy, when his cavalry should get there.

During the halt at Greensboro' most of us lodged day and night in the very uncomfortable railway cars we had arrived in. The possessor of a large house in the town, and perhaps the richest and most conspicuous of the residents, came indeed effusively to the train, but carried off only Mr. Trenholm, the Secretary of the Treasury. This hospitality was explained by the information that the host was the alarmed owner of many of the bonds, and of much of the currency, of the Confederate States, and that he hoped to cajole the Secretary into exchanging a part of the "Treasury gold" for some of those securities. It appeared that we were reputed to have many millions of gold with us. Mr. Trenholm was ill during most or all of the time at the house of his warm-hearted host, and the symptoms were said to be greatly aggravated, if not caused, by importunities with regard to that gold.

Colonel John Taylor Wood, of our staff, had, some time before, removed his family to Greensboro' from Richmond, and took the President (who would otherwise have probably been left with us in the cars) to share his quarters near by. The Woods were boarding, and their rooms were few and small. The entertainment they were able to offer their guest was meager, and was distinguished by very little comfort either to him or to them, the people of the house continually and vigorously insisting to the colonel and his wife, the while, that Mr. Davis must go away, saying they were unwilling to have the vengeance of Stoneman's cavalry brought upon them by his presence in their house.

That route through North Carolina had been for some time the only line of communication between Virginia and Georgia and the Gulf States. The roads and towns were full of officers and privates from those Southern States, belonging to the Army of Northern Virginia. Many of them had been home on furlough, and were returning to the army when met by the news of General Lee's surrender; others were stragglers from their commands. All were now going home, and, as some of the bridges south of Greensboro' had been burned by the enemy's cavalry, and the railways throughout the southern country generally were interrupted, of course everybody wanted the assistance of a horse or mule on his journey. Few had any scruples as to how to get one.

*   *   *

We moved southward on, I think, the day following the council of war held with General Johnston, starting from Greensboro' in the afternoon. The President, those of us who constituted his immediate staff, and some members of the cabinet, were mounted.

By good fortune, I was able to secure an ambulance; but the horses were old and broken down, of a dirty gray color, and with spots like fly-bites all over them,—and the harness was not good. There was no choice, however, and into that ambulance got Mr. Judah P. Benjamin (Secretary of State), General Samuel Cooper (Adjutant General, and ranking officer of the whole army), Mr. George Davis (of North Carolina, Attorney-General), and Mr. Jules St. Martin, Benjamin's brother-in-law.

By the time they got off, the front of our column had been some time in motion, and the President had ridden down the road. Heavy rains had recently fallen, the earth was saturated with water, the soil was a sticky red clay, the mud was awful, and the road, in places, almost impracticable. Having been kept latterly in the rear by something detaining me, I observed, as I rode forward, the tilted hind-part of an ambulance stuck in the mud in the middle of the road, and recognized the voices inside, as I drew rein for a moment to chuckle at their misfortunes. The horses were blowing like two rusty fog-horns; Benjamin was scolding the driver for not going on; that functionary was stoically insisting they could proceed no whit further, because the horses were broken down; and General Cooper (faithful old gentleman, he had been in Richmond throughout our war, and had not known since the Seminole war what it is to "rough it") was grumbling about the impudence of a subordinate officer ("only a brigadier-general, sir"). It seems the offender had thrust himself into the seat in another ambulance drawn by good horses, that was intended for the Adjutant-General. Mud and water were deep all around them, and their plight was pitiful indeed! They plucked up their spirits only when I offered to get somebody to pull them out. Riding forward, I found an artillery camp, where some of the men volunteered to go back with horses and haul the ambulance up the hill; and, returning to them again, I could see from afar the occasional bright glow of Benjamin's cheerful cigar. While the others of the party were perfectly silent, Benjamin's silvery voice was presently heard as he rhythmically intoned, for their comfort, verse after verse of Tennyson's ode on the death of the Duke of Wellington!

*   *   *

In Lexington and in Salisbury we experienced the same cold indifference on the part of the people, first encountered at Greensboro', except that at Salisbury Mr. Davis was invited to the house of a clergyman, where he slept. Salisbury had been entered a few days before by a column of the enemy's cavalry (said to be Stoneman's), and the streets showed many evidences of the havoc they had wrought. With one or two others, I passed the night on the clergyman's front piazza as a guard for the President.

During all this march Mr. Davis was singularly equable and cheerful; he seemed to have had a great load taken from his mind, to feel relieved of responsibilities, and his conversation was bright and agreeable. He talked of men and of books, particularly of Walter Scott and Byron; of horses and dogs and sports; of the woods and the fields; of trees and many plants; of roads, and how to make them; of the habits of birds, and of a variety of other topics. His familiarity with, and correct taste in, the English literature of the last generation, his varied experiences in life, his habits of close observation, and his extraordinary memory, made him a charming companion when disposed to talk.

His cheerfulness continued in Charlotte, and I remember his there saying to me, "I *cannot* feel like a beaten man!" The halt at Charlotte was to await information from the army of General Johnston. After a few days, the President became nervously anxious about his wife and family. He had as yet heard nothing of their whereabouts, but asked me to proceed into South Carolina in search of them, suggesting that I should probably find them at Abbeville.

Mrs. Davis insisted upon starting without delay for the sea-coast, to get out of the reach of capture. She and her sister had heard dreadful stories of the treatment ladies had been subjected to in Georgia and the Carolinas by men in Sherman's army, and thought with terror of the possibility of falling into the hands of the enemy; indeed, she understood it to be the President's wish that she should hasten to seek safety in a foreign country. I explained to her the difficulties and hardships of the journey to the sea-coast, and suggested that we might be captured on the road, urging her to remain where she was until the place should be quietly occupied by United States troops, assuring her that some officer would take care that no harm should befall her, and adding that she would then be able to rejoin her friends. But she persisted in her purpose, and begged me to be off immediately. It was finally decided to make our way to the neighborhood of Madison, Florida, as fast as possible, there to determine how best to get to sea.

*   *   *

I halted my party on the western bank of the Ocmulgee River as the darkness came on, immediately after getting the wagons through the difficult bottom-lands on the eastern side, and after crossing the ferry. About the middle of the night I was aroused by a courier sent back by the President with the report that the enemy was at or near Hawkinsville (about twenty-five miles to the north of us), and the advice that I had better move on at once to the southward, though, it was added, the enemy at Hawkinsville seemed to be only intent upon appropriating the quartermaster's supplies supposed to be there. I started my party promptly, in a terrible storm of thunder, lightning, and rain. As we passed through the village of Abbeville, I dismounted and had a conversation with the President in the old house, where he was lying on the floor wrapped in a blanket. He urged me to move on, and said he should overtake us during the night, after his horses had had more rest. We kept to the southward all night, the rain pouring in torrents most of the time, and the darkness such that, as we went through the woods where the road was not well marked, in a light, sandy soil, but wound about to accommodate the great pines left standing, the wagons were frequently stopped by fallen trees and other obstructions. In such a situation, we were obliged to wait until a flash of lightning enabled the drivers to see the way.

In the midst of that storm and darkness the President overtook us. He was still with us when, about five o'clock in the afternoon (not having stopped since leaving Abbeville, except for the short time, about sunrise, required to cook breakfast), I halted my party for the night, immediately after crossing the little creek just north of Irwinville, and went into camp. My teams were sadly in need of rest, and having now about fifty miles between us and Hawkinsville, where the enemy had been reported to be, and our information being, as stated, that they did not seem to be on the march or likely to move after us, we apprehended no immediate danger.

After arranging the tents and wagons for the night, and without waiting for anything to eat (being still the worse for my dysentery and fever), I lay down upon the ground and fell into a profound sleep. Captain Moody afterward kindly stretched a canvas as a roof over my head, and laid down beside me, though I knew nothing of that until the next day. I was awakened by the coachman, James Jones, running to me about day-break with the announcement that the enemy was at hand! I sprang to my feet, and in an instant a rattling fire of musketry commenced on the north side of the creek. Almost at the same moment Colonel Pritchard [Lt. Col. Benjamin D. Pritchard, commander of the 4th Michigan Cavalry] and his regiment charged up the road from the south upon us. We were taken by surprise, and not one of us exchanged a shot with the enemy. Colonel Johnston tells me he was the first prisoner taken. In a moment, Colonel Pritchard rode directly to me and, pointing across the creek, said, "What does that mean? Have you any men with you?" Supposing the firing was done by our teamsters, I replied, "Of course we have—don't you hear the firing?" He seemed to be nettled at the reply, gave the order, "Charge," and boldly led the way himself across the creek, nearly every man in his command following. Our camp was thus left deserted for a few minutes, except by one mounted soldier near Mrs. Davis's tent (who was afterward said to have been stationed there by Colonel Pritchard in passing) and by the few troopers who stopped to plunder our wagons. I had been sleeping upon the same side of the road with the tent occupied by Mrs. Davis, and was then standing very near it. Looking there, I saw her come out and heard her say something to the soldier mentioned; perceiving she wanted him to move off, I approached and actually persuaded the fellow to ride away. As the soldier moved into the road, and I walked beside his horse, the President emerged for the first time from the tent, at the side farther from us, and walked away into the woods to the eastward, and at right angles to the road.

Presently, looking around and observing somebody had come out of the tent, the soldier turned his horse's head and, reaching the spot he had first occupied, was again approached by Mrs. Davis, who engaged him in conversation. In a minute, this trooper was joined by one or perhaps two of his comrades, who either had lagged behind the column and were just coming up the road, or had at that moment crossed over from the other (the west) side, where a few of them had fallen to plundering, as I have stated, instead of charging over the creek. They remained on horseback and soon became violent in their language with Mrs. Davis. The order to "halt" was called out by one of them to the President. It was not obeyed, and was quickly repeated in a loud voice several times. At least one of the men then threatened to fire, and pointed a carbine at the President. Thereupon, Mrs. Davis, overcome with terror, cried out in apprehension, and the President (who had now walked sixty or eighty paces away into the unobstructed woods) turned around and came back rapidly to his wife near the tent. At least one of the soldiers continued his violent language to Mrs. Davis, and the President reproached him for such conduct to her, when one of them, seeing the face of the President, as he stood near and was talking, said, "Mr. Davis, surrender! I recognize you, sir." Pictures of the President were so common that nearly or quite every man in both armies knew his face.

It was, as yet, scarcely daylight.

During the confusion of the next few minutes, Colonel John Taylor Wood escaped, first inducing the soldier who halted him to go aside into the bushes on the bank of the creek, and there bribing the fellow with some gold to let him get away altogether. As Wood was an officer of the navy, as well as an officer of the army, had commanded cruisers along the Atlantic coast, had captured and sunk a number of New York and New England vessels, and was generally spoken of in the Northern newspapers as a "pirate," he not unnaturally apprehended that, if he remained in the enemy's hands, he would be treated with special severity.

All of the other members of the President's party, except Colonel Thorburn, and all those of my own party, remained as prisoners—unless, indeed, one or two of the teamsters escaped, as to which I do not recollect.

The business of plundering commenced immediately after the capture; and we were soon left with only what we had on and what we had in our pockets.

While it was going on, I emptied the contents of my haversack into a fire where some of the enemy were cooking breakfast, and there saw the papers burn. They were chiefly love-letters, with a photograph of my sweetheart,—though with them chanced to be a few telegrams and perhaps some letters relating to public affairs, of no special interest.

[DIARY]

MARY CHESNUT'S WINDOW

Mary Chesnut (1823-1886), a close friend to Mr. and Mrs. Jefferson Davis, kept a diary recording her views and observations from February 15, 1861, to August 2, 1865. Upon losing her home in Richmond during the evacuations of the spring of 1865, she drifted south as a refugee, temporarily settling into makeshift quarters in Chester, South Carolina, where she heard tales of the fall of Richmond (April 2) and the surrender of Lee (April 9).

March 29, 1865.

It is very late. The wind flaps my curtain. It seems to moan "too late." All this will end by making a nervous lunatic [of me].

March 30, 1865.

I said to General Preston, "I pass my days and nights partly at this window. I am sure our army is silently dispersing. Men are passing the *wrong way*—all the time they slip by. No songs nor shouts now. They have given the thing up. See for yourself—look there!" For a while the streets were thronged with soldiers, and then they were empty again. The marching now is without tap of drum. I told him of the woman in the cracker bonnet at the depot at Charlotte who signaled to her husband as they dragged him off. "Take it easy, Jake—you desert agin, quick as you kin—come back to your wife and children." And she continued to yell, "Desert, Jake! desert agin, Jake!"

April 3, 1865.

Saw Mr. Preston ride off. He came to tell me goodbye. Told him he looked like a crusader on his great white horse and William his squire at his heels.

How different these men look on horseback—they are all consummate riders, with their servants as well mounted behind them carrying cloaks and traps —from the same men packed like sardines in dirty RR cars. Which cars are usually floating inch deep in liquid tobacco juice.

*   *   *

Yesterday it was a tête-à-tête dinner with General Preston—today Governor Bonham. The latter, as we sat at that window which overlooks two thoroughfares:

"All this marching and countermarching, changing of generals and all that— it is but Caesar's death scene—drawing his mantle around him to die decently."

"See how the stream westward never ceases. Lee's army must be melting like a Scotch mist."

"Mist—mist," he answered. "Yes, these men will be missed if there is another battle soon."

April 5, 1865.

One day Isabella and I met Mr. Clarke from Columbia, and from him I derived my first real idea of the ruin this war had brought—or Sherman, rather. Mr. Clarke all unshaven and shorn was brandishing a chair, holding it aloft, like a banner, by its one remaining rung. "This is all I have left of my Columbia house and all my earthly possessions!" Mr. Clarke was one of the rich men of Columbia.

April 7, 1865.

Richmond has fallen—and I have no heart to write about it. Grant broke through our lines. Sherman cut through them. Stoneman is this side of Danville.

They are too many for us.

Everything lost in Richmond, even our archives.

Blue-black is our horizon.

Poor Mrs. Middleton—paralysis. Has she not had trouble enough? How much she has had to bear. Their plantation and home on Edisto destroyed. Their house in Charleston burned. Her children scattered, starvation, almost, in Lincolnton, and all as nothing to the one dreadful blow—her only son killed in Virginia.

April 19, 1865.

Just now Mr. Clay dashed upstairs, pale as a sheet.

"General Lee has capitulated."

I saw it reflected in Mary Darby's face before I heard him. She staggered to the table, sat down, and wept aloud. Clay's eyes were not dry.

Quite beside herself, Mary shrieked, "Now we belong to negroes and Yankees!" Buck said, "I do not believe it."

[MEMOIR]

The Revival

While the cabinet members of the Confederate States of America looked for ways to reach safety, the less senior members of the cause bore the full weight of defeat. George Cary Eggleston (1839-1911), a junior officer commanding troops garrisoned at Richmond, published his A Rebel's Recollections *in 1875, ten years after Lee's surrender.*

It is impossible to say precisely when the conviction became general in the South that we were to be beaten. I cannot even decide at what time I myself began to think the cause a hopeless one, and I have never yet found one of my fellow-Confederates, though I have questioned many of them, who could tell me with any degree of certainty the history of his change from confidence to despondency. We never gave verbal expression to the doubts we felt, or even to the longing, which must have been universal, for the end.

If General Grant had failed to break our power of resistance by his sledge-hammer blows, it speedily became evident that he would be more successful in wearing it away by the constant friction of a siege [at Richmond]. Without fighting a battle he was literally destroying our army. The sharp-shooting was incessant, and the bombardment hardly less so, and under it all our numbers visibly decreased day by day. During the first two months of the siege my own company, which numbered about a hundred and fifty men, lost sixty, in killed and wounded, an average of a man a day.

There was no longer any room for hope except in a superstitious belief that Providence would in some way interfere in our behalf, and to that very many betook themselves for comfort. This shifting upon a supernatural power the task we had failed to accomplish by human means rapidly bred many less worthy superstitions among the troops. The general despondency, which amounted almost to despair, doubtless helped to bring about this result, and the great religious "revival" contributed to it in no small degree. I think hardly any man entertained a thought of coming out of the struggle alive. The only question with each was when his time was to come, and a sort of gloomy fatalism took possession of many minds.

Meantime the revival went on. Prayer-meetings were held in every tent. Testaments were in every hand, and a sort of religious ecstasy took possession of the army. The men had ceased to rely upon the skill of their leaders or the strength of our army for success, and not a few of them hoped now for a miraculous interposition of supernatural power in our behalf. Men in this mood make the best of soldiers, and at no time were the fighting qualities of the Southern army better than during the siege. What cared they for the failure of mere human efforts, when they were persuaded that through such failures God was leading us to ultimate victory? Disaster seemed only to strengthen the faith of many.

When at last the beginning of the end came, in the evacuation of Richmond and the effort to retreat, everything seemed to go to pieces at once. The best disciplinarians in the army relaxed their reins. The best troops became disorganized, and hardly any command marched in a body. Flying citizens in vehicles of every conceivable sort accompanied and embarrassed the columns. Many commands marched heedlessly on without orders, and seemingly without a thought of whither they were going. Others mistook the meaning of their orders, and still others had instructions which it was impossible to obey in any case.

At Amelia Court House we should have found a supply of provisions. General Lee had ordered a train load to meet him there, but the interests of the starving army had been sacrificed to the convenience or the cowardice of the president and his personal following. The train had been hurried on to Richmond and its precious cargo of food thrown out there, in order that Mr. Davis and his people might retreat rapidly and comfortably from the abandoned capital.

"The Expropriators Are Expropriated"

Karl Marx (1818-1883) foresaw the end of the world in the end of a means of production. The prophecy appeared as an abstraction in Das Kapital, *first published in Hamburg in 1867; fifty years later in St. Petersburg, it acquired the form of a revolution.*

As the antithesis to social, collective property, private property exists only where the means of labour and the external conditions of labour belong to private individuals. The private property of the labourer in his means of production is the foundation of petty industry, whether agricultural, manufacturing, or both. This petty mode of production exists also under slavery, serfdom, and other states of dependence. But it flourishes, it lets loose its whole energy, it attains its adequate classical form, only where the labourer is the private owner of his own means of labour set in action by himself: the peasant of the land which he cultivates, the artisan of the tool which he handles as a virtuoso. This mode of production presupposes parcelling of the soil, and scattering of the other means of production. As it excludes the concentration of these means of production, so also it excludes co-operation, division of labour within each separate process of production, the control over, and the productive application of the forces of Nature by society, and the free development of the social productive powers. It is compatible only with a system of production, and a society, moving within narrow and more or less primitive bounds. To perpetuate it would be, as Pecqueur rightly says, "to decree universal mediocrity." At a certain stage of development it brings forth the material agencies for its own dissolution. From that moment new forces and new passions spring up in the bosom of society; but the old social organisation fetters them and keeps them down. It must be annihilated; it is annihilated. Its annihilation, the transformation of the individualised and scattered means of production into socially concentrated ones, of the pigmy property of the many into the huge property of the few, the expropriation of the great mass of the people from the soil, from the means of subsistence, and from the means of labour, this fearful and painful expropriation of the mass of the people forms the prelude to the history of capital. It comprises a series of forcible methods, under the stimulus of passions the most infamous, the most sordid, the pettiest, the most meanly odious.

As soon as this process of transformation has sufficiently decomposed the old society from top to bottom, as soon as the labourers are turned into proletarians, and their means of labour into capital, then the further socialisation of labour and the further expropriation of private proprietors, takes a new form. That which is now to be expropriated is no longer the labourer working for himself, but the capitalist exploiting many labourers. This expropriation is accomplished by the action of the immanent laws of capitalistic production itself, by the centralisation of capital. One capitalist always kills many. Hand in hand with this expropriation of many capitalists by few, there develops, on an ever-extending scale, the economising of all means of production by their use as the means of production of combined, socialised labour, the entanglement of all peoples in the net of the world-market, and with this, the international character of the capitalistic régime. Along with the constantly diminishing number of the magnates of capital, who usurp and monopolise all advantages of this process of transformation, grows the mass of misery, oppression, slavery, degradation, exploitation; but with this too grows the revolt of the working class, a class always increasing in numbers, and disciplined, united, organised by the very mechanism of the process of capitalist production itself. The monopoly of capital becomes a fetter upon the mode of production, which has sprung up and flourished along with, and under it. Centralisation of the means of production and socialisation of labour at last reach a point where they become incompatible with their capitalist integument. This integument is burst asunder. The knell of capitalist private property sounds. The expropriators are expropriated.

The capitalist mode of appropriation, the result of the capitalist mode of production, produces capitalist private property. This is the first negation of individual private property, as founded on the labour of the proprietor. But capitalist production begets, with the inexorability of a law of Nature, its own negation. It is the negation of negation. This does not re-establish private property for the producer, but gives him individual property based on the acquisitions of the capitalist era: *i.e.*, on co-operation and the possession in common of the land and of the means of production.

The transformation of scattered private property, arising from individual labour, into capitalist private property is, naturally, a process, incomparably more protracted, violent, and difficult, than the transformation of capitalistic private property, already practically resting on socialised production, into socialised property. In the former case, we had the expropriation of the mass of the people by a few usurpers; in the latter, we have the expropriation of a few usurpers by the mass of the people.

PARIS (III), 1870-71

The Empress Eugénie, consort of Napoleon III of France, learned by telegram on September 4, 1870, that the German army at the battle of Sedan had captured her husband and 100,000 of his troops. A generation later, Robert Sencourt (a pseudonym for Robert Esmonde Gordon George, 1894-1969) wrote his account of her subsequent flight from the palace of the Tuileries by drawing on contemporary sources.

[I]

The Empress waited in her suite in the Tuileries to hear the result of the conference with General de Palikao, and what steps the Assembly would take. From moment to moment fresh dispatches arrived, now from the Ministry of the Interior, now from the War Ministry, now from the Prefecture of Police. Each was more ominous than the last. The mob had invaded the Chamber of Deputies, and the insignia of the Empire were everywhere being defaced or destroyed. At last a messenger arrived to say that the eagles on the great gates of the gardens that opened on the Place de la Concorde had been torn down, and that the rioters were forcing their way into the enclosed garden of the Palace. The Empress remained unmoved.

At last her attendants in the Palace became seriously alarmed. Trochu had abandoned her, perhaps betrayed her. The shouts of the insurgents became clearer and clearer, and the Guard might at any moment be overwhelmed.

At last three of the Ministers arrived: Busson-Billault, Jérome David, and Henri Chevreau. Entering the salon where the Empress was still standing, they reported that the mob had taken possession of the Chamber of Deputies, and that the Deputies themselves were going over to the Revolution. Paris was already in the hands of the mob. "Ah," said the Empress, "in France one has no longer the right to be unfortunate." In terror for her safety, they implored her to leave the Tuileries at once. Her firmness was still unshakable. She considered that the war depended on her maintaining a firm front. "Here I have been placed by the Emperor," she said, "and here I will stay. To abandon my post will weaken the power to resist the invasion. Unless there is some recognised authority, the disorganisation will be complete, and France at the mercy of Bismarck."

It was now nearly three o'clock in the afternoon. Hurling themselves on the enclosed garden with the shout *"Aux Tuileries! Aux Tuileries!"* the mob sounded more and more ominous, nearer and nearer, into the big salon of the Empress. At this moment Nigra entered with Metternich, and demanded an immediate audience with her. They insisted that she was in the greatest danger. The mob that had assaulted the Chamber of Deputies was now ready to attack the Imperial Palace. Resistance was impossible, and if she stayed longer, it would be to risk her life. Indeed, had they but known it, the mob was at that moment being held back by the argument that she was no longer there, and General de Mellinet, accompanied by Ferdinand de Lesseps, was arguing with the crowd that all were responsible for what was a national possession. Neither Ambassadors nor Ministers found the Empress easy to convince. When Léon Chevreau entered, he found her still arguing. *"Venez, venez,"* she said, "here are these gentlemen pressing me to leave Paris—to flee!"

"Madame," the Minister answered, "it is all over; the Revolution has won."

" It is all over," echoed she; "then that poor General Trochu must be dead!"

Metternich, usually so calm, grew excited, noisy, even abrupt; Nigra, who did not know her so well, retained the tone of formality, but he was equally insistent. The Empress went so far as to say she would consult Pietri, the Prefect of Police and one of her most faithful liegemen. "What do you think of the situation?" she asked him. "Are the Tuileries in danger?" Pietri, who arrived towards three o'clock, was as clear as the others. As he came over from the Prefecture he had seen the mob storming the gates of the Palace. They might force their way in at any moment. If they did, they might massacre any one they met, and the Empress would endanger not only her own life but that of her suite. She sent for Mellinet. "General," she asked, "do you think the Palace can be defended without bloodshed?" "Madame," he answered, "I do not think so." "Then there is nothing more to do, for I cannot have civil war." She had already given orders that the Guard should on no account fire on the people. Pietri had used the one argument which would weaken the Empress. In the face of fear she never quavered. But she could not argue that she must endanger her attendants. Her ladies, the lovely creatures whom Winterhalter had painted, pressed farewells upon her—Vicomtesse Aguado, her mother's Spanish friend; Maréchale Canrobert and Maréchale Pelissier, Madame de Bourgoing, Madame de la Bédoyère. But there was no time for emotional farewells. She turned to Chevreau:

"*Est-ce possible?*" she asked. "*Avez vous bien vu? Avez vous bien entendu? On n'a donc plus d'amis en France quand on est malheureux.*" [Is it possible? Have you really seen? Have you really heard? Then one has no more friends in France when one is unfortunate.]

"*Madame,*" answered Chevreau, falling on his knee, "*mon frère et moi vous montrerons qu'il y a des gens que le malheur attache plus que la toute puissance! Où vous irez, nous irons.*" [My brother and I will show you that there are those whom misfortune makes more faithful than any power. Where you go, we will go.]

The Empress could not bring herself to move: her eyes caressed the thousand loved objects she had gathered there. "You must hurry," urged the Italian Ambassador; "in a few minutes escape may be impossible." They drew her away with them, saying, "We will be responsible for her."

"But where are you going?" cried Chevreau.

"Metternich will tell you," answered the poor woman. She bowed to all present. "Thank you," she said; "goodbye"—and the door closed behind her.

A cloak, a hat, a veil were held out by Madame Lebreton in the next room. She was offered no time for packing or for plans. They felt that she must leave the Palace at once, and as she was. Half an hour had gone by since the two Ambassadors arrived. She walked out of her private room and through her apartments. As she looked round at a hundred objects that were dear to her, she asked herself, "Is this the last time?" And then, taking the lead, she went down the great staircase to take her carriage. But Metternich feared for the livery and the crown which marked it.

He offered his own carriage instead. As young Conneau went off to fetch it, the mob pressed nearer and clamoured at the gates of the courtyard. No one, he saw, could pass out that way. Admiral Jurien de la Gravière, who was with them, went across to the gates to hold the mob in play. Meanwhile the little procession had been climbing the great staircase to escape through the Louvre. Passing again through the apartments of the Empress, they entered the long suite of rooms which led from the Pavillion de Flore to the galleries of pictures. When they came to the door of the gallery, however, they found it locked. They knocked, but there was no answer. As they waited, they heard still louder the savage cries of the crowd around the Palace. It looked as if their only retreat had been cut off. There was a general feeling of dismay. But after a few minutes Charles Thélin, who had opened the prison gates at Ham for Louis Napoleon to escape, and had been made Treasurer of the Emperor's household, appeared with a bunch of keys. Among them was one that would open any door in the Palace.

The Empress now led the way through the long gallery of the Louvre to the Salon Carré, and thence to the Salle des Sept Cheminées. The little procession had been increased by attendants from the Louvre till it had become dangerously large. The Empress, with the force that always marked her character, decided that it must disperse, and thanking them all for the loyalty they had shown her, she turned with Metternich and Nigra to the room containing the Greek antiquities. As she looked she found herself facing an immense canvas. It was the masterpiece of Géricault, the *Wreck of the Medusa*, one of those pictures which aims not at being beautiful, but at telling a whole story. On wild seas, over which storm-clouds were blown fiercely by the wind, some twenty figures, some of them naked, were crowded on a raft beneath a bellying sail. While some had sunk in exhaustion or death, another group with feverish energy had torn off their garments to wave to a schooner on the horizon. Never was the conflict between despair and effort conveyed with more passionate drama. The Empress, looking at it, saw in it the picture of her country's crisis—and her own.

Descending the three great flights of steps that lead to the Egyptian remains, they passed through the funeral monuments of the Pharaohs to the door opening on the arched passage which leads from the Inner Court of the Louvre to the Place St. Germain-l'Auxerrois. But here a new danger faced them. The crowd was surging through the archway into the courtyard of the Louvre.

From time to time the Ambassadors opened the door to spy through. Wild shouts against the Empire and the Empress came through the aperture. *"Vive la République! A bas l'Espagnole!"* The Ambassadors feared for the Empress. Was she afraid? "Not in the least," she answered. "Why do you ask me? You are holding my arm. Do you feel me tremble?" She asked the very question which Louis XVI had asked when the mob invaded the Tuileries in 1792.

When the crowd had passed through the archway, the Empress saw her opportunity, and said, "Now let us go."

"I think we had better wait a little longer," pleaded Nigra.

"No, no," the Empress answered. *"Il faut de l'audace,"* and as she spoke she pulled open the door and stepped out in the archway. "The dignity, courage, and firmness," wrote the British Ambassador, "which Her Majesty had displayed in so remarkable a manner during the whole of the trying period of a month which she had gone through, did not fail her at the last."

Hurrying out into the Place St. Germain, Metternich came on a closed fiacre [taxi] drawn by one horse. Facing the passers-by, they went across to it, and as they went, a boy recognised her. *"Voilà l'Impératrice!"* he called out. Nigra silenced him. Metternich meanwhile hurried the two ladies into the fiacre, and Madame Lebreton gave the address of M. Besson in the Boulevard Hausmann. The two Ambassadors had thought of nothing but getting the Empress out of the Palace. Their chivalry, which might better be called panic, ended in placing her in a common cab. They knew no more. And the remnant of the Court remained in absolute ignorance of what had happened to her.

The cab turned into the Rue de Rivoli and, passing the Louvre and the Tuileries, it drove alone into a great mob who poured down the street; and so on into the Rue de la Paix, and across the Central Boulevards to the quieter quarters between the Madeleine and the Gare St. Lazare, to the Boulevard Hausmann.

[II]

During the winter of 1870-1871, the Germans laid siege to the city of Paris. Becoming increasingly radical under the privations of the siege and then dissatisfied with the terms of peace reached with the Germans, the Parisians

declared themselves the Paris Commune and engaged in open civil war with
the French government set up after Napoleon III's defeat at Sedan (Versaillists
in the account below). In April and May, the remnants of the emperor's troops
returned to Paris, wrested control of the capital from the Commune, and
slaughtered 18,000 ill-organized communards. The account is assembled
from Archibald Forbes' (1838-1900) dispatches to the London Daily News.

The Daily News (London), May 26, 1871

THE FIGHTING IN PARIS
SCENES AND INCIDENTS
OF THE STRUGGLE
(FROM OUR SPECIAL CORRESPONDENT)

PARIS, TUESDAY, MAY 23—In the evening, soon after eight o'clock, the firing died out almost everywhere, and there was a dead calm. The barricades—there were barricades everywhere—had for the most part been finished, and one might pass most of them without fearing to be requisitioned as a navvy. I made my way down the Rue Lafayette, making occasional detours for strategical reasons. What strange people these Parisians are! It was a fine evening, and the scene in the narrow streets was like Duke's Place in Aldgate on a summer Sunday afternoon. Men and women were placidly sitting on chairs by their street doors, gossiping leisurely about the events of the day. The children played round the barricades; their mothers scarcely looked up as the *générale* beat or the distant report of the bursting of a shell came on the light night wind.

Reaching the Hôtel de la Chaussée d'Antin, where I have quarters, I found, as I had expected, that it had been a very hot corner during the afternoon. It is close to the Boulevard Haussmann, which had been continuously swept with shell all the afternoon. A fragment had invaded the privacy of a friend whom I had left in the Hôtel, and had fallen before him on his desk as he wrote. The reason of the temporary lull was not very apparent—perhaps the Versaillists [French moderates opposed to the Commune] were eating a late dinner. About ten the din began again. Shell after shell burst close to us in the

Boulevard Haussmann, and there came the loud noise of a more distant fire, which seemed to be sweeping the barricade. In the intervals of the shellfire was audible the steady grunt of the mitrailleuses [machine guns], and I could distinctly hear the pattering of the balls as they rained down the adjacent Boulevard Haussmann. This dismal din, so perplexing and bewildering, continued all night. A friend sleeping in the room above me was awakened by the smashing of the button of a shell through his window. It dented a hole in the roof above his bed and fell on his pillow.

Daybreak brought no cessation of the noise. Looking out, and cautiously, up the Boulevard Haussmann, I saw before me a strange spectacle of desolation. Lampposts, kiosks, and trees were shattered and torn down. The road was strewn with the green boughs of trees which had been cut by the storm of shot and shell.

About ten there came the sound of a terrible fire behind [Forbes'] hotel, and I managed, at some risk, to obtain ocular proof that the Versaillists had carried the Church of Notre-Dame-de-Lorette and the mantrap barricades in which I had got involved yesterday, and were now fighting their way along the Rue de Châteaudun, so as to get into the Rue de Lafayette, on the eastward considerably of my hotel. Meanwhile a heavy fire was maintained down the Boulevard Haussmann, so that our hotel seemed imminently about to be surrounded. As I returned to its front, and prowled forward cautiously into the Rue de Lafayette, and looked up eastward to the barricades across the Rue de Lafayette, and continued across the Rue de Châteaudun, I saw the Federals firing furiously down the latter street. After considerable resistance they broke, and the Versaillists gained the barricade. I saw the red breeches surrounding it as they poured out of the Rue de Châteaudun.

Now they are (one o'clock) firing westward along the Rue de Lafayette into the Boulevard Haussmann, while other Versaillist troops are pressing down the Boulevard Haussmann, firing like furies, and covered by a shellfire falling in their front. Thus the Federals in the Boulevard Haussmann, a mere handful but very obstinate, are taken front and rear, and must slide out of the crux, to all appearance by the New Opera, from the summit of which still flies the red flag. They are taken in flank, too, for a fire is pouring down on them by the Rue de la Chaussée d'Antin, from the Church of the Trinity. Balls are whistling past my window; a shell has just shattered the lamppost at the junction of the Rue de Lafayette with the Boulevard Haussmann. I see Federal after Federal sneaking away by the cover afforded by the Opera House. Every minute I expect to see the Versaillists come in sight round the corner, marching down the Boulevard Haussmann. One thing is certain, I can't get away eastward anyhow, I am hemmed in between three fires, if not four. There is not a soul in the street, even the women, who are so fond of shell fragments, are under cover now. I hear the bugle sounding, whether it is a Versaillist or a Federal bugle, I cannot tell.

Half-past two P.M.

Contrary to my anticipation, the Versaillists are not yet round the corner; that is, they have not got so far down the Boulevard Haussmann as the corner of the Rue de Lafayette, where I am writing, and the red flag still waves from the top of the New Opera House. The shells and mitrailleuses are whistling past the corner where I am ensconced, in one continual whistle, and the clash of broken glass is incessant. It is impossible to define the situation. All is chaos, at least for the moment. What a beautiful day it is! Such a day as one would like to be lying on the grass, under a hawthorn hedge, looking at the young lambs skipping about; not cowering in a corner, dodging shot and shell, in this undignified manner, and without any matches wherewith to light one's pipe.

Half-past three

They have got a cannon and a mitrailleuse off the Boulevard des Italiens, and they are not giving these pieces much time to cool. Their courage is something surprising. The house at the right-hand corner of the Boulevard Haussmann and the Rue de Lafayette has caught fire. Pleasant prospect, if the fire gains head, for one who is sheltered by its gable, as I am. The red flag is still flying over against us on the top of the Opera House, but I fear its lease is a short one.

Five o'clock

The firing is furious and confusing all round. At the Opera House it is especially strong. I see troops and man after man skulking along the parapet of its roof. They have packs on, so I think they are Versaillists; but I cannot see their breeches and so cannot be certain. The *drapeau rouge* still waves from the statue on the summit of the New Opera House.

Twenty minutes past five

They were Versaillists that I saw on the parapet of the New Opera. There is a cheer; the people rush out into the fire and clap their hands. The tricolor is waving on the hither end of the Opera House. I saw the man stick it up. The red flag still waves at the other end. A ladder is needed to remove it. Ha! you are a good plucky one, if all the rest were cowards. You deserve to give the army a good name. A little grig of a fellow in red breeches, he is one of the old French linesman breed. He scuttles forward to the corner of the Rue Halévy in the Boulevard Haussmann, takes up his post behind a tree, and fires along the Boulevard Haussmann towards the Rue Taitbout. When is a Frenchman not dramatic? He fires with an air; he loads with an air; he fires again with a flourish, and is greeted with cheering and clapping of hands. Then he beckons us back dramatically, for he meditates firing up the Rue de Lafayette, but changes his mind and blazes away again up Haussmann. Then he turns and waves on his fellows as if he were on the boards of a theater, the Federal bullets cutting the bark and leaves all around him. He is down. The woman and I dart out from our corner and carry him in. He is dead, with a bullet through the forehead.

Twenty-five minutes to six

The scene is intensely dramatic. A Versaillist has got a ladder and is mounting the statue of Apollo on the front elevation of the New Opera House. He tears down the *drapeau rouge* just as the Versailles troops stream out of the Chaussée d'Antin across the Boulevard Haussmann, and down the Rue Meyerbeer and the continuation of the Chaussée d'Antin. The people rushed from their houses with bottles of wine; money was showered into the streets. The women fell on the necks of the sweaty, dusty men in red breeches, and hugged them amid shouts of *"Vive la ligne."* The soldiers fraternized warmly; drank and pressed forward. Their discipline was admirable. They formed in companies behind the next barricade and obeyed the officer at once when he called them from conviviality. Now the wave of Versaillists is over us for good, and the red breeches are across the Great Boulevard and going at the Place Vendôme. Everybody seems wild with joy, and Communist cards of citizenship are being torn up wholesale. It is not *citoyen* now under pain of suspicion. You may say *monsieur* if you like.

Wednesday

And so evening wore into night, and night became morning. Ah! this morning! Its pale flush of aurora bloom was darkest, most somber night for the once proud, now stricken and humiliated, city. Great God! that men should be so mad as to strive to make universal ruin because their puny course of factiousness is run! The flames from the Palace of the Tuileries, kindled by damnable petroleum, insulted the soft light of the morning and cast lurid rays on the grimy recreant Frenchmen who skulked from their dastardly incendiarism to pot at countrymen from behind a barricade. How the place burned! The flames reveled in the historical palace, whipped up the rich furniture, burst out the plate-glass windows, brought down the fantastic roof. It was in the Prince Imperial's wing facing the Tuileries Gardens where the demon of fire first had his dismal sway. By eight o'clock the whole of the wing was nearly burned out. As I reached the end of the Rue Dauphine the red belches of flames were bursting out from the corner of the Tuileries facing the private gardens and the Rue de Rivoli: the rooms occupied by the King of Prussia and his suite on the visit to France the year of the Exhibition. There is a furious jet of flame pouring out of the window where Bismarck used to sit and smoke.

I turn from the spectacle sad and sick, to be sickened yet further by another spectacle. The Versaillist troops collected about the foot of the Rue Saint-

Honoré were enjoying the fine game of Communist hunting. The Parisians of civil life are caitiffs to the last drop of their thin, sour, white blood. But yesterday they had cried *"Vive la Commune!"* and submitted to be governed by this said Commune. Today they rubbed their hands with livid currish joy to have it in their power to denounce a Communist and reveal his hiding place. Very eager at this work are the dear creatures of women. They know the ratholes into which the poor devils have got, and they guide to them with a fiendish glee which is a phase of the many-sided sex. *Voilà!* the braves of France returned to a triumph after a shameful captivity! They have found him, the miserable! Yes, they drag him out from one of the purlieus which Haussmann had not time to sweep away, and a guard of six of them hem him round as they march him into the Rue Saint-Honoré. A tall, pale, hatless man, with something not ignoble in his carriage. His lower lip is trembling, but his brow is firm, and the eye of him has some pride and defiance in it. They yell—the crowd—"Shoot him; shoot him!"—the demon women most clamorous, of course. An arm goes into the air; there are on it the stripes of a noncommissioned officer, and there is a stick in the fist. The stick falls on the head of the pale man in black. Ha! the infection has caught; men club their rifles, and bring them down on that head, or clash them into splinters in their lust for murder. He is down; he is up again; he is down again; the thuds of the gunstocks on him sounding just as the sound when a man beats a cushion with a stick. A certain British impulse, stronger than consideration for self, prompts me to run forward. But it is useless. They are firing into the flaccid carcass now, thronging about it like blowflies on a piece of meat. His brains spurt on my boot and plash into the gutter, whither the carrion is bodily chucked, presently to be trodden on and rolled on by the feet of multitudes and wheels of gun carriages.

Womanhood, then, is not quite dead in that band of bedlamites who had clamored "Shoot him." Here is one in hysterics; another, with wan, scared face, draws out of the press an embryo bedlamite, her offspring, and, let us hope, goes home. But surely all manhood is dead in the soldiery of France to do a deed like this. An officer—one with a bull throat and the eyes of Algiers—stood by and looked on at the sport, sucking a cigar meanwhile.

It is hard to breathe in an atmosphere mainly of petroleum smoke. There is a sun, but his heat is dominated by the heat of the conflagrations. His rays are obscured by the lurid, blue-black smoke that is rising with a greasy fatness everywhere into the air. Let us out of it, for goodness' sake. I take horse, and ride off by the river brink toward the Point-du-Jour, leaving at my back the still loud rattle of the firing and the smoke belches. I ride on to the Point-du-Jour through Dombrowski's "second line of defense" by the railway viaduct. Poor Dombrowski! a good servant to bad masters. I should like to know his fate for certain. Versaillists have told me that they saw him taken prisoner yesterday morning, dragged on to the Trocadéro, and there shot in cold blood in the face of day, looking dauntlessly into the muzzles of the chassepots. Others say he is wounded and a prisoner.

As I ride up the broad slope of the avenue between Viroflay and Versailles, I pass a very sorrowful and dejected company. In file after file of six each march the prisoners of the Commune—there are over two thousand of them together— patiently, and it seems to me with some consciousness of pride they march, linked closely arm in arm. Among them are many women, some of them the fierce barricade Hecates, others mere girls, soft and timid, who are here seemingly because a parent is here too. All are bareheaded and foul with dust, many powder-stained too, and the burning sun beats down on bald foreheads. Not the sun alone beats down, but the flats of sabers wielded by the dashing Chasseurs d'Afrique, who are the escort of these unfortunates. Their experiences might have taught them decency to the captives. No saber blades had descended on their pates in that long, dreary march from Sedan to their German captivity; they were the prisoners of soldiers. But they are prisoners now no longer, as they caper on their wiry Arab stallions, and in their pride of cheap victory, they belabor unmercifully the miserables of the Commune. In front are three or four hundred prisoners, lashed together with ropes, and among these are not a few men in red breeches, deserters taken red-handed. I marvel that they are here at all, and not dead in the streets of Paris.

As I drive along the green margin of the placid Seine to Saint-Denis, the spectacle which the capital presents is one never to be forgotten. On its white houses the sun still smiles. But up through the sunbeams struggle and surge ghastly swart waves and folds and pillars of dense smoke; not one or two, but

I reckon them on my fingers till I lose the count. Ha! there is a sharp crack, and then a dull thud on the air. No artillery that, surely some great explosion, which must have rocked Paris to its base. There rises a convolvulus-shaped volume of whiter smoke, with a jetlike spurt, such as men describe when Vesuvius bursts into eruption, and then it breaks into fleecy waves and eddies away to the horizon all round as the ripple of a stone thrown into a pool spreads to the margin of the water. The crowds of Germans who sit by the Seine, stolidly watching, are startled into a burst of excitement—the excitement might well be worldwide. "Paris the beautiful" is Paris the ghastly, Paris the battered, Paris the burning, Paris the blood-spattered, now. And this is the nineteenth century, and Europe professes civilization, and France boasts of culture, and Frenchmen are braining one another with the butt ends of muskets, and Paris is burning. We want but a Nero to fiddle.

[LYRICS]

THE GHOST DANCE

In January of 1889 Wovoka (c. 1856-1932), a Paiute, dreamed that the gods revealed to him a future where the age of misery would come to an abrupt conclusion, the dead would return, and men would treat one another with civility. The gods charged him with teaching his people a ritual dance that would speed the coming of the new dispensation. The Ghost Dance spread with a starling rapidity to diverse tribes across the whole of the great plains. In early 1890, it reached the Sioux during the outbreak of the Sioux uprising and was vigorously suppressed by the United States military. This effort culminated in the massacre of Wounded Knee, on December 29, 1890.

A slender antelope, a slender antelope.
A slender antelope, a slender antelope.
He is wallowing upon the ground,
He is wallowing upon the ground,
He is wallowing upon the ground.

The black rock, the black rock,
The black rock, the black rock.
The rock is broken, the rock is broken,
The rock is broken, the rock is broken.

The wind stirs the willows,
The wind stirs the willows,
The wind stirs the willows.
The wind stirs the grasses,
The wind stirs the grasses,
The wind stirs the grasses.

Fog! Fog!
Lightning! Lightning!
Whirlwind! Whirlwind!

The whirlwind! The whirlwind!
The whirlwind! The whirlwind!
The snowy earth comes gliding, the snowy earth comes gliding,
The snowy earth comes gliding, the snowy earth comes gliding.

There is dust from the whirlwind,
There is dust from the whirlwind,
There is dust from the whirlwind.
The whirlwind on the mountain,
The whirlwind on the mountain,
The whirlwind on the mountain.

The rocks are ringing,
The rocks are ringing,
The rocks are ringing.
They are ringing in the mountains,
They are ringing in the mountains,
They are ringing in the mountains.

The cottonwoods are growing tall,
The cottonwoods are growing tall,
The cottonwoods are growing tall.
They are growing tall and verdant,
They are growing tall and verdant,
They are growing tall and verdant.

[POEM]

WAITING FOR THE BARBARIANS

(1898)

C. P. Cavafy (1863-1933)

What are we waiting for, assembled in the forum?

The barbarians are due here today.

Why isn't anything happening in the senate?
Why do the senators sit there without legislating?

Because the barbarians are coming today.
What laws can the senators make now?
Once the barbarians are here, they'll do the legislating.

Why did our emperor get up so early,
and why is he sitting at the city's main gate
on his throne, in state, wearing the crown?

Because the barbarians are coming today
and the emperor is waiting to receive their leader.
He has even prepared a scroll to give him,
replete with titles, with imposing names.

Why have our two consuls and praetors come out today
wearing their embroidered, their scarlet togas?
Why have they put on bracelets with so many amethysts,
and rings sparkling with magnificent emeralds?
Why are they carrying elegant canes
beautifully worked in silver and gold?

Because the barbarians are coming today
and things like that dazzle the barbarians.

Why don't our distinguished orators come forward as usual
to make their speeches, say what they have to say?

Because the barbarians are coming today
and they're bored by rhetoric and public speaking.

Why this sudden restlessness, this confusion?
(How serious people's faces have become.)
Why are the streets and squares emptying so rapidly,
everyone going home so lost in thought?

Because night has fallen and the barbarians have not come.
And some who have just returned from the border say
there are no barbarians any longer.

And now, what's going to happen to us without barbarians?
They were, those people, a kind of solution.

PART III

THE TWENTIETH CENTURY:
THE END IN A VOID

SAN FRANCISCO, 1906

━┝━◆━◦━◇━┥━

On April 17, 1906, San Francisco was engulfed by earthquake and fire. Jack London (1876-1916) described the catastrophe for Collier's Weekly, *in the issue of May 5.*

The earthquake shook down in San Francisco hundreds of thousands of dollars' worth of walls and chimneys. But the conflagration that followed burned up hundreds of millions of dollars' worth of property. There is no estimating within hundreds of millions the actual damage wrought. Not in history has a modern imperial city been so completely destroyed. San Francisco is gone! Nothing remains of it but memories and a fringe of dwelling houses on its outskirts. Its industrial section is wiped out. Its social and residential section is wiped out. The factories and warehouses, the great stores and newspaper buildings, the hotels and the palaces of the nabobs, are all gone. Remains only the fringe of dwelling houses on the outskirts of what was once San Francisco.

Within an hour after the earthquake shock the smoke of San Francisco's burning was a lurid tower visible a hundred miles away. And for three days and nights this lurid tower swayed in the sky, reddening the sun, darkening the day, and filling the land with smoke.

On Wednesday morning at a quarter past five came the earthquake. A minute later the flames were leaping upward. In a dozen different quarters south of Market Street, in the working-class ghetto, and in the factories, fires started. There was no opposing the flames. There was no organization, no communication. All the cunning adjustments of a twentieth-century city had been smashed by the earthquake. The streets were humped into ridges and depressions and piled with debris of fallen walls. The steel rails were twisted into perpendicular and horizontal angles. The telephone and telegraph systems were disrupted. And the great water mains had burst. All the shrewd contrivances and safeguards of man had been thrown out of gear by thirty seconds' twitching of the earth crust.

By Wednesday afternoon, inside of twelve hours, half the heart of the city was gone. At that time I watched the vast conflagration from out on the bay. It was dead calm. Not a flicker of wind stirred. Yet from every side wind was pouring in upon the city. East, west, north, and south, strong winds were blowing upon the doomed city. The heated air rising made an enormous suck. Thus did the fire of itself build its own colossal chimney through the atmosphere. Day and night this dead calm continued, and yet, near to the flames, the wind was often half a gale, so mighty was the suck.

The edict which prevented chaos was the following proclamation by Mayor E. E. Schmitz:

"The Federal Troops, the members of the Regular Police Force, and all Special Police Officers have been authorized to KILL any and all persons found engaged in looting or in the commission of any other crime.

"I have directed all the Gas and Electric Lighting Companies not to turn on gas or electricity until I order them to do so; you may therefore expect the city to remain in darkness for an indefinite time.

"I request all citizens to remain at home from darkness until daylight of every night until order is restored.

"I warn all citizens of the danger of fire from damaged or destroyed chimneys, broken or leaking gas pipes or fixtures, or any like cause."

Wednesday night saw the destruction of the very heart of the city. Dynamite was lavishly used, and many of San Francisco's proudest structures were crumbled by man himself into ruins, but there was no withstanding the onrush of the flames. Time and again successful stands were made by the fire fighters, and every time the flames flanked around on either side, or came up from the rear, and turned to defeat the hard-won victory.

An enumeration of the buildings destroyed would be a directory of San Francisco. An enumeration of the buildings undestroyed would be a line and several addresses. An enumeration of the deeds of heroism would stock a library and bankrupt the Carnegie medal fund. An enumeration of the dead—will never be made. All vestiges of them were destroyed by the flames. The number of the victims of the earthquake will never be known. South of Market Street, where the loss of life was particularly heavy, was the first to catch fire.

Remarkable as it may seem, Wednesday night, while the whole city crashed and roared into ruin, was a quiet night. There were no crowds. There was no shouting and yelling. There was no hysteria, no disorder. I passed Wednesday night in the part of the advancing flames, and in all those terrible hours I saw not one woman who wept, not one man who was excited, not one person who was in the slightest degree panic-stricken.

Before the flames, throughout the night, fled tens of thousands of homeless ones. Some were wrapped in blankets. Others carried bundles of bedding and dear household treasures. Sometimes a whole family was harnessed to a carriage or delivery wagon that was weighted down with their possessions. Baby buggies, toy wagons, and gocarts were used as trucks, while every other person was dragging a trunk. Yet everybody was gracious. The most perfect courtesy obtained. Never in all San Francisco's history were her people so kind and courteous as on this night of terror.

All the night these tens of thousands fled before the flames. Many of them, the poor people from the labor ghetto, had fled all day as well. They had left their homes burdened with possessions. Now and again they lightened up, flinging out upon the street clothing and treasures they had dragged for miles.

They held on longest to their trunks, and over these trunks many a strong man broke his heart that night. The hills of San Francisco are steep, and up these hills, mile after mile, were the trunks dragged. Everywhere were trunks, with across them lying their exhausted owners, men and women. Before the march of the flames were flung picket lines of soldiers. And a block at a time, as the flames advanced, these pickets retreated. One of their tasks was to keep the trunk pullers moving. The exhausted creatures, stirred on by the menace of bayonets, would arise and struggle up the steep pavements, pausing from weakness every five or ten feet.

Often after surmounting a heartbreaking hill, they would find another wall of flame advancing upon them at right angles and be compelled to change anew the line of their retreat. In the end, completely played out, after toiling for a dozen hours like giants, thousands of them were compelled to abandon their trunks. Here the shopkeepers and soft members of the middle class were at a disadvantage. But the workingmen dug holes in vacant lots and back yards and buried their trunks.

At nine o'clock Wednesday evening I walked down through miles and miles of magnificent buildings and towering skyscrapers. Here was no fire. All was in perfect order. The police patrolled the streets. Every building had its watchman at the door. And yet it was doomed, all of it. There was no water. The dynamite was giving out. And at right angles two different conflagrations were sweeping down upon it.

At one o'clock in the morning I walked down through the same section. Everything still stood intact. There was no fire. And yet there was a change. A rain of ashes was falling. The watchmen at the doors were gone. The police had been withdrawn. There were no firemen, no fire engines, no men fighting with dynamite. The district had been absolutely abandoned. I stood at the corner of Kearney and Market, in the very innermost heart of San Francisco. Kearney Street was deserted. Half a dozen blocks away it was burning on both sides. The street was a wall of flame. And against this wall of flame, silhouetted sharply, were two United States cavalrymen sitting their horses, calmly watching. That was all. Not another person was in sight. In the intact heart of the city two troopers sat their horses and watched.

Surrender was complete. There was no water. The sewers had long since been pumped dry. There was no dynamite. At half-past one in the morning three sides of Union Square were in flames. The fourth side, where stood the great St.

Francis Hotel, was still holding out. An hour later, ignited from top and sides, the St. Francis was flaming heavenward. Union Square, heaped high with mountains of trunks, was deserted. Troops, refugees, and all had retreated.

It was at Union Square that I saw a man offering a thousand dollars for a team of horses. He was in charge of a truck piled high with trunks from some hotel. It had been hauled here into what was considered safety, and the horses had been taken out. The flames were on three sides of the square, and there were no horses.

Also, at this time, standing beside the truck, I urged a man to seek safety in flight. He was all but hemmed in by several conflagrations. He was an old man and he was on crutches. Said he: "Today is my birthday. Last night I was worth thirty thousand dollars. I bought five bottles of wine, some delicate fish, and other things for my birthday dinner. I have had no dinner, and all I own are these crutches."

I convinced him of his danger and started him limping on his way. An hour later, from a distance, I saw the truckload of trunks burning merrily in the middle of the street.

On Thursday morning, at a quarter past five, just twenty-four hours after the earthquake, I sat on the steps of a small residence of Nob Hill. With me sat Japanese, Italians, Chinese, and Negroes—a bit of the cosmopolitan flotsam of the wreck of the city. All about were the palaces of the nabob pioneers of Forty-nine. To the east and south, at right angles, were advancing two mighty walls of flame.

Day was trying to dawn through the smoke pall. A sickly light was creeping over the face of things. Once only the sun broke through the smoke pall, blood-red, and showing quarter its usual size. The smoke pall itself, viewed from beneath, was a rose color that pulsed and fluttered with lavender shades. Then it turned to mauve and yellow and dun. There was no sun. And so dawned the second day on stricken San Francisco.

Here and there through the smoke, creeping warily under the shadows of tottering walls, emerged occasional men and women. It was like the meeting of the handful of survivors after the day of the end of the world.

On Mission Street lay a dozen steers, in a neat row stretching across the street, just as they had been struck down by the flying ruins of the earthquake. The fire had passed through afterward and roasted them.

San Francisco, at the present time, is like the crater of a volcano, around which are camped tens of thousands of refugees. At the Presidio alone are at least twenty thousand. All the surrounding cities and towns are jammed with the homeless ones, where they are being cared for by the relief committees. The refugees were carried free by the railroads to any point they wished to go, and it is estimated that over one hundred thousand people have left the peninsula on which San Francisco stood.

ENTROPY

Accepting the logic of the scientific law of entropy, the American historian and educator Henry Adams (1838-1918) observed that civilization had regressed into lower and lower phases of history. He provoked his readers by suggesting that it was likely to reach its terminus well before the end of the 20th century. Some of his speculations on the subject appreared in 1910, in A Letter to American Teachers of History.

In the earlier scientific commentaries on the Law of Dissipation, astronomers and physicists commonly took some little pains to soften the harshness of their doom by assurances that the prospect was not so black as it seemed, but that the sun would adapt itself to man's convenience by allowing some thousands or millions of years to elapse before its extinction. This pleasing thoughtfulness has vanished. Geologists, when most generous, scarcely allow more than thirty thousand years since the last ice-cap began its partial recession; while, quite commonly, they insist that their most careful and elaborate estimates do not justify them in granting more than a quarter that time to the very incomplete process of clearing away the ice and snow from the streets of primitive New York and

Boston. The cataclysmic ruin that spread over all the most populous parts of the northern hemisphere while the accomplished and highly educated architects of Nippur were laying the arched foundations of their city, has, it is true, been partially covered or disguised under new vegetation; but even this brief retrospective reprieve is darkened by the earnest assurances of the most popular textbooks and teachers that they can hold out no good reason for hoping that the exemption will last. The sun is ready to condense again at any moment, causing another violent disequilibrium, to be followed by another great outburst and waste of its expiring heat.

The humor of these prophecies seldom strikes a reader `with its full force in America, but in Europe the love of dramatic effect inspires every line. Compared with the superficial and self-complacent optimism which seems to veneer the surface of society, the frequent and tragic outbursts of physicists, astronomers, geologists, biologists, and sociological socialists announcing the end of the world, surpass all that could be conceived as a natural product of the time. The note of warning verges on the grotesque; it is hysterically solemn; a little more, and it would sound like that of a Salvation army; a small natural shock might easily turn it to a panic. Naturally a historian is most interested in what concerns primitive history, and all the relations of primitive man to nature. He takes up the last work on the subject, which happens in 1910, to be "Les Premières Civilisations," by M. J. de Morgan, published in June, 1909. M. de Morgan is one of the highest authorities—possibly quite the highest authority—on his subject, and this volume contains the whole result of his vast study. Unconscious of thermodynamics, he treats primitive man as a sort of function of the glacial epoch, and ends by telling his readers (p. 97):—

"The glacial period is far from being ended; our times, which still make an integral part of it, are characterized by an important retreat of the glaciers, started long before the beginnings of history. It is to be supposed that this retreat of the ice is not definitive, but that the cold will return, and with it the depopulation of a part of our globe. Nothing can enable us to foretell the amplitude of this future oscillation, or the lot which the laws of nature destine to humanity. During this cataclysm revolutions will occur which the most fecund imagination cannot conceive,—disasters the more horrible because, while the population of the earth goes on increasing every day, and even the less favored districts little by little become inhabited, the different human groups, crowded back one on another, and finding no more space for existence, will be driven to internecine destruction."

M. de Morgan belongs to the most serious class of historians, while M. Camille Flammarion, the distinguished director of the Meudon observatory, besides being a serious astronomer, is also one of the most widely read, and most highly intelligent, vulgarizers of science. When he reaches the point of describing the solar catastrophe in his popular astronomy, he lays bare an enormous field for harrowing horrors ("Astronomie Populaire," 102, 103, Paris, 1905): —

"Life and human activity will insensibly be shut up within the tropical zones. Saint Petersburg, Berlin, London, Paris, Vienna, Constantinople, Rome, will successively sink to sleep under their eternal cerements. During many centuries, equatorial humanity will undertake vain arctic expeditions to rediscover under the ice the sites of Paris, of Bordeaux, of Lyons, of Marseilles. The seashores will have changed and the map of the earth will be transformed. No longer will man live,—no longer will he breathe,—except in the equatorial zone, down to the day when the last tribe, already expiring in cold and hunger, shall camp on the shores of the last sea in the rays of a pale sun which will henceforward illumine an earth that is only a wandering tomb, turning around a useless light and a barren heat. Surprised by the cold, the last human family has been touched by the finger of death, and soon their bones will be buried under the shroud of eternal ice. The historian of nature would then be able to write:—'Here lies the entire humanity of a world which has lived! Here lie all the dreams of ambition, all the conquests of military glory, all the resounding affairs of finance, all the systems of an imperfect science, and also all the oaths of mortals' love! Here lie all the beauties of earth!'—But no mortuary stone will mark the spot where the poor planet shall have rendered its last sigh!"

As though to assure the public that he knows what he is talking about, M. Flammarion, who is a practical astronomer, goes on with a certain sombre exaltation, like a religious prophet, to say that the terrors he predicts are of common occurrence in astronomy, and leaves his scholars to infer that nature regards her end as attained only when she has treated man as an enemy to be crushed.

Volumes would be needed if a writer should attempt to follow the track of this idea through all the branches of present thought; but, without unnecessarily disturbing the labors of anthropology and biology, the merest insect might be excused for asking what happens to fellow insects, who, like himself, are enjoying the precarious hospitality of these numerous solar systems.

All energies which are convertible into heat must suffer degradation; among these, as the physicists expressly insist, are all vital processes; the mere temporary approach to a final equilibrium would be fatal; and, among all the infinite possibilities of evolution, the only absolute certainty in physics is that the earth every day approaches it. No one can be trusted to express so much as an opinion about the moment when any special vital process may expect to be reduced in energy; man and beast can, at the best, look forward only to a diversified agony of twenty million years; but at no instant of this considerable period can the professor of mathematics flatter either himself or his students with an exclusive or extended hope of escaping imbecility.

According to some geologists, this view is extravagantly—almost ridiculously—optimistic; but with the scientific correctness of these opinions, the historian is not concerned. He asks only how far the teaching of his colleagues contradicts his own, and how far society sides with his contradictors. His question is difficult to answer. At first sight he is conscious of no divergence. Society has the air of taking for granted its indefinite progress towards perfection. Yet the same society has acquired a growing habit of feeling its own pulse, and registering its own temperature, from day to day; of prescribing to itself new régimes from year to year; and of doubting its own health like a nervous invalid. Keeping Europe still in view for illustration and assuming for the moment that America does not exist, every reader of the French or German papers knows that not a day passes without producing some uneasy discussion of supposed social decrepitude;—falling off of the birth rate;—decline of rural population;—lowering of army standards;—multiplication of suicides;—increase of insanity or idiocy,—of cancer,—of tuberculosis;—signs of nervous exhaustion,—of enfeebled vitality,—"habits" of alcoholism and drugs,—failure of eye-sight in the young,—and so on, without end.

"The anarchist, the esthete, the mystic, the revolutionary socialist, even if they do not despair of the future, agree with the pessimist in the same sentiment of hatred and disgust for whatever is; in the same need of destroying the real, and escaping from it. The collective melancholy would not have invaded consciousness to that point unless it has taken morbid development; and in consequence the development of suicide which results from it, is of the same nature. All the proofs unite in causing us to regard the enormous increase which has shown itself within a century in the number of voluntary deaths, as a pathological phenomenon which becomes every day more menacing." (Émile Durkheim, "Le Suicide." Paris, 1897) At the rate of progress since 1870, the press might soon learn to blacken the prospects of humanity with all the picturesque genius of Camille Flammarion. A little more superficial knowledge is all it needs; the general disposition is already excellent.

LOUVAIN, 1914

Writing in the New York Tribune *of August 31, 1914, Richard Harding Davis (1864-1916), the most famous newspaper correspondent of his day, described the burning of Louvain in the first month of World War I.*

LONDON, AUGUST 30—I left Brussels on Thursday afternoon and have just arrived in London. For two hours on Thursday night I was in what for six hundred years has been the city of Louvain. The Germans were burning it, and to hide their work kept us locked in the railroad carriages. But the story was written against the sky, was told to us by German soldiers incoherent with excesses; and we could read it in the faces of women and children being led to concentration camps and of citizens on their way to be shot.

The Germans sentenced Louvain on Wednesday to become a wilderness, and with the German system and love of thoroughness they left Louvain an empty blackened shell. The reason for this appeal to the torch and the execution of noncombatants, as given to me on Thursday morning by General von Lutwitz, military governor of Brussels, was this: on Wednesday while the German military commander of the troops of Louvain was at the Hôtel de Ville talking to the Burgomaster, a son of the Burgomaster with an automatic pistol shot the chief of staff and German staff surgeons.

Lutwitz claims this was the signal for the civil guard, in civilian clothes on roofs, to fire upon the German soldiers in the open square below. He said also the Belgians had quick-firing guns, brought from Antwerp. As for a week the Germans had occupied Louvain and closely guarded all approaches, the story that there was any gunrunning is absurd.

Fifty Germans were killed and wounded. For that, said Lutwitz, Louvain must be wiped out. So in pantomime with his fist he swept the papers across his table.

"The Hôtel de Ville," he added, "was a beautiful building; it is a pity it must be destroyed."

Ten days ago I was in Louvain when it was occupied by Belgian troops and King Albert and his staff. The city dates from the eleventh century, and the population was 42,000. The citizens were brewers, lacemakers, and manufacturers of ornaments for churches. The university once was the most celebrated in European cities, and still is, or was, headquarters of the Jesuits.

In the Louvain college many priests now in America have been educated, and ten days ago over the green walls of the college, I saw hanging two American flags. I found the city clean, sleepy, and pretty, with narrow twisting streets and smart shops and cafés set in flower gardens of the houses, with red roofs, green shutters, and white walls.

Over those that faced south had been trained pear trees, their branches heavy with fruit spread out against the walls like branches of candelabra. The Town Hall was very old and very beautiful, an example of Gothic architecture, in detail and design more celebrated even than the Town Hall of Bruges or Brussels. It was five hundred years old, and lately had been repaired with great taste and at great cost.

Opposite was the Church of St. Pierre, dating from the fifteenth century, a very noble building, with many chapels filled with carvings of the time of the

Renaissance in wood, stone, and iron. In the university were 150,000 volumes.

Near it was the bronze statue of Father Damien, priest of the leper colony in the South Pacific, of which Robert Louis Stevenson wrote. All these buildings now are empty, exploded cartridges. Statues, pictures, carvings, parchments, archives—all are gone.

No one defends the sniper. But because ignorant Mexicans when their city was invaded fired upon our sailors, we did not destroy Vera Cruz. Even had we bombarded Vera Cruz, money could have restored it. Money can never restore Louvain. Great architects, dead these six hundred years, made it beautiful, and their handiwork belonged to the world. With torch and dynamite the Germans have turned these masterpieces into ashes, and all the Kaiser's horses and all his men cannot bring them back again.

When by troop train we reached Louvain, the entire heart of the city was destroyed and fire had reached the Boulevard Tirlemont, which faces the railroad station. The night was windless, and the sparks rose in steady, leisurely pillars, falling back into the furnace from which they sprang. In their work the soldiers were moving from the heart of the city to the outskirts, street by street, from house to house.

In each building, so German soldiers told me, they began at the first floor, and when that was burning steadily passed to the one next. There were no exceptions—whether it was a store, chapel, or private residence it was destroyed. The occupants had been warned to go, and in each deserted shop or house the furniture was piled, the torch was stuck under it, and into the air went the savings of years, souvenirs of children, of parents, heirlooms that had passed from generation to generation.

The people had time only to fill a pillowcase and fly. Some were not so fortunate, and by thousands, like flocks of sheep, they were rounded up and marched through the night to concentration camps. We were not allowed to speak to any citizen of Louvain, but the Germans crowded the windows, boastful, gloating, eager to interpret.

We were free to move from one end of the train to the other, and in the two hours during which it circled the burning city war was before us in its most hateful aspect.

In other wars I have watched men on one hilltop, without haste, without heat, fire at men on another hill, and in consequence on both sides good men were wasted. But in those fights there were no women and children, and the shells struck only vacant stretches of veldt or uninhabited mountainsides.

At Louvain it was war upon the defenseless, war upon churches, colleges, shops of milliners and lacemakers; war brought to the bedside and fireside; against women harvesting in the fields, against children in wooden shoes at play in the streets.

At Louvain that night the Germans were like men after an orgy.

There were fifty English prisoners, erect and soldierly. In the ocean of gray the little patch of khaki looked pitifully lonely, but they regarded the men who had outnumbered but not defeated them with calm but uncurious eyes. In one way I was glad to see them there. Later they will bear witness as to how the enemy makes a wilderness and calls it war. It was a most weird picture.

On the high ground rose the broken spires of the Church of St. Pierre and the Hôtel de Ville, and descending like steps were row beneath row of houses, those on the Boulevard de Jodigne. Some of these were already cold, but others sent up steady, straight columns of flame. In others at the third and fourth stories the window curtains still hung, flowers still filled the window boxes, while on the first floor the torch had just passed and the flames were leaping. Fire had destroyed the electric plant, but at times the flames made the station so light that you could see the second hand of your watch, and again all was darkness, lit only by candles.

You could tell when an officer passed by the electric torch he carried strapped to his chest. In the darkness the gray uniforms filled the station with an army of ghosts. You distinguished men only when pipes hanging from their teeth glowed red or their bayonets flashed.

Outside the station in the public square the people of Louvain passed in an unending procession, women bareheaded, weeping, men carrying the children asleep on their shoulders, all hemmed in by the shadowy army of gray wolves. Once they were halted, and among them were marched a line of men. They well knew their fellow townsmen. These were on their way to be shot. And better to point the moral an officer halted both processions and, climbing to a cart, explained why the men were to die. He warned others not to bring down upon themselves a like vengeance.

As those being led to spend the night in the fields looked across to those marked for death they saw old friends, neighbors of long standing, men of their own household. The officer bellowing at them from the cart was illuminated by the headlights of an automobile. He looked like an actor held in a spotlight on a darkened stage.

It was all like a scene upon the stage, so unreal, so inhuman, you felt that it could not be true, that the curtain of fire, purring and crackling and sending up hot sparks to meet the kind, calm stars, was only a painted backdrop; that the reports of rifles from the dark rooms came from blank cartridges, and that these trembling shopkeepers and peasants ringed in bayonets would not in a few minutes really die, but that they themselves and their homes would be restored to their wives and children.

You felt it was only a nightmare, cruel and uncivilized. And then you remembered that the German Emperor has told us what it is. It is his Holy War.

THE HINDENBURG TRENCH, 1917

Siegfried Sassoon (1886-1967) was a poet who served as a British officer in World War I. His public statements of pacifism after the war were attributed to shell shock, and he was temporarily institutionalized. He published Memoirs of an Infantry Officer *in 1930.*

At 9 p.m. the Company fell in at the top of the ruined street of St. Martin. Two guides from the outgoing battalion awaited us. We were to relieve some Northumberland Fusiliers in the Hindenburg Trench—the companies going up independently.

It was a grey evening, dry and windless. The village of St. Martin was a shattered relic; but even in the devastated area one could be conscious of the arrival of spring, and as I took up my position in the rear of the moving column there was something in the sober twilight which could remind me of April evenings in England and the Butley cricket field where a few of us had been having our first knock at the nets. The cricket season had begun . . . . But the Company had left the shell-pitted road and was going uphill across open ground. Already the guides were making the pace too hot for the rear platoon; like most guides they were inconveniently nimble owing to their freedom from accoutrement, and insecurely confident that they knew the way. The muttered message "pass it along—steady the pace in front" was accompanied by the usual muffled clinkings and rattlings of arms and equipment. Unwillingly retarded, the guides led us into the deepening dusk. We hadn't more than two miles to go, but gradually the guides grew less authoritative. Several times they stopped to get their bearings. Leake fussed and fumed and they became more and more flurried. I began to suspect that our progress was circular.

At a midnight halt the hill still loomed in front of us; the guides confessed that they had lost their way, and Leake decided to sit down and wait for daylight. (There were few things more uncomfortable in the life of an officer than to be walking in front of a party of men all of whom knew that he was leading them in the wrong direction.) With Leake's permission I blundered experimentally into the gloom, fully expecting to lose both myself and the Company. By a lucky accident, I soon fell headlong into a sunken road and found myself among a small party of Sappers who could tell me where I was. It was a case of "Please, can you tell me the way to the Hindenburg Trench?" Congratulating myself on my cleverness I took one of the Sappers back to poor benighted B Company, and we were led to our Battalion rendezvous.

We were at the end of a journey which had begun twelve days before, when we started from Camp 13. Stage by stage, we had marched to the life-denying region which from far away had threatened us with the blink and growl of its bombardments. Now we were groping and stumbling along a deep ditch to the place appointed for us in the zone of inhuman havoc. There must have been some hazy moonlight, for I remember the figures of men huddled against the sides of communication trenches; seeing them in some sort of ghastly glimmer (was it, perhaps, the diffused whiteness of a sinking flare beyond the ridge?) I was doubtful whether they were asleep or dead, for the attitudes of many were like death, grotesque and distorted. But this is nothing new to write about, you will say; just a weary company, squeezing past dead or drowsing men while it sloshes and stumbles to a front-line trench. Nevertheless that night relief had its significance for me, though in human experience it had been multiplied a millionfold. I, a single human being with my little stock of earthly experience in my head, was entering once again the veritable gloom and disaster of the thing called Armageddon. And I saw it then, as I see it now—a dreadful place, a place of horror and desolation which no imagination could have invented. Also it was a place where a man of strong spirit might know himself utterly powerless against death and destruction, and yet stand up and defy gross darkness and stupefying shell-fire, discovering in himself the invincible resistance of an animal or an insect, and an endurance which he might, in after days, forget or disbelieve.

Anyhow, there I was, leading that little procession of Flintshire Fusiliers many of whom had never seen a front-line trench before. At that juncture they asked no compensation for their efforts except a mug of hot tea. The tea would have been a miracle, and we didn't get it till next morning, but there was some comfort in the fact that it wasn't raining.

It was nearly four o'clock when we found ourselves in the Hindenburg Main Trench. After telling me to post the sentries, Leake disappeared down some stairs to the Tunnel (which will be described later on). The Company we were relieving had already departed, so there was no one to give me any information. At first I didn't even know for certain that we were in the Front Line. The trench was a sort of gully, deep, wide, and unfinished looking. The sentries had to clamber up a bank of loose earth before they could see over the top. Our Company was only about eighty strong and its sector was fully 600 yards. The distance between the sentry-posts made me aware of our inadequacy in that wilderness. I had no right to feel homeless, but I did; and if I had needed to be reminded of my forlorn situation as a living creature I could have done it merely by thinking of a Field Cashier. Fifty franc notes were comfortable things, but they were no earthly use up here, and the words "Field Cashier" would have epitomized my remoteness from snugness and security, and from all assurance that I should be alive and kicking the week after next. But it would soon be Sunday morning; such ideas weren't wholesome, and there was a certain haggard curiosity attached to the proceedings; combined with the self-dramatizing desperation which enabled a good many of us to worry our way through much worse emergencies than mine.

Out in no-man's-land there was no sign of any German activity. The only remarkable thing was the unbroken silence. I was in a sort of twilight, for there was a moony glimmer in the low-clouded sky; but the unknown territory in front was dark, and I stared out at it like a man looking from the side of a ship. Returning to my own sector I met a runner with a verbal message from Battalion H.Q. B Company's front was to be thoroughly patrolled at once. Realizing the futility of sending any of my few spare men out on patrol (they'd been walking about for seven hours and were dead beat) I lost my temper, quietly and inwardly. Shirley and Rees were nowhere to be seen and it wouldn't have been fair to send them out, inexperienced as they were. So I stumped along to our right-flank post, told them to pass it along that a patrol was going out from right to left, and then started sulkily out for a solitary stroll in no-man's-land. I felt more annoyed with Battalion Headquarters than with the enemy. There was no wire in front of the trench, which was, of course, constructed for people facing the other way. I counted my steps; 200 steps straight ahead; then I began to walk the presumptive 600 steps to the left. But it isn't easy to count your steps in the dark among shell-holes, and after a problematic 400 I lost confidence in my automatic pistol, which I was grasping in my right-hand breeches pocket. Here I am, I thought, alone out in this god-forsaken bit of ground, with quite a good chance of bumping into a Boche strong-post. Apparently there was only one reassuring action which I could perform; so I expressed my opinion of the War by relieving myself (for it must be remembered that there are other reliefs beside Battalion reliefs). I insured my sense of direction by placing my pistol on the ground with its muzzle pointing the way I was going. Feeling less lonely and afraid, I finished my patrol without having met so much as a dead body, and regained the trench exactly opposite our left-hand post, after being huskily challenged by an irresolute sentry, who, as I realized at the time, was the greatest danger I had encountered. It was now just beginning to be more daylight than darkness, and when I stumbled down a shaft to the underground trench I left the sentries shivering under a red and rainy-looking sky.

By ten o'clock I was above ground again, in charge of a fatigue party. We went half-way back to St. Martin, to an ammunition dump, whence we carried up boxes of trench mortar bombs. I carried a box myself, as the conditions were vile and it seemed the only method of convincing the men that it had to be done. We were out nearly seven hours; it rained all day and the trenches were a morass of glue-like mud. The unmitigated misery of that carrying party was a typical infantry experience of discomfort without actual danger. Even if the ground had been dry the boxes would have been too heavy for most of the men; but we were lucky in one way; the wet weather was causing the artillery to spend an inactive Sunday. It was a yellow corpse-like day, more like November than April, and the landscape was desolate and treeless. What we were doing was quite unexceptional; millions of soldiers endured the same sort of thing and got badly shelled into the bargain. Nevertheless I can believe that my party, staggering and floundering under its loads, would have made an impressive picture of "Despair". The background, too, was appropriate. We were among the débris of the intense bombardment of ten days before, for we were passing along and across the Hindenburg Outpost Trench, with its belt of wire (fifty yards deep in places); here and there these rusty jungles had been flattened by tanks. The Outpost Trench was about 200 yards from the Main Trench, which was now our front line. It had been solidly made, ten feet deep, with timbered fire-steps, splayed sides, and timbered steps at intervals to front and rear and to machine-gun emplacements. Now it was wrecked as though by earthquake and eruption. Concrete strong-posts were smashed and tilted sideways; everywhere the chalky soil was pocked and pitted with huge shell-holes; and wherever we looked the mangled effigies of the dead were our *memento mori*. Shell-twisted and dismembered, the Germans maintained the violent attitudes in which they had died. The British had mostly been killed by bullets or bombs, so they looked more resigned. But I can remember a pair of hands (nationality unknown) which protruded from the soaked ashen soil like the roots of a tree turned upside down; one hand seemed to be pointing at the sky with an accusing gesture. Each time I passed that place the protest of those fingers became more expressive of an appeal to God in defiance of those who made the War. Who made the War? I laughed hysterically as the thought passed through my mud-stained mind. But I only laughed mentally, for my box of Stokes gun ammunition left me no breath to spare for an angry guffaw. And the dead were the dead; this was no time to be pitying them or asking silly questions about their outraged lives. Such sights must be taken for granted, I thought, as I gasped and slithered and stumbled with my disconsolate crew. Floating on the surface of the flooded trench was the mask of a human face which had detached itself from the skull.

St. Petersburg, 1917

John Reed (1887-1920), a young American sympathetic to the Communist cause, witnessed the seizure of the Winter Palace on November 7. He published his account two years later in Ten Days That Shook the World. *Indicted for treason, he escaped to the Soviet Union and died of typhus. He was subsequently buried with other Bolshevik heroes beside the Kremlin wall.*

Wednesday, November 7, I rose very late. The noon cannon boomed from Peter-Paul as I went down the Nevsky. It was a raw, chill day. In front of the State Bank some soldiers with fixed bayonets were standing at the closed gates.

"What side do you belong to?" I asked. "The government?"

"No more government," one answered with a grin, "*Slava Bogu!* Glory to God!" That was all I could get out of him.

The streetcars were running on the Nevsky, men, women, and small boys hanging on every projection. Shops were open, and there seemed even less uneasiness among the street crowds than there had been the day before. A whole crop of new appeals against insurrection had blossomed out on the walls during the night—to the peasants, to the soldiers at the front, to the workmen of Petrograd.

I bought a copy of *Rabotchi Put*, the only newspaper which seemed on sale, and a little later paid a soldier fifty kopecks for a secondhand copy of *Dien*. The Bolshevik paper, printed on large-sized sheets in the conquered office of the *Russkaya Volia*, had huge headlines: ALL POWER—TO THE SOVIETS OF WORKERS, SOLDIERS, AND PEASANTS! PEACE! BREAD! LAND!

Just at the corner of the Ekaterina Canal, under an arc light, a cordon of armed sailors was drawn across the Nevsky, blocking the way to a crowd of people in columns of fours. There were about three or four hundred of them, men in frock coats, well-dressed women, officers—all sorts and conditions of people.

Like a black river, filling all the streets, without song or cheer we poured through the Red Arch, where the man just ahead of me said in a low voice: "Look out, comrades! Don't trust them. They will fire, surely!" In the open we began to run, stooping low and bunching together, and jammed up suddenly behind the pedestal of the Alexander Column.

After a few minutes' huddling there, some hundreds of men, the army seemed reassured and without any orders suddenly began again to flow forward. By this time, in the light that streamed out of all the Winter Palace windows, I could see that the first two or three hundred men were Red Guards, with only a few scattered soldiers. Over the barricade of firewood we clambered, and leaping down inside gave a triumphant shout as we stumbled on a heap of rifles thrown down by the *yunkers* who had stood there. On both sides of the main gateway the doors stood wide open, light streamed out, and from the huge pile came not the slightest sound.

Carried along by the eager wave of men, we were swept into the right-hand entrance, opening into a great bare vaulted room, the cellar of the east wing, from which issued a maze of corridors and staircases. A number of huge packing cases stood about, and upon these the Red Guards and soldiers fell furiously, battering them open with the butts of their rifles, and pulling out carpets, curtains, linens, porcelain plates, glassware. One man went strutting around with a bronze clock perched on his shoulder; another found a plume of ostrich feathers, which he stuck in his hat. The looting was just beginning when somebody cried, "Comrades! Don't touch anything! Don't take anything! Property of the people!" Many hands dragged the spoilers down. Damask and tapestry were snatched from the arms of those who had them; two men took away the bronze clock. Roughly and hastily the things were crammed back in their cases, and self-appointed sentinels stood guard. It was all utterly spontaneous. Through corridors and up staircases the cry could be heard growing fainter and fainter in the distance, "Revolutionary discipline! Property of the people."

We crossed back over to the left entrance, in the west wing. There order was also being established. "Clear the palace!" bawled a Red Guard, sticking his head through an inner door. "Come, comrades, let's show that we're not thieves and bandits. Everybody out of the palace except the Commissars, until we get sentries posted."

Two Red Guards, a soldier and an officer, stood with revolvers in their hands. Another soldier sat at a table behind them, with pen and paper. Shouts of "All out! All out!" were heard far and near within, and the army began to pour through the door, jostling, expostulating, arguing. As each man appeared he was seized by the self-appointed committee, who went through his pockets and looked under his coat. Everything that was plainly not his property was taken away, the man at the table noted it on his paper, and it was carried into a little room. The most amazing assortment of objects were thus confiscated; statuettes, bottles of ink, bedspreads worked with the imperial monogram, candles, a small oil painting, desk blotters, gold-handled swords, cakes of soap, clothes of every description, blankets. One Red Guard carried three rifles, two of which he had taken away from *yunkers*; another had four portfolios bulging with written documents. The culprits either sullenly surrendered or pleaded like children. All talking at once, the committee explained that stealing was not worthy of the people's champions; often those who were caught turned around and began to help go through the rest of the comrades.

We asked if we might go inside. The committee was doubtful, but the big Red Guard answered firmly that it was forbidden. "Who are you anyway?" he asked. "How do I know that you are not all Kerenskys?" (There were five of us, two women.)

In the meanwhile unrebuked we walked into the palace. There was still a great deal of coming and going, of exploring newfound apartments in the vast edifice, of searching for hidden garrisons of *yunkers* which did not exist. We went upstairs and wandered through room after room. This part of the palace had been entered also by other detachments from the side of the Neva. The paintings, statues, tapestries, and rugs of the great state apartments were unharmed; in the offices, however, every desk and cabinet had been ransacked, the papers scattered over the floor, and in the living rooms beds had been stripped of their coverings and wardrobes wrenched open. The most highly prized loot was clothing, which the working people needed. In a room where furniture was stored we came upon two soldiers ripping the elaborate Spanish leather upholstery from chairs. They explained it was to make boots with.

The old palace servants in their blue and red and gold uniforms stood nervously about, from force of habit repeating, "You can't go in there, *barin!* It is forbidden—"

All this time, it must be remembered, although the Winter Palace was surrounded, the government was in constant communication with the front and with provincial Russia. The Bolsheviki had captured the Ministry of War early in the morning, but they did not know of the military telegraph office in the attic, nor of the private telephone line connecting it with the Winter Palace. In that attic a young officer sat all day, pouring out over the country a flood of appeals and proclamations; and when he heard that the palace had fallen, put on his hat and walked calmly out of the building.

Interested as we were, for a considerable time we didn't notice a change in the attitude of the soldiers and Red Guards around us. As we strolled from room to room a small group followed us, until by the time we reached the great picture gallery where we had spent the afternoon with the *yunkers*, about a hundred men surged in after us. One giant of a soldier stood in our path, his face dark with sullen suspicion.

"Who are you?" he growled. "What are you doing here?" The others massed slowly around, staring and beginning to mutter. "*Provocatori!*" I heard somebody say. "Looters!" I produced our passes from the Military Revolutionary Committee. The soldier took them gingerly, turned them upside down, and looked at them without comprehension. Evidently he could not read. He handed them back and spat on the floor. "*Bumagi!* Papers!" said he with contempt. The mass slowly began to close in, like wild cattle around a cowpuncher on foot. Over their heads I caught sight of an officer, looking helpless, and shouted to him. He made for us, shouldering his way through.

"I'm the Commissar," he said to me. "Who are you? What is it?" The others held back, waiting. I produced the papers.

"You are foreigners?" he rapidly asked in French. "It is very dangerous." Then he turned to the mob, holding up our documents. "Comrades!" he cried. "These people are foreign comrades—from America. They have come here to be able to tell their countrymen about the bravery and the revolutionary discipline of the proletarian army!"

"How do you know that?" replied the big soldier. "I tell you they are provocators! They say they have come here to observe the revolutionary discipline of the proletarian army, but they have been wandering freely through the palace, and how do we know they haven't got their pockets full of loot?"

"*Pravilno!*" snarled the others, pressing forward.

"Comrades! Comrades!" appealed the officer, sweat standing out on his forehead. "I am Commissar of the Military Revolutionary Committee. Do you trust me? Well, I tell you that these passes are signed with the same names that are signed to my pass!"

He led us down through the palace and out through a door opening onto the Neva quay, before which stood the usual committee going through pockets. "You have narrowly escaped," he kept muttering, wiping his face.

We came out into the cold, nervous night, murmurous with obscure armies on the move, electric with patrols. From across the river, where loomed the darker mass of Peter-Paul, came a hoarse shout. Underfoot the sidewalk was littered with broken stucco, from the cornice of the palace where two shells from the battleship *Aurora* had struck; that was the only damage done by the bombardment.

It was now about three in the morning. On the Nevsky all the street lights were again shining, the cannon gone, and the only signs of war were Red Guards and soldiers squatting around fires. The city was quiet—probably never so quiet in its history; on that night not a single holdup occurred, not a single robbery.

ALLES VERGÄNGLICHE

Oswald Spengler (1880-1936), a German philosopher and social theorist, attributed the end of civilizations to an inevitable law of cultural history. Societies were like people. They lived and they died. In The Decline of the West *(1918), Spengler argued that the West's time had run its course, and the next phase of history belonged to the races of the Orient.*

Every thing-become is mortal. Not only peoples, languages, races and Cultures are transient. In a few centuries from now there will no more be a Western Culture, no more be German, English or French than there were Romans in the time of Justinian. Not that the sequence of human generations failed; it was the inner form of a people, which had put together a number of these generations as a single gesture, that was no longer there. The *Civis Romanus*, one of the most powerful symbols of Classical being, had nevertheless, as a form, only a duration of some centuries. But the primitive phenomenon of the great Culture will itself have disappeared some day, and with it the drama of world-history; aye, and man himself, and beyond man the phenomenon of plant and animal existence on the earth's surface, the earth, the sun, the whole world of sun-systems. All art is mortal, not merely the individual artifacts but the arts themselves. One day the last portrait of Rembrandt and the last bar of Mozart will have ceased to be—though possibly a coloured canvas and a sheet of notes may remain—because the last eye and the last ear accessible to their message will have gone. Every thought, faith and science dies as soon as the spirits in whose worlds their "eternal truths" were true and necessary are extinguished. Dead, even, are the star-worlds which "appeared," a proper world to the proper eye, to the astronomers of the Nile and the Euphrates, for our eye is different from theirs; and our eye in its turn is mortal. All this we know. The beast does not know, and what he does not know does not exist in his experienced world-around. But if the image of the past vanishes, the longing to give a deeper meaning to the passing vanishes also. And so it is with reference to the purely human macrocosm that we apply the oft-quoted line, which shall serve as motto for all that follows: *Alles Vergängliche ist nur ein Gleichnis.* [Everything transient is only a likeness.]

BERLIN (I), 1918-19

In his Diaries, *Count Harry Kessler (1868-1937), a German soldier and diplomat, describes the revolution in Berlin that followed the German defeat in World War I.*

Monday, 11 November 1918

Today the dreadful armistice terms have been signed. Langwerth says that anything else was out of the question: our Front has cracked completely. The Emperor has fled to Holland.

Tuesday, 12 November 1918

Although entry to the Reichstag is now under strict control (it is impossible to get in without the Soldiers' Council red pass), its appearance inside has not altered since the first night of the revolution except for the even greater accumulation of filth. Cigarette butts everywhere; waste paper, dust, and dirt from the streets litter the carpets. The corridors and lobby teem with armed civilians, soldiers and sailors. In the lobby rifles are piled on the carpet and sailors lounge in the easy chairs. The disorder is vast, but quiet reigns. The old attendants, in their parliamentary livery, flit about, helplessly and shyly, last relics of the former regime. The members of the bourgeois parties have completely disappeared.

In the city everything is peaceful today and the factories are working again. Nothing has been heard of shootings. Noteworthy is that during the days of revolution the trams, irrespective of street-fighting, ran regularly. Nor did the electricity, water, or telephone services break down for a moment. The revolution never created more than an eddy in the ordinary life of the city which flowed calmly along on its customary course. Moreover, though there was so much shooting, there were remarkably few dead or wounded. The colossal, world-shaking upheaval has scurried across Berlin's day-to-day life much like an incident in a crime film.

Tuesday, 24 December 1918

This morning Christmas Eve began with an artillery action. Government troops tried to bombard the sailors out of the Palace and the Imperial Stables.

At eleven I went to the Ministry and found Meyer exultant. The Government, he said, is at last taking a stern line. Let them put a few sailors up against the wall! He was mildly reproachful at my not sharing this counter-revolutionary mood.

Towards noon I walked up Unter den Linden. The Republican Security Guard had thrown a barrier across the street from Friedrichstrasse, but it was possible to circumvent this. There was a fairly large crowd in front of the University. Otherwise all was quiet. But large, pallid patches on the Palace walls, traces of the artillery bombardment, were visible at this distance already. An immense crowd swarmed unimpeded in the Lustgarten. Shellfire had very badly damaged the main Palace portal facing the Lustgarten. One of the pillars lay shattered on the ground and both wings of the iron doorway, riddled with holes, hung crooked on their hinges. The balcony over it, from which the Emperor made his speech on 4 August 1914, was smashed to pieces and remnants dangled down. The windows of the façade were no more than dark cavities, no panes, the sills splintered. The most grievous damage had been sustained by the balcony's beautiful caryatids, where a Michelangelo-like arm was shot away and their expressive heads were bowed still more movingly than before. Sailors were on guard in front of the portal.

Spartacus [Communist] agitators started small meetings all over the square. People argued with them, but they listened too. A tall, fanatical-looking fellow, with flickering eyes and a malevolent look shouted down a decently dressed man who was trying to convince him. Action, he snarled, is what is wanted, not simply words all the time. The Government has talked enough. Let it take socialism seriously or it will find its shilly-shallying cut short. Elsewhere a tatterdemalion old man, collarless, preached reason: Always let reason take its course, a little reason on both sides and mutual understanding will prevail. Every speaker had his audience. These small assemblies, with their sometimes frantic, sometimes balanced manner of discussion reminded me of Hyde Park on a Sunday evening.

The Christmas Fair carried on throughout the blood-letting. Hurdy-gurdies played in the Friedrichstrasse while street-vendors sold indoor fireworks, gingerbread, and silver tinsel. Jewellers' shops in Unter den Linden remained unconcernedly open, their windows brightly lit and glittering. In the Leipziger Strasse the usual Christmas crowds thronged the big stores. In thousands of homes the Christmas tree was lit and the children played around it with their presents from Daddy, Mummy and Auntie dear. In the Imperial Stables lay the dead, and the wounds freshly inflicted on the Palace and on Germany gaped into the Christmas night.

Saturday, 28 December 1918

Before the lunch I went over the Palace. The damage done by the shelling is surprisingly small. A grenade landed in the Hall of Pillars and, tearing to shreds a Skarbina painting, pierced the rear wall. The private apartments of the Emperor and the Empress, especially the dressing-rooms, have been pretty badly looted. With a single exception, the Empress's wardrobes have been emptied and deep inroads made into those belonging to the Emperor. The handles of his walking-sticks have been screwed off, the staffs smashed and thrown away. Photographs, powder-boxes, and mementoes have been scattered around. The Empress's writing-desk has been broken open. Rumour says that the contents, including correspondence between the Emperor and old Queen Victoria, are being hawked around the town. The Emperor's trinket stands, their glass shattered, have been cleaned out. It seems difficult to say how far the sailors have been responsible for the pillage. But these private apartments, the furniture, the articles of everyday use, and what remains of the Emperor's and Empress's mementoes and *objets d'art* are so insipid and tasteless, so philistine, that it is difficult to feel much indignation against the pilferers. Only astonishment that the wretched, timid, unimaginative creatures who liked this trash, and frittered away their life in this precious palatial haven, amidst lackeys and sycophants, could ever make any impact on history. Out of this atmosphere was born the World War, or as much of the guilt for it as falls on the Emperor. In this rubbishy, trivial, unreal microcosm, furnished with nothing but false values which deceived him and others, he made his judgements, plans, and decisions. Morbid taste and a pathologically excitable character in charge of an all too well-oiled machine of state. Now the symbols of his futile animating spirit lie strewn around here in the shape of doltish odds and ends. I feel no sympathy, only aversion and complicity when I reflect that this world was not done away with long ago, but on the contrary still continues to exist, in somewhat different forms, elsewhere.

It was a shock to be confronted with the dead sailors, some in coffins, others on stretchers, laid out in a ground-floor doorway that I often used when attending Court functions. Some relatives, small folk, were having the lids lifted for identification. A stale smell of corpses hung in the cold air. The prosiness of the relatives' almost business-like behaviour befitted the senselessness of these deaths. Nobody could really say why these youngsters were sacrificed or to what purpose they themselves threw their lives away.

Monday, 6 January 1919

Eleven o'clock, corner of Siegesallee and Viktoriastrasse. Two processions meet, the one is going in the direction of Siegesallee, the other in that of Wilhelmstrasse. They are made up of the same sort of people, artisans and factory girls, dressed in the same sort of clothes, waving the same red flags, and moving in the same sort of shambling step. But they carry slogans, jeer at each other as they pass, and perhaps will be shooting one another down before the day is out. At this hour the Sparticists are still fairly thin on the ground in

Siegesallee. Ten minutes later, when I reach Brandenburger Tor, vast masses of them are coming down Unter den Linden from the east. At Wilhelmstrasse they encounter just as immense a throng of Social Democrats. For the moment everything is peaceful.

Suddenly, shortly after one, a tremendous uproar: "Liebknecht, Liebknecht! Liebknecht is here!" I see a slender, fair-haired youth running away from a mob. They catch up with him, strike at him. He keeps on running. I can see the fair-haired head, with the breathless, flushed boy's face, amidst the fists and brandished sticks. From all sides there are shouts of "The young Liebknecht! Liebknecht's son!" He stumbles, disappears under the seething mob. I feel sure that they will beat him to death. But suddenly he is visible again, his face mangled and blood-stained, exhausted but supported by Spartacists who have rushed in and now drag him away.

Meanwhile a hansom cab is surrounded by the mob, which tries to drag out the occupants. One of them is supposed to be Liebknecht himself, but I can see pretty clearly that he is just an elderly man with spectacles and a soft hat. The crowd nevertheless rocks the cab from side to side. The old nag staggers from one side to the other as though drunk. But rescue arrives here too in the shape of Spartacists who punch their way through the throng and run off in triumph with the wearily trotting chestnut bay and its rickety cab.

Now Spartacus approaches in serried ranks. Towards half past one I find myself behind their lines. Here and there a cry of "Home, the women and children!" But nothing happens as yet. Going back through Leipziger Strasse, I meet a crowd of armed civilians lined up in front of a department-store. Impossible to tell whether they are on the Government or Spartacus side. A strong detachment of Government troops moves across Potsdamer Platz at the double. There is shouting all the time. Berlin has become a witches' cauldron wherein opposing forces and ideas are being brewed together. Today history is in the making and the issue is not only whether Germany shall continue to exist in the shape of the Reich or the democratic republic, but whether East or West, war or peace, an exhilarating vision of Utopia or the humdrum everyday world shall have the upper hand. Not since the great days of the French Revolution has humanity depended so much on the outcome of street-fighting in a single city.

Shortly after four (it was still reasonably light) I looked for a moment into the Ministry of Foreign Affairs. Empty. No clerks, no attendants, let alone senior officials; just soldiers at the windows. As I left, some shots were fired. Nobody knew why.

Wednesday, 8 January 1919

The Wilhelmstrasse is impassable. A gun has been mounted in front of the Chancellery. At intervals a machine-gun fires from the balcony of the Ministry of the Interior to prevent Spartacists from bringing a machine-gun into position on the roof of a house at the corner of the Neue Wilhelmstrasse. I made my way to the upper part of Unter den Linden. To the rat-tat-tat of distant machine-guns life proceeded almost normally. A fair amount of traffic, some shops and cafés open, street-vendors peddling their wares, and barrel-organs grinding away as usual.

On my way back I found Pariser Platz barricaded, but I was allowed through. Beyond Brandenburger Tor a vast crowd could be seen in the Tiergarten area. I was crossing the square when shooting broke out. The machine-gun on top of Brandenburger Tor was firing into the Tiergarten crowd, which dispersed amidst agonized screams. Then silence. It was a quarter to one. When the shooting began again, I was proceeding towards the Reichstag. That was also Spartacus's line of fire. Bullets whizzed past my ear.

At four o'clock I was in the Friedrichstrasse. There was a good deal of traffic and a lot of people stood discussing matters in small groups when suddenly there was a sound of shooting from the Unter den Linden end. Yet the Leipziger Strasse, except for its closed shops, looked perfectly normal and the big cafés on Potsdamer Platz were open, brightly lit and doing business as usual.

According to an evening paper, Haase and Breitscheid are making a last effort at negotiations. If it fails, a catastrophe will probably follow. Today's fighting gives the impression of being merely a prologue to the real tragedy. At half past seven I had a meal in the Fürstenhof. The iron gates were just being shut because a Spartacus attack was expected on the Potsdamer Railway Station opposite. Single shots were dropping all the time. As I left, about nine, street vendors with cigarettes, malt goodies, and soap were still crying their wares. I looked for a moment into the boldly lit Café Vaterland. Despite the fact that at any moment bullets might whistle through the windows, the band was playing, the tables were full, and the lady in the cigarette-booth smiled as winsomely at her customers as in the sunniest days of peace.

Friday, 17 January 1919

Today they started taking down from the Brandenburger Tor the decorations, the laurel wreaths, the red streamers and banners, and the mottoes "Peace and Freedom" which were put up for the entry of the troops into the city from the Front. The whole Spartacus rising, centred on the area between Brandenburger Tor and Wilhelmstrasse, was enacted within this festooned setting. Now there stands at the corner of Unter den Linden and Wilhelmstrasse a 105 mm gun, its crew wearing steel helmets.

In the evening I went to a cabaret in the Bellevuestrasse. The sound of a shot cracked through the performance of a fiery Spanish dancer. Nobody took any notice. It underlined the slight impression that the revolution has made on metropolitan life. I only began to appreciate the Babylonian, unfathomably deep, primordial and titanic quality of Berlin when I saw how this historic, colossal event has caused no more than local ripples on the even more colossally eddying movement of Berlin existence. An elephant stabbed with a penknife shakes itself and strides on as if nothing has happened.

TOKYO, 1923

From the "News of the Week," The Spectator (London), week ending
Saturday, September 8, 1923.

The whole world has been shocked by the news of the earthquake in Japan on
last Saturday afternoon which practically obliterated the great cities of Tokyo
and Yokohama and which, so far as one can judge, was the worst earthquake
in history. The famous earthquakes at Lisbon, Martinique, Valparaiso,
Messina, San Francisco, and the Abruzzi seem small by comparison. The slow-
ness with which the details have come through is in itself a sign of the appalling
severity of this cataclysm. Japan has been stricken with paralysis at the centre.
The deep concern and the sympathy with Japan felt by everyone here is patent.
Relief funds have at once been opened. The China Squadron of the British
Navy has been sent to Japanese waters to help in the work of relief. It is said
that at Yokohama no building remains standing. It is estimated that in the districts of Yokohama and Tokyo 240,000 lives have been lost and that the total
casualties may amount to nearly half a million.

The terror inspired by the repeated shocks and the falling of houses was
magnified by the breaking out of fires in all directions, and at Yokohama and
other points on the Bay of Tokyo by the inrush of seismic waves. Bridges fell
and railways were snapped and twisted out of shape. It is said that one or two
islands in the Bay much frequented by summer visitors disappeared and that
new islands rose to the surface. The fires could be checked only by blowing
up belts of the ruined houses. Most of the food supplies were destroyed and
order (though only partial order) could be maintained among desperate people only by the proclamation of martial law. Nobody from the outside was
allowed to enter the capital. The acute famine was made more terrible by the
absence of water, as the whole water system had been destroyed. The cause
of the fires was the breaking of the gas pipes through the collapse of the houses and the explosion of the oil tanks. Although Tokyo did not suffer so much
as Yokohama all the Government buildings were demolished as well as the

Foreign Embassies, including the British Embassy. An instance of the appalling completeness of the catastrophe is the fate which is reported to have overtaken the Fuji spinning mills near the famous Mount Fuji. The mills crashed to the ground and some eight thousand operatives perished. According to a report published in the *Daily Chronicle* of Thursday, the great docks at Yokohama are a jumble of ruins. Apparently the bottom of the harbour has been considerably raised and relief ships have to feel their way in with much caution.

The probable effect of these awful events upon the whole fabric of life in Japan is a pitiful subject for speculation. It has been said that the loss in terms of money to Japan cannot be much less than £1,000,000,000. How long will Japan take to recover from such a stupendous shock?

[EDITORIAL]

The Market Goes South

From The New Yorker, *"Talk of the Town," November 2, 1929.*

FEAR, running through the jungle like flame, strong as ever. Doom still makes a crackling sound, like summer thunder. Thousands of minor clerks and small tradespeople, hearing faint noises of railroads they had never seen, mines they had never worked, steel they had never tempered, fled before the terror of dark. Then came the voices. Two hundred and five for twenty-five thousand steel, said a Morgan, gritting his teeth. The fundamental business of the country is on a sound and prosperous basis, said President Hoover. No buildings were burned down, no industries have died, no mines, no railroads have vanished, crooned Arthur Brisbane. The great comforters. There, there, my children. Try and catch a little sleep. Mother is near.

THE collapse of the market, over and above the pain, couldn't help but be amusing. It is amusing to see a fat land quivering in paunchy fright. The quake, furthermore, verified our suspicion that our wise and talky friends hadn't known for months what they were talking about when they were discussing stocks. Forcing us to breakfast on copper and oil, dine on sugar and food products, and sleep with rails and motors, they had succeeded in boring us to the breaking point. Uninformed dreamers, running a fever. Then came the debacle. They still talked, in husky voices; but we at least had the satisfaction of knowing that it was costing them anywhere from a hundred to two hundred and fifty dollars a word every time they opened their mouths. Many of them have gone quietly back to work. They may not be the most useful citizens in the world, but from now on when they talk they'll talk about their business or their love affairs and know a little something of what they're talking about.

THE DEATH INSTINCT

Sigmund Freud (1856-1939) argued that the "death instinct" drives all living things to return to their origin—which is an inorganic state. The instinct exists in constant tension with that of "Eros," which drives all living things to reproduce and multiply. In Civilization and Its Discontents *(1930) Freud broadened the dialectic to apply to whole civilizations and left unanswered the question as to which instinct would prove the stronger.*

The element of truth behind all this, which people are so ready to disavow, is that men are not gentle creatures who want to be loved; they are, on the contrary, creatures among whose instinctual endowments is to be reckoned a powerful share of aggressiveness. As a result, their neighbour is for them not only a potential helper or sexual object, but also someone who tempts them to satisfy their aggressiveness on him, to exploit his capacity for work without compensation, to use him sexually without his consent, to seize his possessions, to humiliate him, to cause him pain, to torture and to kill him. *Homo homini lupus*. [Man is a wolf to man.] Who, in the face of all his experience of life and of history, will have the courage to dispute this assertion? As a rule this cruel aggressiveness waits for some provocation or puts itself at the service of some other purpose, whose goal might also have been reached by milder measures. In circumstances that are favourable to it, when the mental counter-forces which ordinarily inhibit it are out of action, it also manifests itself spontaneously and reveals man as a savage beast to whom consideration towards his own kind is something alien. Anyone who calls to mind the atrocities committed during the racial migrations or the invasions of the Huns, or by the people known as Mongols under Jenghiz Khan and Tamerlane, or at the capture of Jerusalem by the pious Crusaders, or even, indeed, the horrors of the recent World War—anyone who calls these things to mind will have to bow humbly before the truth of this view.

In consequence of this primary mutual hostility of human beings, civilized society is perpetually threatened with disintegration. The interest of work in common would not hold it together; instinctual passions are stronger than reasonable interests. Civilization has to use its utmost efforts in order to set limits to man's aggressive instincts and to hold the manifestations of them in check by psychical reaction-formations. Hence, therefore, the use of methods intended to incite people into identifications and aim-inhibited relationships of love, hence the restriction upon sexual life, and hence too the ideal's commandment to love one's neighbour as oneself—a commandment which is really justified by the fact that nothing else runs so strongly counter to the original nature of man. In spite of every effort, these endeavours of civilization have not so far achieved very much. It hopes to prevent the crudest excesses of brutal violence by itself assuming the right to use violence against criminals, but the law is not able to lay hold of the more cautious and refined manifestations of human aggressiveness. The time comes when each one of us has to give up as illusions the expectations which, in his youth, he pinned upon his fellow-men, and when he may learn how much difficulty and pain has been added to his life by their ill-will.

* * *

The name "libido" can once more be used to denote the manifestation of the power of Eros in order to distinguish it from the energy of the death instinct. Civilization is a process in the service of Eros, whose purpose is to combine single human individuals, and after that families, then races, peoples and nations, into one great unity, the unity of mankind. Why this has to happen, we do not know; the work of Eros is precisely this. These collections of men are to be libidinally bound to one another. Necessity alone, the advantages of work in common, will not hold them together. But man's natural aggressive instinct, the hostility of each against all and of all against each, opposes this progam of civilization. This aggressive instinct is the derivative and the main representative of the death instinct which we have found alongside of Eros and which shares world-dominion with it. And now, I think, the meaning of the evolution of civilization is no longer obscure to us. It must present the struggle between Eros and Death, between the instinct of life and the instinct of destruction, as it works itself out in the human species. This struggle is what all life essentially consists of, and the evolution of civilization may therefore be simply described as the struggle for life of the human species. And it is this battle of the giants that our nurse-maids try to appease with their lullaby about Heaven.

* * *

For a wide variety of reasons, it is very far from my intention to express an opinion upon the value of human civilization. I have endeavoured to guard myself against the enthusiastic prejudice which holds that our civilization is the most precious thing that we possess or could acquire and that its path will necessarily lead to heights of unimagined perfection. I can at least listen without indignation to the critic who is of the opinion that when one surveys the aims of cultural endeavour and the means it employs, one is bound to come to the conclusion that the whole effort is not worth the trouble, and that the outcome of it can only be a state of affairs which the individual will be unable to tolerate. My impartiality is made all the easier to me by my knowing very little about all these things. One thing only do I know for certain and that is that man's judgements of value follow directly his wishes for happiness— that, accordingly, they are an attempt to support his illusions with arguments. I should find it very understandable if someone were to point out the obligatory nature of the course of human civilization and were to say, for instance, that the tendencies to a restriction of sexual life or to the institution of a humanitarian ideal at the expense of natural selection were developmental trends which cannot be averted or turned aside and to which it is best for us to yield as though they were necessities of nature. I know, too, the objection that can be made against this, to the effect that in the history of mankind, trends such as these, which were considered unsurmountable, have often been thrown aside and replaced by other trends. Thus I have not the courage to rise up before my fellow-men as a prophet, and I bow to their reproach that I can offer them no consolation: for at bottom that is what they are all demanding—the wildest revolutionaries no less passionately than the most virtuous believers.

The fateful question for the human species seems to me to be whether and to what extent their cultural development will succeed in mastering the disturbance of their communal life by the human instinct of aggression and self-destruction. It may be that in this respect precisely the present time deserves a special interest. Men have gained control over the forces of nature to such an extent that with their help they would have no difficulty in exterminating one another to the last man. They know this, and hence comes a large part of their current unrest, their unhappiness and their mood of anxiety. And now it is to be expected that the other of the two "Heavenly Powers," eternal Eros, will make an effort to assert himself in the struggle with his equally immortal adversary. But who can foresee with what success and with what result?

[COLUMN]

THE GREAT DEPRESSION

H. L. Mencken (1880-1956), American satirist, newspaperman, and liter-
ary critic, wrote comfortably in many voices. His column "The End of an
Era," appeared in the Baltimore Evening Sun, *September 14, 1931.*

On September 4, 476, a gang of ruffians commanded by Odoacer the barbarian
seized young Romulus Augustulus, the last Roman Emperor, and clapped him into
a dungeon. This was at 10:40 in the forenoon. At the same instant the Roman
Empire blew up with a bang, and the Middle Ages began. The curious thing is that
no one knew it. People went about their business as if nothing had happened. They
complained that the times were hard, but that was all. Not even the learned were
aware that a great epoch in history had come to a close, and another begun.

We of today may be just as blind. It may be that the so-called Modern Period
is falling into chaos around our heads—that an entirely new epoch is beginning
for mankind. It may be that the capitalistic system is blowing up, as the Roman
system blew up. It may be that the new era is beginning in Russia, or somewhere
else, or even here at home. If so, I can only say that I regret it extremely. The capitalistic system suits me precisely. I am aware of its defects, but on the whole it
agrees with my prejudices and interests. If Communism is on the way I hope to
be stuffed and on exhibition in the Smithsonian before it hits Maryland.

But all this is beside the point. The simple question is, can capitalism survive its present appalling attack of boils? Will it prevail against Bolshevism, or
will it succumb? The question is by no means easy to answer. Capitalism is
plainly wobbling, but is Bolshevism really any stronger? If it were as hard hit,
wouldn't it wobble too? Only time can tell, and time tells slowly, even in a
frantic age. Meanwhile, let us ponder two facts. The first is that in England the
greatest trading corporation in history, the very pearl and model of the capitalistic system, is plainly bankrupt. The other is that in the United States,
where capitalism has been elevated to the august estate of a national religion

with fifty Popes and 10,000 gaudy Cardinals, the whole pack of these inspired brethren, though the God of Rotary is in hourly communication with them, face a similar bankruptcy with blank faces, and haven't the slightest notion what to do.

[EPITAPH]

The last Heath Hen, a species of bird indigenous to Martha's Vineyard, was seen alive on March 11, 1932. Henry Beetle Hough, editor of the island's Vineyard Gazette, *wrote its much-quoted obituary.*

We are looking upon the utmost finality which can be written, glimpsing the darkness which will not know another ray of light. We are in touch with the reality of extinction.

[PAINTING]

GUERNICA

(1937)

by Pablo Picasso (1881-1973)

AUSCHWITZ, 1944

Tadeusz Borowski (1922-1951), a Polish poet and writer of fiction, was sent to Auschwitz for publishing books that the German occupiers found objectionable.

A cheerful little station, very much like any other provincial railway stop: a small square framed by tall chestnuts and paved with yellow gravel. Not far off, beside the road, squats a tiny wooden shed, uglier and more flimsy than the ugliest and flimsiest railway shack; farther along lie stacks of old rails, heaps of wooden beams, barracks parts, bricks, paving stones. This is where they load freight for Birkenau: supplies for the construction of the camp, and people for the gas chambers. Trucks drive around, load up lumber, cement, people—a regular daily routine.

And now the guards are being posted along the rails, across the beams, in the green shade of the Silesian chestnuts, to form a tight circle around the ramp. They wipe the sweat from their faces and sip out of their canteens. It is unbearably hot; the sun stands motionless at its zenith.

"Fall out!"

We sit down in the narrow streaks of shade along the stacked rails. The hungry Greeks (several of them managed to come along, God only knows how) rummage underneath the rails. One of them finds some pieces of mildewed bread, another a few half-rotten sardines. They eat.

"*Schweinedreck,*" spits a young, tall guard with corn-coloured hair and dreamy blue eyes. "For God's sake, any minute you'll have so much food to stuff down your guts, you'll bust!" He adjusts his gun, wipes his face with a handkerchief.

"Hey you, fatso!" His boot lightly touches Henri's shoulder. "*Pass mal auf,* want a drink?"

"Sure, but I haven't got any marks," replies the Frenchman with a professional air.

"*Schade,* too bad."

"Come, come, Herr Posten, isn't my word good enough any more? Haven't we done business before? How much?"

"One hundred. *Gemacht?*"

"*Gemacht.*"

We drink the water, lukewarm and tasteless. It will be paid for by the people who have not yet arrived.

"Now you be careful," says Henri, turning to me. He tosses away the empty bottle. It strikes the rails and bursts into tiny fragments. "Don't take any money, they might be checking. Anyway, who the hell needs money? You've got enough to eat. Don't take suits, either, or they'll think you're planning to escape. Just get a shirt, silk only, with a collar. And a vest. And if you find some-thing to drink, don't bother calling me. I know how to shift for myself, but you watch your step or they'll let you have it."

"Do they beat you up here?"

"Naturally. You've got to have eyes in your ass. *Arschaugen.*"

Around us sit the Greeks, their jaws working greedily, like huge human insects. They munch on stale lumps of bread. They are restless, wondering what will happen next. The sight of the large beams and the stacks of rails has them worried. They dislike carrying heavy loads.

"*Was wir arbeiten?*" they ask.

"*Niks. Transport kommen, alles Krematorium, compris?*"

"*Alles verstehen,*" they answer in crematorium Esperanto. All is well—they will not have to move the heavy rails or carry the beams.

In the meantime, the ramp has become increasingly alive with activity, increasingly noisy. The crews are being divided into those who will open and unload the arriving cattle cars and those who will be posted by the wooden steps. They receive instructions on how to proceed most efficiently. Motor cycles drive up, delivering S.S. officers, bemedalled, glittering with brass, beefy men with highly polished boots and shiny, brutal faces. Some have brought their briefcases, others hold thin, flexible whips. This gives them an air of mil-itary readiness and agility. They walk in and out of the commissary—for the miserable little shack by the road serves as their commissary, where in the summertime they drink mineral water, *Studentenquelle,* and where in winter they can warm up with a glass of hot wine. They greet each other in the state-approved way, raising an arm Roman fashion, then shake hands cordially, exchange warm smiles, discuss mail from home, their children, their families. Some stroll majestically on the ramp. The silver squares on their collars glitter, the gravel crunches under their boots, their bamboo whips snap impatiently.

We lie against the rails in the narrow streaks of shade, breathe unevenly, occasionally exchange a few words in our various tongues, and gaze listlessly at the majestic men in green uniforms, at the green trees, and at the church steeple of a distant village.

"The transport is coming," somebody says. We spring to our feet, all eyes turn in one direction. Around the bend, one after another, the cattle cars begin rolling in. The train backs into the station, a conductor leans out, waves his hand, blows a whistle. The locomotive whistles back with a shrieking noise, puffs, the train rolls slowly alongside the ramp. In the tiny barred windows appear pale, wilted, exhausted human faces, terror-stricken women with tangled hair, unshaven men. They gaze at the station in silence. And then, suddenly, there is a stir inside the cars and a pounding against the wooden boards.

"Water! Air!"—weary, desperate cries.

Heads push through the windows, mouths gasp frantically for air. They draw a few breaths, then disappear; others come in their place, then also disappear. The cries and moans grow louder.

A man in a green uniform covered with more glitter than any of the others jerks his head impatiently, his lips twist in annoyance. He inhales deeply, then with a rapid gesture throws his cigarette away and signals to the guard. The guard removes the automatic from his shoulder, aims, sends a series of shots along the train. All is quiet now. Meanwhile, the trucks have arrived, steps are being drawn up, and the Canada men[1] stand ready at their posts by the train doors. The S.S. officer with the briefcase raises his hand.

"Whoever takes gold, or anything at all besides food, will be shot for stealing Reich property. Understand? *Verstanden?*"

"*Jawohl!*" we answer eagerly.

"*Also los!* Begin!"

The bolts crack, the doors fall open. A wave of fresh air rushes inside the train. People . . . inhumanly crammed, buried under incredible heaps of luggage, suitcases, trunks, packages, crates, bundles of every description (everything that had been their past and was to start their future). Monstrously squeezed together, they have fainted from heat, suffocated, crushed one another. Now they push towards the opened doors, breathing like fish cast out on the sand.

----

[1]Canada stood for wealth and well-being in the camps. The Canada men were members of a labor gang that unloaded incoming transports of people heading for the gas chambers.

"Attention! Out, and take your luggage with you! Take out everything. Pile all your stuff near the exits. Yes, your coats too. It is summer. March to the left. Understand?"

"Sir, what's going to happen to us?" they jump from the train on to the gravel, anxious, worn-out.

"Where are you people from?"

"Sosnowiec-Będzin. Sir, what's going to happen to us?" They repeat the question stubbornly, gazing into our tired eyes.

"I don't know, I don't understand Polish."

It is the camp law: people going to their death must be deceived to the very end. This is the only permissible form of charity. The heat is tremendous. The sun hangs directly over our heads, the white, hot sky quivers, the air vibrates, an occasional breeze feels like a sizzling blast from a furnace. Our lips are parched, the mouth fills with the salty taste of blood, the body is weak and heavy from lying in the sun. Water!

A huge, multicoloured wave of people loaded down with luggage pours from the train like a blind, mad river trying to find a new bed. But before they have a chance to recover, before they can draw a breath of fresh air and look at the sky, bundles are snatched from their hands, coats ripped off their backs, their purses and umbrellas taken away.

"But please, sir, it's for the sun, I cannot . . ."

"*Verboten!*" one of us barks through clenched teeth. There is an S.S. man standing behind your back, calm, efficient, watchful.

"*Meine Herrschaften*, this way, ladies and gentlemen, try not to throw your things around, please. Show some goodwill," he says courteously, his restless hands playing with the slender whip.

"Of course, of course," they answer as they pass, and now they walk along-side the train somewhat more cheerfully. A woman reaches down quickly to pick up her handbag. The whip flies, the woman screams, stumbles, and falls under the feet of the surging crowd. Behind her, a child cries in a thin little voice "Mamele!"—a very small girl with tangled black curls.

The heaps grow. Suitcases, bundles, blankets, coats, handbags that open as they fall, spilling coins, gold, watches; mountains of bread pile up at the exits, heaps of marmalade, jams, masses of meat, sausages; sugar spills on the gravel. Trucks, loaded with people, start up with a deafening roar and drive off amidst the wailing and screaming of the women separated from their children, and the stupefied silence of the men left behind. They are the ones who had been ordered to step to the right—the healthy and the young who will go to the camp. In the end they too will not escape death, but first they must work.

Trucks leave and return, without interruption, as on a monstrous conveyor belt. A Red Cross van drives back and forth, back and forth, incessantly: it transports the gas that will kill these people. The enormous cross on the hood, red as blood, seems to dissolve in the sun.

The Canada men at the trucks cannot stop for a single moment, even to catch their breath. They shove the people up the steps, pack them in tightly, sixty per truck, more or less. Near by stands a young, cleanshaven "gentleman," an S.S. officer with a notebook in his hand. For each departing truck he enters a mark; sixteen gone means one thousand people, more or less. The gentleman is calm, precise. No truck can leave without a signal from him, or a mark in his notebook: *Ordnung muss sein*. The marks swell into thousands, the thousands into whole transports, which afterwards we shall simply call "from Salonica," "from Strasbourg," "from Rotterdam." This one will be called "Sosnowiec-Będzin." The new prisoners from Sosnowiec-Będzin will receive serial numbers 131-2—thousand, of course, though afterwards we shall simply say 131-2, for short. The transports swell into weeks, months, years. When the war is over, they will count up the marks in their notebooks—all four and a half million of them. The bloodiest battle of the war, the greatest victory of the strong, united Germany. *Ein Reich, ein Volk, ein Führer*—and four crematoria.

The train has been emptied. A thin, pock-marked S.S. man peers inside, shakes his head in disgust and motions to our group, pointing his finger at the door.

"*Rein*. Clean it up!"

We climb inside. In the corners amid human excrement and abandoned wrist-watches lie squashed, trampled infants, naked little monsters with enormous heads and bloated bellies. We carry them out like chickens, holding several in each hand.

"Don't take them to the trucks, pass them on to the women," says the S.S.

man, lighting a cigarette. His cigarette lighter is not working properly; he examines it carefully.

"Take them, for God's sake!" I explode as the women run from me in horror, covering their eyes.

The name of God sounds strangely pointless, since the women and the infants will go on the trucks, every one of them, without exception. We all know what this means, and we look at each other with hate and horror.

"What, you don't want to take them?" asks the pockmarked S.S. man with a note of surprise and reproach in his voice, and reaches for his revolver.

"You mustn't shoot, I'll carry them." A tall, gray-haired woman takes the little corpses out of my hands and for an instant gazes straight into my eyes.

"My poor boy," she whispers and smiles at me. Then she walks away, staggering along the path. I lean against the side of the train. I am terribly tired. Someone pulls at my sleeve.

"*En avant*, to the rails, come on!"

I look up, but the face swims before my eyes, dissolves, huge and transparent, melts into the motionless trees and the sea of people . . . I blink rapidly: Henri.

"Listen, Henri, are we good people?"

"That's stupid. Why do you ask?"

"You see, my friend, you see, I don't know why, but I am furious, simply furious with these people—furious because I must be here because of them. I feel no pity. I am not sorry they're going to the gas chamber. Damn them all! I could throw myself at them, beat them with my fists. It must be pathological, I just can't understand . . . "

"Ah, on the contrary, it is natural, predictable, calculated. The ramp exhausts you, you rebel—and the easiest way to relieve your hate is to turn against someone weaker. Why, I'd even call it healthy. It's simple logic, *compris?*" He props himself up comfortably against the heap of rails. "Look at the Greeks, they know how to make the best of it! They stuff their bellies with anything they find. One of them has just devoured a full jar of marmalade."

"Pigs! Tomorrow half of them will die of the shits."

"Pigs? You've been hungry."

"Pigs!" I repeat furiously. I close my eyes. The air is filled with ghastly cries, the earth trembles beneath me, I can feel sticky moisture on my eyelids. My throat is completely dry.

The morbid procession streams on and on—trucks growl like mad dogs. I shut my eyes tight, but I can still see corpses dragged from the train, trampled infants, cripples piled on top of the dead, wave after wave . . . freight cars roll in, the heaps of clothing, suitcases and bundles grow, people climb out, look at the sun, take a few breaths, beg for water, get into the trucks, drive away. And again freight cars roll in, again people . . . The scenes become confused in my mind—I am not sure if all of this is actually happening, or if I am dreaming. There is a humming inside my head; I feel that I must vomit.

Henri tugs at my arm.

"Don't sleep, we're off to load up the loot."

*   *   *

We proceed to load the loot. We lift huge trunks, heave them on to the trucks. There they are arranged in stacks, packed tightly. Occasionally somebody slashes one open with a knife, for pleasure or in search of vodka and perfume. One of the crates falls open; suits, shirts, books drop out on the ground . . . I pick up a small, heavy package. I unwrap it—gold, about two handfuls, bracelets, rings, brooches, diamonds . . .

"*Gib hier*," an S.S. man says calmly, holding up his briefcase already full of gold and colourful foreign currency. He locks the case, hands it to an officer, takes another, an empty one, and stands by the next truck, waiting. The gold will go to the Reich.

It is hot, terribly hot. Our throats are dry, each word hurts. Anything for a sip of water! Faster, faster, so that it is over, so that we may rest. At last we are done, all the trucks have gone. Now we swiftly clean up the remaining dirt: there must be "no trace left of the *Schweinerei*." But just as the last truck disappears behind the trees and we walk, finally, to rest in the shade, a shrill whistle sounds around the bend. Slowly, terribly slowly, a train rolls in, the engine whistles back with a deafening shriek. Again weary, pale faces at the windows, flat as though cut out of paper, with huge, feverishly burning eyes. Already trucks are pulling up, already the composed gentleman with the notebook is at his post, and the S.S. men emerge from the commissary carrying briefcases for the gold and money. We unseal the train doors.

It is impossible to control oneself any longer. Brutally we tear suitcases from their hands, impatiently pull off their coats. Go on, go on, vanish! They go, they vanish. Men, women, children. Some of them know.

*   *   *

I go back inside the train; I carry out dead infants; I unload luggage. I touch corpses, but I cannot overcome the mounting, uncontrollable terror. I try to escape from the corpses, but they are everywhere: lined up on the gravel, on the cement edge of the ramp, inside the cattle cars. Babies, hideous naked women, men twisted by convulsions. I run off as far as I can go, but immediately a whip slashes across my back. Out of the corner of my eye I see an S.S. man, swearing profusely. I stagger forward and run, lose myself in the Canada group. Now, at last, I can once more rest against the stack of rails. The sun has leaned low over the horizon and illuminates the ramp with a reddish glow; the shadows of the trees have become elongated, ghostlike. In the silence that settles over nature at this time of day, the human cries seem to rise all the way to the sky.

Only from this distance does one have a full view of the inferno on the teeming ramp. I see a pair of human beings who have fallen to the ground locked in a last desperate embrace. The man has dug his fingers into the woman's flesh and has caught her clothing with his teeth. She screams hysterically, swears, cries, until at last a large boot comes down over her throat and she is silent. They are pulled apart and dragged like cattle to the truck. I see four Canada men lugging a corpse: a huge, swollen female corpse. Cursing, dripping wet from the strain, they kick out of their way some stray children who have been running all over the ramp, howling like dogs. The men pick them up by the collars, heads, arms, and toss them inside the trucks, on top of the heaps. The four men have trouble lifting the fat corpse on to the car, they call others for help, and all together they hoist up the mound of meat. Big, swollen, puffed-up corpses are being collected from all over the ramp; on top of them are piled the invalids, the smothered, the sick, the unconscious. The heap seethes, howls, groans. The driver starts the motor, the truck begins rolling.

"Halt! Halt!" an S.S. man yells after them. "Stop, damn you!"

They are dragging to the truck an old man wearing tails and a band around his arm. His head knocks against the gravel and pavement; he moans and wails in an uninterrupted monotone: "*Ich will mit dem Herrn Kommandanten sprechen*—I wish to speak with the commandant . . . " With senile stubbornness he keeps repeating these words all the way. Thrown on the truck, trampled by others, choked, he still wails: "*Ich will mit dem . . . *"

"Look here, old man!" a young S.S. man calls, laughing jovially. "In half an hour you'll be talking with the top commandant! Only don't forget to greet him with a *Heil Hitler!*"

Several other men are carrying a small girl with only one leg. They hold her by the arms and the one leg. Tears are running down her face and she whispers faintly: "Sir, it hurts, it hurts . . . " They throw her on the truck on top of the corpses. She will burn alive along with them.

The evening has come, cool and clear. The stars are out. We lie against the rails. It is incredibly quiet. Anaemic bulbs hang from the top of the high lamp posts; beyond the circle of light stretches an impenetrable darkness. Just one step, and a man could vanish for ever. But the guards are watching, their automatics ready.

"Did you get the shoes?" asks Henri.

"No."

"Why?"

"My God, man, I am finished, absolutely finished!"

"So soon? After only two transports? Just look at me, I . . . since Christmas, at least a million people have passed through my hands. The worst of all are the transports from around Paris—one is always bumping into friends."

"And what do you say to them?"

"That first they will have a bath, and later we'll meet at the camp. What would you say?"

I do not answer. We drink coffee with vodka; somebody opens a tin of cocoa and mixes it with sugar. We scoop it up by the handful, the cocoa sticks to the lips. Again coffee, again vodka.

"Henri, what are we waiting for?"

"There'll be another transport."

"I'm not going to unload it! I can't take any more."

"So, it's got you down? Canada is nice, eh?" Henri grins indulgently and disappears into the darkness. In a moment he is back again.

"All right. Just sit here quietly and don't let an S.S. man see you. I'll try to find you your shoes."

"Just leave me alone. Never mind the shoes." I want to sleep. It is very late.

Another whistle, another transport. Freight cars emerge out of the darkness, pass under the lamp-posts, and again vanish in the night. The ramp is small, but the circle of lights is smaller. The unloading will have to be done gradually. Somewhere the trucks are growling. They back up against the steps, black, ghostlike, their searchlights flash across the trees. *Wasser! Luft!* The same all over again, like a late showing of the same film: a volley of shots, the train falls silent. Only this time a little girl pushes herself halfway through the small window and, losing her balance, falls out on to the gravel. Stunned, she lies still for a moment, then stands up and begins walking around in a circle, faster and faster, waving her rigid arms in the air, breathing loudly and spasmodically, whining in a faint voice. Her mind has given way in the inferno inside the train. The whining is hard on the nerves: an S.S. man approaches calmly, his heavy boot strikes between her shoulders. She falls. Holding her down with his foot, he draws his revolver, fires once, then again. She remains face down, kicking the gravel with her feet, until she stiffens. They proceed to unseal the train.

I am back on the ramp, standing by the doors. A warm, sickening smell gushes from inside. The mountain of people filling the car almost halfway up to the ceiling is motionless, horribly tangled, but still steaming.

"*Ausladen!*" comes the command. An S.S. man steps out from the darkness. Across his chest hangs a portable searchlight. He throws a stream of light inside.

"Why are you standing about like sheep? Start unloading!" His whip flies and falls across our backs. I seize a corpse by the hand; the fingers close tightly around mine. I pull back with a shriek and stagger away. My heart pounds, jumps up to my throat. I can no longer control the nausea. Hunched under the train I begin to vomit. Then, like a drunk, I weave over to the stack of rails.

I lie against the cool, kind metal and dream about returning to the camp, about my bunk, on which there is no mattress, about sleep among comrades who are not going to the gas tonight. Suddenly I see the camp as a haven of peace. It is true, others may be dying, but one is somehow still alive, one has enough food, enough strength to work . . .

The lights on the ramp flicker with a spectral glow, the wave of people—feverish, agitated, stupefied people—flows on and on, endlessly. They think that now they will have to face a new life in the camp, and they prepare themselves emotionally for the hard struggle ahead. They do not know that in just a few moments they will die, that the gold, money, and diamonds which they have so prudently hidden in their clothing and on their bodies are now useless to them. Experienced professionals will probe into every recess of their flesh, will pull the gold from under the tongue and the diamonds from the uterus and the colon. They will rip out gold teeth. In tightly sealed crates they will ship them to Berlin.

The S.S. men's black figures move about, dignified, businesslike. The gentleman with the notebook puts down his final marks, rounds out the figures: fifteen thousand.

Many, very many, trucks have been driven to the crematoria today.

It is almost over. The dead are being cleared off the ramp and piled into the last truck. The Canada men, weighed down under a load of bread, marmalade and sugar, and smelling of perfume and fresh linen, line up to go. For several days the entire camp will live off this transport. For several days the entire camp will talk about "Sosnowiec-Będzin." "Sosnowiec-Będzin" was a good, rich transport.

The stars are already beginning to pale as we walk back to the camp. The sky grows translucent and opens high above our heads—it is getting light.

Great columns of smoke rise from the crematoria and merge up above into a huge black river which very slowly floats across the sky over Birkenau and disappears beyond the forests in the direction of Trzebinia. The "Sosnowiec-Będzin" transport is already burning.

[ESSAY]

THE DROWNED AND THE SAVED

Primo Levi (1919-1987), an Italian writer and chemist, was one of a very few Jews to survive the Nazi death camps. He wrote Survival in Auschwitz *in 1947 "to furnish documentation for a quiet study of certain aspects of the human mind."*

The Lager [Auschwitz] was pre-eminently a gigantic biological and social experiment.

Thousands of individuals, differing in age, condition, origin, language, culture and customs, are enclosed within barbed wire: there they live a regular, controlled life which is identical for all and inadequate to all needs, and which is more rigorous than any experimenter could have set up to establish what is essential and what adventitious to the conduct of the human animal in the struggle for life.

We do not believe in the most obvious and facile deduction: that man is fundamentally brutal, egoistic and stupid in his conduct once every civilized institution is taken away, and that the Häftling [prisoner] is consequently nothing but a man without inhibitions. We believe, rather, that the only conclusion to be drawn is that in the face of driving necessity and physical disabilities many social habits and instincts are reduced to silence.

But another fact seems to us worthy of attention: there comes to light the existence of two particularly well differentiated categories among men—the saved and the drowned. Other pairs of opposites (the good and the bad, the wise and the foolish, the cowards and the courageous, the unlucky and the fortunate) are considerably less distinct, they seem less essential, and above all they allow for more numerous and complex intermediary gradations.

This division is much less evident in ordinary life; for there it rarely happens that a man loses himself. A man is normally not alone, and in his rise or fall is tied to the destinies of his neighbours; so that it is exceptional for anyone to acquire unlimited power, or to fall by a succession of defeats into utter ruin. Moreover, everyone is normally in possession of such spiritual, physical and even financial resources that the probabilities of a shipwreck, of total inadequacy in the face of life, are relatively small. And one must take into account a definite cushioning effect exercised both by the law, and by the moral sense which constitutes a self-imposed law; for a country is considered the more civilized the more the wisdom and efficiency of its laws hinder a weak man from becoming too weak or a powerful one too powerful.

But in the Lager things are different: here the struggle to survive is without respite, because everyone is desperately and ferociously alone. If some Null Achtzehn[1] vacillates, he will find no one to extend a helping hand; on the contrary, someone else will knock him aside, because it is in no one's interest that there will be one more "musselman"[2] dragging himself to work every day; and if someone, by a miracle of savage patience and cunning, finds a new method of avoiding the hardest work, a new art which yields him an ounce of bread, he will try to keep his method secret, and he will be esteemed and respected for this, and will derive from it an exclusive, personal benefit; he will become stronger and so will be feared, and who is feared is, ipso facto, a candidate for survival.

In history and in life one sometimes seems to glimpse a ferocious law which states: "to he that has, will be given; from he that has not, will be taken away." In the Lager, where man is alone and where the struggle for life is reduced to its primordial mechanism, this unjust law is openly in force, is recognized by all. With the adaptable, the strong and astute individuals, even the leaders willingly keep contact, sometimes even friendly contact, because they hope later to perhaps derive some benefit. But with the musselmans, the men in decay, it is not even worth speaking, because one knows already that they will complain

---

[1] 0,18—the last digits in the entry number of a prisoner Levi knew who had lost the will to live. [Ed.]

[2] This word, "*Muselmänn*," I do not know why, was used by the old ones of the camp to describe the weak, the inept, those doooomed to selection. [Levi]

and will speak about what they used to eat at home. Even less worthwhile is it to make friends with them, because they have no distinguished acquaintances in camp, they do not gain any extra rations, they do not work in profitable Kommandos and they know no secret method of organizing. And in any case, one knows that they are only here on a visit, that in a few weeks nothing will remain of them but a handful of ashes in some near-by field and a crossed-out number on a register. Although engulfed and swept along without rest by the innumerable crowd of those similar to them, they suffer and drag themselves along in an opaque intimate solitude, and in solitude they die or disappear, without leaving a trace in anyone's memory.

The result of this pitiless process of natural selection could be read in the statistics of Lager population movements. At Auschwitz, in 1944, of the old Jewish prisoners (we will not speak of the others here, as their condition was different), "*kleine Nummer*," low numbers less than 150,000, only a few hundred had survived; not one was an ordinary Häftling, vegetating in the ordinary Kommandos, and subsisting on the normal ration. There remained only the doctors, tailors, shoemakers, musicians, cooks, young attractive homosexuals, friends or compatriots of some authority in the camp; or they were particularly pitiless, vigorous and inhuman individuals, installed (following an investiture by the SS command, which showed itself in such choices to possess satanic knowledge of human beings) in the posts of Kapos, *Blockältester*, etc.; or finally, those who, without fulfilling particular functions, had always succeeded through their astuteness and energy in successfully organizing, gaining in this way, besides material advantages and reputation, the indulgence and esteem of the powerful people in the camp. Whosoever does not know how to become an "Organisator," "Kombinator," "Prominent" (the savage eloquence of these words!) soon becomes a "musselman." In life, a third way exists, and is in fact the rule; it does not exist in the concentration camp.

To sink is the easiest of matters; it is enough to carry out all the orders one receives, to eat only the ration, to observe the discipline of the work and the camp. Experience showed that only exceptionally could one survive more than three months in this way. All the musselmans who finished in the gas chambers have the same story, or more exactly, have no story; they followed the slope down to the bottom, like streams that run down to the sea. On their entry into the camp, through basic incapacity, or by misfortune, or through some banal incident, they are overcome before they can adapt themselves; they are beaten by time, they do not begin to learn German, to disentangle the infernal knot of laws and prohibitions until their body is already in decay, and nothing can save them from selections or from death by exhaustion. Their life is short, but their number is endless; they, the *Muselmänner*, the drowned, form the backbone of the camp, an anonymous mass, continually renewed and always identical, of non-men who march and labour in silence, the divine spark dead within them, already too empty to really suffer. One hesitates to call them living: one hesitates to call their death death, in the face of which they have no fear, as they are too tired to understand.

They crowd my memory with their faceless presences, and if I could enclose all the evil of our time in one image, I would choose this image which is familiar to me: an emaciated man, with head dropped and shoulders curved, on whose face and in whose eyes not a trace of a thought is to be seen.

If the drowned have no story, and single and broad is the path to perdition, the paths to salvation are many, difficult and improbable.

The most travelled road, as we have stated, is the *"Prominenz."* *"Prominenten"* is the name for the camp officials, from the Häftling-director (*Lagerältester*) to the Kapos, the cooks, the nurses, the night-guards, even to the hut-sweepers and to the *Scheissminister* and *Bademeister* (superintendents of the latrines and showers). We are more particularly interested in the Jewish prominents, because while the others are automatically invested with offices as they enter the camp in virtue of their natural supremacy, the Jews have to plot and struggle hard to gain them.

The Jewish prominents form a sad and notable human phenomenon. In them converge present, past and atavistic sufferings, and the tradition of hostility towards the stranger makes of them monsters of asociality and insensitivity.

They are the typical product of the structure of the German Lager: if one offers a position of privilege to a few individuals in a state of slavery, exacting in exchange the betrayal of a natural solidarity with their comrades, there will certainly be someone who will accept. He will be withdrawn from the common law and will become untouchable; the more power that he is given, the more he will be consequently hateful and hated. When he is given the command of a group of unfortunates, with the right of life or death over them, he will be cruel and tyrannical, because he will understand that if he is not sufficiently so, someone else, judged more suitable, will take over his post. Moreover, his capacity for hatred, unfulfilled in the direction of the oppressors, will double back, beyond all reason, on the oppressed; and he will only be satisfied when he has unloaded on to his underlings the injury received from above.

We are aware that this is very distant from the picture that is usually given of the oppressed who unite, if not in resistance, at least in suffering. We do not deny that this may be possible when oppression does not pass a certain limit, or perhaps when the oppressor, through inexperience or magnanimity, tolerates or favours it. But we state that in our days, in all countries in which a foreign people have set foot as invaders, an analogous position of rivalry and hatred among the subjected has been brought about; and this, like many other human characteristics, could be experienced in the Lager in the light of particularly cruel evidence.

About the non-Jewish prominents there is less to say, although they were far and away the most numerous (no "Aryan" Häftling was without a post, however modest). That they were stolid and bestial is natural when one thinks that the majority were ordinary criminals, chosen from the German prisons for the very purpose of their employment as superintendents of the camps for Jews; and we maintain that it was a very apt choice, because we refuse to believe that the squalid human specimens whom we saw at work were an average example, not of Germans in general, but even of German prisoners in particular. It is difficult to explain how in Auschwitz the political German, Polish and Russian prominents rivalled the ordinary convicts in brutality. But it is known that in Germany the qualification of political crime also applied to such acts as clandestine trade, illicit relations with Jewish women, theft from Party officials. The "real" politicals lived and died in other camps, with names now sadly famous, in notoriously hard conditions, which, however, in many aspects differed from those described here.

But besides the officials in the strict sense of the word, there is a vast category of prisoners, not initially favoured by fate, who fight merely with their own strength to survive. One has to fight against the current; to battle every day and every hour against exhaustion, hunger, cold and the resulting inertia; to resist enemies and have no pity for rivals; to sharpen one's wits, build up one's patience, strengthen one's will-power. Or else, to throttle all dignity and kill all conscience, to climb down into the arena as a beast against other beasts, to let oneself be guided by those unsuspected subterranean forces which sustain families and individuals in cruel times. Many were the ways devised and put into effect by us in order not to die: as many as there are different human characters. All implied a weakening struggle of one against all, and a by no means small sum of aberrations and compromises. Survival without renunciation of any part of one's own moral world—apart from powerful and direct interventions by fortune—was conceded only to very few superior individuals, made of the stuff of martyrs and saints.

HIROSHIMA, 1945

On August 6, 1945, a United States aircraft dropped an atomic bomb on the Japanese city of Hiroshima and killed 100,000 people, almost all of them civilians. John Hersey (1914-1993) interviewed the survivors and subsequently published their collected memories of the bombing as a book entitled Hiroshima.

All day, people poured into Asano Park. This private estate was far enough away from the explosion so that its bamboos, pines, laurel, and maples were still alive, and the green place invited refugees—partly because they believed that if the Americans came back, they would bomb only buildings; partly because the foliage seemed a center of coolness and life, and the estate's exquisitely precise rock gardens, with their quiet pools and arching bridges, were very Japanese, normal, secure; and also partly (according to some who were there) because of an irresistible, atavistic urge to hide under leaves. Mrs. Nakamura and her children were among the first to arrive, and they settled in the bamboo grove near the river. They all felt terribly thirsty, and they drank from the river. At once they were nauseated and began vomiting, and they retched the whole day. Others were also nauseated; they all thought (probably because of the strong odor of ionization, an "electric smell" given off by the bomb's fission) that they were sick from a gas the Americans had dropped. When Father Kleinsorge and the other priests came into the park, nodding to their friends as they passed, the Nakamuras were all sick and prostrate. A woman named Iwasaki, who lived in the neighborhood of the mission and who was sitting near the Nakamuras, got up and asked the priests if she should stay where she was or go with them. Father Kleinsorge said, "I hardly know where the safest place is." She stayed there, and later in the day, though she had no visible wounds or burns, she died.

When Mr. Tanimoto, with his basin still in his hand, reached the park, it was very crowded, and to distinguish the living from the dead was not easy, for most of the people lay still, with their eyes open. To Father Kleinsorge, an Occidental, the silence in the grove by the river, where hundreds of gruesomely wounded suffered together, was one of the most dreadful and awesome phenomena of his whole experience. The hurt ones were quiet; no one wept, much less screamed in pain; no one complained; none of the many who died did so noisily; not even the children cried; very few people even spoke. And when Father Kleinsorge gave water to some whose faces had been almost blotted out by flash burns, they took their share and then raised themselves a little and bowed to him, in thanks.

Mr. Tanimoto greeted the priests and then looked around for other friends. He saw Mrs. Matsumoto, wife of the director of the Methodist School, and asked her if she was thirsty. She was, so he went to one of the pools in the Asano's rock gardens and got water for her in his basin. Then he decided to try to get back to his church. He went into Noboricho by the way the priests had taken as they escaped, but he did not get far; the fire along the streets was so fierce that he had to turn back. He walked to the river bank and began to look for a boat in which he might carry some of the most severely injured across the river from Asano Park and away from the spreading fire. Soon he found a good-sized pleasure punt drawn up on the bank, but in and around it was an awful tableau—five dead men, nearly naked, badly burned, who must have expired more or less all at once, for they were in attitudes which suggested that they had been working together to push the boat down into the river. Mr. Tanimoto lifted them away from the boat, and as he did so, he experienced such horror at disturbing the dead—preventing them, he momentarily felt, from launching their craft and going on their ghostly way—that he said out loud, "Please forgive me for taking this boat. I must use it for others, who are alive." The punt was heavy, but he managed to slide it into the water. There were no oars, and all he could find for propulsion was a thick bamboo pole. He worked the boat upstream to the most crowded part of the park and began to ferry the wounded. He could pack ten or twelve into the boat for each crossing, but as the river was too deep in the center to pole his way across, he had to paddle with the bamboo, and consequently each trip took a very long time. He worked several hours that way.

Early in the afternoon, the fire swept into the woods of Asano Park. The first Mr. Tanimoto knew of it was when, returning in his boat, he saw that a great number of people had moved toward the riverside. On touching the bank, he went up to investigate, and when he saw the fire, he shouted, "All the young men who are not badly hurt come with me!" Father Kleinsorge moved Father Schiffer and Father LaSalle close to the edge of the river and asked people there to get them across if the fire came too near, and then joined Tanimoto's volunteers. Mr. Tanimoto sent some to look for buckets and basins and told others to beat the burning underbrush with their clothes; when utensils were at hand, he formed a bucket chain from one of the pools in the rock gardens. The team fought the fire for more than two hours, and gradually defeated the flames. As Mr. Tanimoto's men worked, the frightened people in the park pressed closer and closer to the river, and finally the mob began to force some of the unfortunates who were on the very bank into the water. Among those driven into the river and drowned were Mrs. Matsumoto, of the Methodist School, and her daughter.

It began to rain. Mrs. Nakamura kept her children under the umbrella. The drops grew abnormally large, and someone shouted, "The Americans are dropping gasoline. They're going to set fire to us!" (This alarm stemmed from one of the theories being passed through the park as to why so much of Hiroshima had burned: it was that a single plane had sprayed gasoline on the city and then somehow set fire to it in one flashing moment.) But the drops were palpably water, and as they fell, the wind grew stronger and stronger, and suddenly—probably because of the tremendous convection set up by the blazing city—a whirlwind ripped through the park. Huge trees crashed down; small ones were uprooted and flew into the air. Higher, a wild array of flat things revolved in the twisting funnel—pieces of iron roofing, papers, doors, strips of matting. Father Kleinsorge put a piece of cloth over Father Schiffer's eyes, so that the feeble man would not think he was going crazy. The gale blew Mrs. Murata, the mission housekeeper, who was sitting close by the river, down the embankment at a shallow, rocky place, and she came out with her bare feet bloody. The vortex moved out onto the river, where it sucked up a waterspout and eventually spent itself.

Late in the afternoon, when he went ashore for a while, Mr. Tanimoto, upon whose energy and initiative many had come to depend, heard people begging for food. He consulted Father Kleinsorge, and they decided to go back into town to get some rice from Mr. Tanimoto's Neighborhood Association shelter and from the mission shelter. Father Cieslik and two or three others went with them. At first, when they got among the rows of prostrate houses, they did not know where they were; the change was too sudden, from a busy city of two hundred and forty-five thousand that morning to a mere pattern of residue in the afternoon. The asphalt of the streets was still so soft and hot from the fires that walking was uncomfortable. They encountered only one person, a woman, who said to them as they passed, "My husband is in those ashes." At the mission, where Mr. Tanimoto left the party, Father Kleinsorge was dismayed to see the building razed. In the garden, on the way to the shelter, he noticed a pumpkin roasted on the vine. He and Father Cieslik tasted it and it was good. They were surprised at their hunger, and they ate quite a bit. They got out several bags of rice and gathered up several other cooked pumpkins and dug up some potatoes that were nicely baked under the ground, and started back. Mr. Tanimoto rejoined them on the way. One of the people with him had some cooking utensils. In the park, Mr. Tanimoto organized the lightly wounded women of his neighborhood to cook. Father Kleinsorge offered the Nakamura family some pumpkin, and they tried it, but they could not keep it on their stomachs. Altogether, the rice was enough to feed nearly a hundred people.

Just before dark, Mr. Tanimoto came across a twenty-year-old girl, Mrs. Kamai, the Tanimotos' next-door neighbor. She was crouching on the ground with the body of her infant daughter in her arms. The baby had evidently been dead all day. Mrs. Kamai jumped up when she saw Mr. Tanimoto and said, "Would you please try to locate my husband?"

Mr. Tanimoto knew that her husband had been inducted into the Army just the day before; he and Mrs. Tanimoto had entertained Mrs. Kamai in the afternoon, to make her forget. Kamai had reported to the Chugoku Regional Army Headquarters—near the ancient castle in the middle of town—where some four thousand troops were stationed. Judging by the many maimed soldiers Mr. Tanimoto had seen during the day, he surmised that the barracks had been badly damaged by whatever it was that had hit Hiroshima. He knew he hadn't a chance of finding Mrs. Kamai's husband, even if he searched, but he wanted to humor her. "I'll try," he said.

"You've got to find him," she said. "He loved our baby so much. I want him to see her once more."

NAGASAKI, 1945

William L. Laurence (1888-1977), a New York Times *reporter, accompanied the United States mission to bomb Nagasaki on August 9, 1945. His account received a Pulitzer prize.*

WITH THE ATOMIC-BOMB MISSION TO JAPAN, AUGUST 9 (Delayed)— We are on our way to bomb the mainland of Japan. Our flying contingent consists of three specially designed B-29 Superforts, and two of these carry no bombs. But our lead plane is on its way with another atomic bomb, the second in three days, concentrating in its active substance an explosive energy equivalent to twenty thousand and, under favorable conditions, forty thousand tons of TNT.

We have several chosen targets. One of these is the great industrial and shipping center of Nagasaki, on the western shore of Kyushu, one of the main islands of the Japanese homeland.

I watched the assembly of this man-made meteor during the past two days and was among the small group of scientists and Army and Navy representatives privileged to be present at the ritual of its loading in the Superfort last night, against a background of threatening black skies torn open at intervals by great lightning flashes.

It is a thing of beauty to behold, this "gadget." Into its design went millions of man-hours of what is without doubt the most concentrated intellectual effort in history. Never before had so much brain power been focused on a single problem.

This atomic bomb is different from the bomb used three days ago with such devastating results on Hiroshima.

I saw the atomic substance before it was placed inside the bomb. By itself it is not at all dangerous to handle. It is only under certain conditions, produced in the bomb assembly, that it can be made to yield up its energy, and even then it gives only a small fraction of its total contents—a fraction, however, large enough to produce the greatest explosion on earth.

The briefing at midnight revealed the extreme care and the tremendous amount of preparation that had been made to take care of every detail of the mission, to make certain that the atomic bomb fully served the purpose for which it was intended. Each target in turn was shown in detailed maps and in aerial photographs.

The briefing period ended with a moving prayer by the chaplain. We then proceeded to the mess hall for the traditional early-morning breakfast before departure on a bombing mission.

A few hours before take-off time, we all went to the flying field and stood around in little groups or sat in jeeps talking rather casually about our mission to the Empire, as the Japanese home islands are known hereabouts.

In command of our mission is Major Charles W. Sweeney, twenty-five, of 124 Hamilton Avenue, North Quincy, Massachusetts. His flagship, carrying the atomic bomb, is named *The Great Artiste*, but the name does not appear on the body of the great silver ship, with its unusually long, four-bladed, orange-tipped propellers. Instead, it carries the number 77, and someone remarks that it was "Red" Grange's winning number on the gridiron.

We took off at 3:50 this morning and headed northwest on a straight line for the Empire. The night was cloudy and threatening, with only a few stars here and there breaking through the overcast. The weather report had predicted storms ahead part of the way but clear sailing for the final and climactic stages of our odyssey.

We were about an hour away from our base when the storm broke.

I noticed a strange eerie light coming through the window high above the navigator's cabin, and as I peered through the dark all around us I saw a startling phenomenon. The whirling giant propellers had somehow become great luminous disks of blue flame. The same luminous blue flame appeared on the plexiglas windows in the nose of the ship, and on the tips of the giant wings. It looked as though we were riding the whirlwind through space on a chariot of blue fire.

It was, I surmised, a surcharge of static electricity that had accumulated on the tips of the propellers and on the di-electric material of the plastic windows. One's thoughts dwelt anxiously on the precious cargo in the invisible ship ahead of us. Was there any likelihood of danger that this heavy electric tension in the atmosphere all about us might set it off?

I expressed my fears to Captain Bock, who seems nonchalant and unperturbed at the controls. He quickly reassured me.

"It is a familiar phenomenon seen often on ships. I have seen it many times on bombing missions. It is known as St. Elmo's fire."

The first signs of dawn came shortly after five o'clock. Sergeant Curry, of Hoopeston, Illinois, who had been listening steadily on his earphones for radio reports, while maintaining a strict radio silence himself, greeted it by rising to his feet and gazing out the window.

"It's good to see the day," he told me. "I get a feeling of claustrophobia hemmed in in this cabin at night."

He is a typical American youth, looking even younger than his twenty years. It takes no mind reader to read his thoughts.

"It's a long way from Hoopeston," I find myself remarking.

"Yep," he replies, as he busies himself decoding a message from outer space.

"Think this atomic bomb will end the war?" he asks hopefully.

"There is a very good chance that this one may do the trick," I assured him, "but if not, then the next one or two surely will. Its power is such that no nation can stand up against it very long." This was not my own view. I had heard it expressed all around a few hours earlier, before we took off. To anyone who had seen this man-made fireball in action, as I had less than a month ago in the desert of New Mexico, this view did not sound over-optimistic.

By 5:50 it was really light outside. Our genial bombardier, Lieutenant Levy, comes over to invite me to take his front-row seat in the transparent nose of the ship, and I accept eagerly. From that vantage point in space, seventeen thousand feet above the Pacific, one gets a view of hundreds of miles on all sides, horizontally and vertically. At that height the vast ocean below and the sky above seem to merge into one great sphere.

I was on the inside of that firmament, riding above the giant mountains of white cumulus clouds, letting myself be suspended in infinite space. One hears the whirl of the motors behind one, but it soon becomes insignificant against the immensity all around and is before long swallowed by it. There comes a point where space also swallows time and one lives through eternal moments filled with an oppressive loneliness, as though all life had suddenly vanished from the earth and you are the only one left, a lone survivor traveling endlessly through interplanetary space.

My mind soon returns to the mission I am on. Somewhere beyond these vast mountains of white clouds ahead of me there lies Japan, the land of our enemy. In about four hours from now one of its cities, making weapons of war for use against us, will be wiped off the map by the greatest weapon ever made by man: In one tenth of a millionth of a second, a fraction of time immeasurable by any clock, a whirlwind from the skies will pulverize thousands of its buildings and tens of thousands of its inhabitants.

But at this moment no one yet knows which one of the several cities chosen as targets is to be annihilated. The final choice lies with destiny. The winds over Japan will make the decision. If they carry heavy clouds over our primary target, that city will be saved, at least for the time being. None of its inhabitants will ever know that the wind of a benevolent destiny had passed over their heads. But that same wind will doom another city.

Our weather planes ahead of us are on their way to find out where the wind blows. Half an hour before target time we will know what the winds have decided.

Does one feel any pity or compassion for the poor devils about to die? Not when one thinks of Pearl Harbor and of the Death March on Bataan.

Captain Bock informs me that we are about to start our climb to bombing altitude.

We reached Yakushima at 9:12 and there, about four thousand feet ahead of us, was *The Great Artiste* with its precious load.

We started circling. We saw little towns on the coastline, heedless of our presence. We kept on circling, waiting for the third ship in our formation.

The winds of destiny seemed to favor certain Japanese cities that must remain nameless. We circled about them again and again and found no opening in the thick umbrella of clouds that covered them. Destiny chose Nagasaki as the ultimate target.

We flew southward down the channel and at 11:33 crossed the coastline and headed straight for Nagasaki, about one hundred miles to the west. Here again we circled until we found an opening in the clouds. It was 12:01 and the goal of our mission had arrived.

We heard the prearranged signal on our radio, put on our arc welder's glasses, and watched tensely the maneuverings of the strike ship about half a mile in front of us.

"There she goes!" someone said.

Out of the belly of *The Great Artiste* what looked like a black object went downward.

Captain Bock swung around to get out of range; but even though we were turning away in the opposite direction, and despite the fact that it was broad daylight in our cabin, all of us became aware of a giant flash that broke through the dark barrier of our arc welder's lenses and flooded our cabin with intense light.

We removed our glasses after the first flash, but the light still lingered on, a bluish-green light that illuminated the entire sky all around. A tremendous blast wave struck our ship and made it tremble from nose to tail. This was followed by four more blasts in rapid succession, each resounding like the boom of cannon fire hitting our plane from all directions.

Observers in the tail of our ship saw a giant ball of fire rise as though from the bowels of the earth, belching forth enormous white smoke rings. Next they saw a giant pillar of purple fire, ten thousand feet high, shooting skyward with enormous speed.

By the time our ship had made another turn in the direction of the atomic explosion the pillar of purple fire had reached the level of our altitude. Only about forty-five seconds had passed. Awe-struck, we watched it shoot upward like a meteor coming from the earth instead of from outer space, becoming ever more alive as it climbed skyward through the white clouds. It was no longer smoke, or dust, or even a cloud of fire. It was a living thing, a new species of being, born right before our incredulous eyes.

At one stage of its evolution, covering millions of years in terms of seconds, the entity assumed the form of a giant square totem pole, with its base about three miles long, tapering off to about a mile at the top. Its bottom was brown, its center was amber, its top white. But it was a living totem pole, carved with many grotesque masks grimacing at the earth.

Then, just when it appeared as though the thing had settled down into a state of permanence, there came shooting out of the top a giant mushroom that increased the height of the pillar to a total of forty-five thousand feet. The mushroom top was even more alive than the pillar, seething and boiling in a white fury of creamy foam, sizzling upward and then descending earthward, a thousand Old Faithful geysers rolled into one.

It kept struggling in an elemental fury, like a creature in the act of breaking the bonds that held it down. In a few seconds it had freed itself from its gigantic stem and floated upward with tremendous speed, its momentum carrying it into the stratosphere to a height of about sixty thousand feet.

But no sooner did this happen when another mushroom, smaller in size than the first one, began emerging out of the pillar. It was as though the decapitated monster was growing a new head.

As the first mushroom floated off into the blue it changed its shape into a flowerlike form, its giant petals curving downward, creamy white outside, rose-colored inside. It still retained that shape when we last gazed at it from a distance of about two hundred miles. The boiling pillar of many colors could also be seen at that distance, a giant mountain of jumbled rainbows, in travail. Much living substance had gone into those rainbows. The quivering top of the pillar was protruding to a great height through the white clouds, giving the appearance of a monstrous prehistoric creature with a ruff around its neck, a fleecy ruff extending in all directions, as far as the eye could see.

DEAD CAT ON OUR RAINBOW

On October 27, 1951, in the early and nervous phase of the Cold War, Collier's *furnished its readers with a fantasy scenario of World War III. The magazine hired a distinguished cast of professors, Pulitzer prize-winning journalists, and government officials to "cover" an unprovoked nuclear strike by the Soviet Union against all of America's principal cities. Hal Boyle (1911-1974), an Associated Press reporter, filed a story on the bombing of Washington, D.C.*

WASHINGTON UNDER THE BOMB

Note to editors: Following is the first eyewitness account of the A-bombing of Washington, D.C., early today by a Soviet plane. Associated Press columnist Hal Boyle sent his story out in a helicopter which evacuated congressmen from the stricken capital.

The American capital is missing in action.

A single enemy atom bomb has destroyed the heart of the city. The rest is rapidly becoming a fire-washed memory. The flames are raging over 18 square miles.

Washington is burning to death. Communications are temporarily disrupted. Help of all kinds is urgently needed from the rest of the country—blood, drugs, bandages, doctors, nurses, food, transportation.

Uncounted thousands are dead. More thousands of injured lie, spread in untended rows, on hospital lawns and parks, or walk unheeded until they fall.

Civil defense has broken down. The few valiant disaster squads are helpless in this homeless flood of agony and misery. Troops are moving in to restore order among maddened masses trying to flee the city.

Fright crowds the rubbled streets and wears the blank face of awe. It couldn't happen here yesterday. It did happen here before dawn today.

The bomb exploded in southwest Washington, midway between the Capitol building and the Jefferson Memorial. It lighted the city as if it were a Roman candle.

For a radius of a mile from the center of the blast the devastation is utter— a huge scorched zero, as if a giant, white-hot hammer had pounded the area into the earth. Blast and fire then reached out in widening waves.

Most of the shrines that unite the American people are casualties. The Lincoln and Jefferson Memorials are in ruins. The top of the Washington Monument is sheared off, but the main part of the shaft still stands.

The White House is gutted. The President and his family are safe. The Secret Service has escorted him from the capital to a secret destination.

The dome of the Capitol itself is a great white shattered teacup. The office building of the House of Representatives is flaming. The Smithsonian Institution, the National Gallery, the archives building, the Department of Justice and the Bureau of Internal Revenue lie in tremendous wreckage. A prank of the bomb: windows melted in the Bureau of Engraving, but a few green leaves still cling to the trees in East Park.

I entered the city, after a five-mile walk along the railroad tracks, just as the roof of the Union Station caved in and shot up a tower of sparks.

A taxi horn sounded frantically, and a voice called: "Get in, you damned fool!"

It was Don Whitehead, a fellow AP war correspondent. He too was back in the States from the European front for a special briefing. The taxi windshield was shattered, and as we drove away I felt blood on the seat.

"The driver," said Whitehead. "Piece of debris got him. I found him dying.

Loaded him on an ambulance truck. Took his cab."

I remember the meter was still ticking. It read $2.60.

"The Reds sure hung a dead cat on our rainbow," said Whitehead. "One edge of the Pentagon, I understand, is on fire. Most of the bridges are down. The people can't get away."

Fallen wires writhed across the street like live grapevines. Abandoned trolleys stood at halt like big dead beetles. Wreckage and bits of flesh littered the streets.

We rode through a river of dazed refugees, burdened with any belongings they had been able to snatch up. One woman held a picture clenched in her hands. Behind her trailed a little girl pushing a doll buggy.

An old man, struggling to bear a crippled son in his tired arms, suddenly collapsed and went down. A young woman, carrying her elderly mother on her back, crawled painfully on hands and knees. A man in charred rags screamed on the pavement. No one stopped.

The heat seared. The entire business district raged in bonfire. It crackled like a million cattle stampeding in a field of potato chips. Shriveled corpses lay where they had fallen. They looked small and lonely.

A fat man wearing nothing but the bottoms of his pajamas stepped out in front of us and called hopefully:

"Taxi, taxi!"

"Poor fool," said Don, as we went by. "There's a man who believes in normal living."

We already had picked up five lost children in the cab, and there wasn't room for anybody else.

Hoping to get the five children in the cab out of danger, we drove toward the Arlington Memorial Bridge. It was broken. The span had dropped into the Potomac. The entrance to the bridge was choked by thousands of refugees, held back by a police line.

"A plane came over about an hour ago," said a sweating policeman. "Somebody hollered, 'It's the Reds again!' That started a panic. They broke through us and rushed out on the bridge. My God! They were pushed right on off into the river and drowned—hundreds of them. Hundreds of them!"

We drove back to the long green mall below the Capitol. Helicopters were landing there and taking away surviving members of Congress to a new meeting place. Ten are known to be dead, at least 30 are missing.

Whitehead has found a congressman who has agreed to fly the story out with him.

Whitehead then showed the congressman, who is a bachelor, the five frightened children in our cab. And he asked him:

"Aren't you taking your family with you, too, sir?"

"Sure," he said, wryly. "They'll vote someday. Start loading."

Before boarding a helicopter, a white-haired senator turned toward the silent Capitol. His eyes streaming, he lifted both fists and shook them fiercely at the bright morning sky, palled by rolling smoke clouds.

A young soldier has just climbed out on the lower roof of the Capitol and tied up an American flag. As it catches the breeze above the ruins, a sigh as of a tremendous wind sweeps through the vast crowd. And now everybody is crying and cheering together.

But to the north the flames are rising higher and spreading fast, as the enemy fire eats away the glory of this show window of America.

In its ashes Washington cries to the nation for help.

Silent Spring

Rachel Carson (1907-1964), an American biologist and one-time government official, published Silent Spring *in 1962. Her conjuring up of the destruction of the biosphere gave rise to the apocalyptic chorus of voices prophesying the ruin of what has come to be known as "the environment."*

The history of life on earth has been a history of interaction between living things and their surroundings. To a large extent, the physical form and the habits of the earth's vegetation and its animal life have been molded by the environment. Considering the whole span of earthly time, the opposite effect, in which life actually modifies its surroundings, has been relatively slight. Only within the moment of time represented by the present century has one species—man—acquired significant power to alter the nature of his world.

During the past quarter century this power has not only increased to one of disturbing magnitude but it has changed in character. The most alarming of all man's assaults upon the environment is the contamination of air, earth, rivers, and sea with dangerous and even lethal materials. This pollution is for the most part irrecoverable; the chain of evil it initiates not only in the world that must support life but in living tissues is for the most part irreversible. In this now universal contamination of the environment, chemicals are the sinister and little-recognized partners of radiation in changing the very nature of the world—the very nature of its life. Strontium 90, released through nuclear explosions into the air, comes to earth in rain or drifts down as fallout, lodges in soil, enters into the grass or corn or wheat grown there, and in time takes up its abode in the bones of a human being, there to remain until his death. Similarly, chemicals sprayed on croplands or forests or gardens lie long in soil, entering into living organisms, passing from one to another in a chain of poisoning and death. Or they pass mysteriously by underground streams until they emerge and, through the alchemy of air and sunlight, combine into new forms that kill vegetation, sicken cattle, and work unknown harm on those who drink from once pure wells. As Albert Schweitzer has said, "Man can hardly even recognize the devils of his own creation."

It took hundreds of millions of years to produce the life that now inhabits the earth—eons of time in which that developing and evolving and diversifying life reached a state of adjustment and balance with its surroundings. The environment, rigorously shaping and directing the life it supported, contained elements that were hostile as well as supporting. Certain rocks gave out dangerous radiation; even within the light of the sun, from which all life draws its energy, there were short-wave radiations with power to injure. Given time—time not in years but in millennia—life adjusts, and a balance has been reached. For time is the essential ingredient; but in the modern world there is no time.

The rapidity of change and the speed with which new situations are created follow the impetuous and heedless pace of man rather than the deliberate pace of nature. Radiation is no longer merely the background radiation of rocks, the bombardment of cosmic rays, the ultraviolet of the sun that have existed before there was any life on earth; radiation is now the unnatural creation of man's tampering with the atom. The chemicals to which life is asked to make its adjustment are no longer merely the calcium and silica and copper and all the rest of the minerals washed out of the rocks and carried in rivers to the sea; they are the synthetic creations of man's inventive mind, brewed in his laboratories, and having no counterparts in nature.

To adjust to these chemicals would require time on the scale that is nature's; it would require not merely the years of a man's life but the life of generations. And even this, were it by some miracle possible, would be futile, for the new chemicals come from our laboratories in an endless stream. . . .

These sprays, dusts, and aerosols are now applied almost universally to farms, gardens, forests, and homes—nonselective chemicals that have the power to kill every insect, the "good" and the "bad," to still the song of birds and the leaping of fish in the streams, to coat the leaves with a deadly film, and to linger on in soil—all this though the intended target may be only a few weeds or insects. Can anyone believe it is possible to lay down such a barrage of poisons on the surface of the earth without making it unfit for all life? They should not be called "insecticides," but "biocides." . . .

Along with the possibility of the extinction of mankind by nuclear war, the central problem of our age has therefore become the contamination of man's total environment with such substances of incredible potential for harm—substances that accumulate in the tissues of plants and animals and even penetrate the germ cells to shatter or alter the very material of heredity upon which the shape of the future depends.

Some would-be architects of our future look toward a time when it will be possible to alter the human germ plasm by design. But we may easily be doing so now by inadvertence, for many chemicals, like radiation, bring about gene mutations. It is ironic to think that man might determine his own future by something so seemingly trivial as the choice of an insect spray. . . .

Nature has introduced great variety into the landscape, but man has displayed a passion for simplifying it. Thus he undoes the built-in checks and balances by which nature holds the species within bounds. . . . Much of the necessary knowledge is now available but we do not use it. We train ecologists in our universities and even employ them in our governmental agencies but we seldom take their advice. We allow the chemical death rain to fall as though there were no alternative, whereas in fact there are many, and our ingenuity could soon discover many more if given opportunity.

Have we fallen into a mesmerized state that makes us accept as inevitable that which is inferior or detrimental, as though having lost the will or the vision to demand that which is good? Such thinking, in the words of the ecologist Paul Shepard, "idealizes life with only its head out of water, inches above the limits of toleration of the corruption of its own environment . . . Why should we tolerate a diet of weak poisons, a home in insipid surroundings, a circle of acquaintances who are not quite our enemies, the noise of motors with just enough relief to prevent insanity? Who would want to live in a world which is just not quite fatal?" . . .

There is still very limited awareness of the nature of the threat. This is an era of specialists, each of whom sees his own problem and is unaware of or intolerant of the larger frame into which it fits. It is also an era dominated by industry, in which the right to make a dollar at whatever cost is seldom challenged. When the public protests, confronted with some obvious evidence of damaging results of pesticide applications, it is fed little tranquilizing pills of half truth. We urgently need an end to these false assurances, to the sugar coating of unpalatable facts. It is the public that is being asked to assume the risks that the insect controllers calculate. The public must decide whether it wishes to continue on the present road, and it can do so only when in full possession of the facts. In the words of Jean Rostand, "The obligation to endure gives us the right to know."

PHNOM PENH, 1975

In Cambodia between 1975 and 1979, the Khmer Rouge exterminated between one and two million of their eight million countrymen. A radical Marxist sect that drew inspiration and material support from the Chinese, the Khmer Rouge felt that they could establish an agrarian utopia by killing the educated classes. Haing S. Ngor (1950-1996), a Cambodian doctor who escaped, made his way to America, and went on to perform in the movie The Killing Fields, *published his memoirs in 1987.*

Thousands and thousands and thousands of people filled the street, plodding south, where the Khmer Rouge told them to go. Thousands more stood in windows and doorways, unwilling to leave, or else came out from their houses offering flowers or bowls of rice, which some of the guerrillas accepted with shy country smiles and others coldly ignored. Car horns blared. From distant parts of the city came the chattering of assault rifles and the occasional boom of artillery. The fighting wasn't over, but white bedsheets hung from the buildings as signs of truce and surrender.

The Khmer Rouge strode through the boulevard, tired and bad-tempered, armed with AK-47 rifles and clusters of round, Chinese-made grenades on their belts. Their black uniforms were dusty and muddy. They had been fighting all night; some had waded through ditches. A few specialists carried the big tubular rocket-propelled grenade launchers on their shoulders, accompanied by soldiers carrying the elongated grenades in backpacks. Here and there were *mit neary*, the female comrades, firing pistols in the air and shouting harshly at the civilians to hurry up and leave. They were young, the Khmer Rouge, most of them in their teens. Their skins were very dark. Racially they were pure Khmers, children of the countryside. To them Phnom Penh was a strange, foreign place.

A Khmer Rouge shouted, "You have to leave the city for at least three hours. You must leave for your own safety, because we cannot trust the Americans. The Americans will drop bombs on us very soon. Go now, and do not bother to bring anything with you!"

Was I supposed to believe him? My instincts told me no. The guerrillas on the street looked totally unlike normal Cambodians, except for their dark, round faces. And yet a part of me wanted to believe that they were telling the truth.

The harsh voice yelled again, "If you have weapons, put them on the sidewalk. Let Angka collect them. The war is over now and there is no more need for weapons. The weapons are the property of Angka!"

I glanced to the side of the street. Sure enough, a few trusting civilians came out of their houses and put their AK-47s, their M-16s, their pistols on the sidewalk. I wondered: Who is Angka? Or what is Angka?

In the Khmer language, *angka* means "organization." Angka was the Organization—logically, I supposed, the Khmer Rouge command group. What did that imply? That the guerrillas were going to try to organize the Cambodians? That wasn't likely. If there was ever a disorganized people, it was us. Peasants who farmed when and where they wanted, employees who were casual about showing up for work, a society so *laissez-faire* that nothing ever got done. Even Sihanouk hadn't been able to organize us when he was our ruler, and he had tried. Where was Sihanouk now? I wondered. Was he part of Angka? Wasn't he the leader of the Khmer Rouge? When was he going to come back to Phnom Penh? Why hadn't they mentioned his name?

All around, people muttered, "Why evacuate the city? We don't want to go. The war is over. The Americans are not going to bomb us. We don't want to leave." They walked and stopped, took two steps and stopped again. Those with motorcycles pushed them by the handlebars, as I did. Those with cars pushed them with the help of friends or relatives. Nobody started their engines. There was no room on the road to drive. There was no gasoline to spare. When could we buy gasoline again?

I trudged south with the flow of the traffic. A contingent of Khmer Rouge approached from the opposite direction. In front of them walked a frightened-looking man whose hands were tied behind his back. Shoving him forward was a *mit neary* with a pistol. As she neared me, she waved the pistol in the air and addressed the crowd:

"The wheel of history is turning," she declared. "The wheel of history rolls on. If you use your hands to try to stop the wheel, they will be caught in the spokes. If you use your feet to try to stop it, you will lose them too. There is no turning back. World history will not wait. The revolution is here. You must make your choice, to follow Angka or not. If you choose not to follow Angka, we will not be responsible for your safety."

She gave the man in front of her another contemptuous shove. He staggered, the whites of his eyes showing his fear. As they went past me, she waved her pistol again and shouted, "Everybody is equal now! Everybody is the same! No more masters and no more servants! The wheel of history is turning! You must follow Angka's rules! "

I pushed on with the Vespa. Whatever hopes I had for the Khmer Rouge were fading fast. They were supposed to liberate us, not tie us up and make threats about obeying Angka's rules. Whoever Angka was.

* * *

As the rainy season began—normally the time when youths from the surrounding villages would shave their heads and join the monkhood—soldiers entered the empty temple of Tonle Bati and began removing the Buddha statues. Rolling the larger statues end over end, they threw them over the side, dumped them on the ground with heads and hands severed from the bodies, or threw them into the reflecting pond. But they could destroy only the outward signs of our religion, not the beliefs within. And even then, as I noticed with bitter satisfaction, there was one statue they did not destroy. It was the bronze Buddha, still gleaming inside the small Angkorian outbuilding. It had taken all my father's ingenuity to maneuver the heavy statue inside the narrow stone entrance. The Khmer Rouge couldn't figure how to get it out, much less smash it. They didn't have the intelligence, or the tools.

In Tonle Bati the Khmer Rouge made us go to *bonns*, or brain-washing sessions. They were always at night and usually in some mosquito-infested clearing in the forest. One evening, however, the Khmer Rouge leaders held a special *bonn* in the *sala* or hall next to the temple itself. We in the audience sat on the cool, smooth wooden floor. Soldiers had rigged a loudspeaker system powered by truck batteries. Standing near the microphone were cadre with the usual black cotton trousers and shirts, plus red headbands and red kramas tied like sashes around their waists. Outside, a light rain fell. One of the costumed men stepped to the microphone and spoke.

"In Democratic Kampuchea, under the glorious rule of Angka," he said, "we need to think about the future. We don't need to think about the past. You 'new' people must forget about the prerevolutionary times. Forget about cognac, forget about fashionable clothes and hairstyles. Forget about Mercedes. Those things are useless now. What can you do with a Mercedes now? You cannot barter for anything with it! You cannot keep rice in a Mercedes, but you can keep rice in a box you make yourself out of palm tree leaf!

"We don't need the technology of the capitalists," he went on. "We don't need any of it at all. Under our new system, we don't need to send our young people to school. Our school is the farm. The land is our paper. The plow is our pen. We will 'write' by plowing. We don't need to give exams or award certificates. Knowing how to farm and knowing how to dig canals—those are our certificates," he said.

"We don't need doctors anymore. They are not necessary. If someone needs to have their intestines removed, I will do it." He made a cutting motion with an imaginary knife across his stomach. "It is easy. There is no need to learn how to do it by going to school.

"We don't need *any* of the capitalist professions! We don't need doctors or engineers. We don't need professors telling us what to do. They were all corrupted. We just need people who want to work hard on the farm!

"And yet, comrades," he said, looking around at our faces, "there are some naysayers and troublemakers who do not show the proper willingness to work hard and sacrifice! Such people do not have the proper revolutionary mentality! Such people are our enemies! And comrades, some of them are right here in our midst!"

There was an uneasy shifting in the audience. Each of us hoped the speaker was talking about somebody else.

"These people cling to the old capitalist ways of thinking," he said. "They cling to the old capitalist fashions! We have some people among us who still wear eyeglasses. And *why* do they *use* eyeglasses? Can't they see me? If I move to slap your face"—he swung his open hand—"and you flinch, then you can see well enough. So you don't need glasses. People wear them to be handsome in the capitalistic style. They wear them because they are vain. We don't need people like that anymore! People who think they are handsome are lazy! They are leeches sucking energy from others!"

I took off my glasses and put them in my pocket. Around me, others with glasses did the same. My eyesight wasn't too bad, just a little nearsighted and astigmatic. I could still recognize people at a distance, but missed some of the details.

The speaker retreated from the microphone and stepped back into the line of cadre dressed like him, with the red kramas around their waists and the red headbands. A hiss in the loudspeaker system gave way to tape-recorded music, a strange march with chimes and gongs finishing out the phrases, the same kind of music I had heard in the exodus from Phnom Penh. Definitely music from Peking, I decided. The cadre began a stylized dance to it, raising their hands and dropping them in unison, as if using hoes. When the second stanza of the music began they changed position and mimed pulling on the handles of giant wrenches, as if tightening bolts on industrial machinery. I watched in surprise. I had never seen a dance that glorified farm work and factory labor.

At the end of the last dance all the costumed cadre, male and female, formed a single line and shouted "BLOOD AVENGES BLOOD!" at the top of their lungs. Both times when they said the word "blood" they pounded their chests with their clenched fists, and when they shouted "avenges" they brought their arms out straight like a Nazi salute, except with a closed fist instead of an open hand.

"BLOOD AVENGES BLOOD! BLOOD AVENGES BLOOD! BLOOD AVENGES BLOOD!" the cadre repeated with fierce, determined faces, thumping their fists on their hearts and raising their fists. They shouted other revolutionary slogans and gave the salutes and finally ended with "Long live the Cambodian revolution!"

It was a dramatic performance, and it left us scared. In our language, "blood" has its ordinary meaning, the red liquid in the body, and another meaning of kinship or family. Blood avenges blood. You kill us, we kill you. We "new" people had been on the other side of the Khmer Rouge in the civil war. Soldiers of the Lon Nol regime, with the help of American weapons and planes, had killed many tens of thousands of Khmer Rouge in battle. Symbolically, the Khmer Rouge had just announced that they were going to take revenge.

BERLIN (II), 1989

The collapse of the Berlin Wall in December 1989, ended the dream of socialist Utopia that had occupied the stage of European thought for nearly the whole of the 20th century. In The German Comedy: Scenes of Life After the Wall, *novelist Peter Schneider (1940-) confronts the intellectual consequences.*

Even before the wall fell, I had begun to wonder how some of my friends and acquaintances were dealing with the chaos of events. Does anyone take advantage of this great opportunity to reflect publicly on an error of judgment? Do I?

I have similar questions for some of the spokespersons from liberal, leftist, and "alternative" political groups. Pretty much everyone was happy about the opening of the Wall. People gave credit where credit was due: much, of course, to Gorbachev, but also to the citizens' rights movements in East Germany and the other Eastern bloc nations. But are these "friends of peace" celebrating now, and in what way? Is there nothing here that needs to be explained, nothing to set right, nothing to remember?

I'm not asking for confessions, lamentations, a literature of suffering and martyrdom. But a word of reflection, maybe even an occasional apology—just a little effort at remembering would prove that people really are looking for insights, not places to hide. Why can't people admit it? Why pretend continuity where none exists?

The watershed year of 1989 can be compared only with 1945, which it surpasses in intellectual significance. Back then, a pseudophilosophy marked from its inception by misanthropy and racism was finally forced to capitulate. The historical turning point of 1989 has a different character. The political embodiment of a utopia that had inspired the best and the brightest of many generations finally gave up the ghost. The great social experiment that had run for seventy years, and more or less forcibly involved over 250 million people, had to be broken off because it was constantly breaking down. This is an event of epochal dimensions, every bit as significant as the cataclysms that ended the Christian Middle Ages following the discoveries by Giordano Bruno and Galileo Galilei. And this failure cannot be explained by arguing that the theory was simply misapplied. In accordance with the wishes of its founders and organizers, socialism was devised as a "scientific" doctrine. And if an experiment continues to fail for seventy years, the source of error must be sought in its original hypothesis as well as in its execution.

You don't have to doubt Mozart because Igor Oistrakh plays him badly. But when every virtuoso makes the same piece sound bad, you have every right to suspect the composer. The flat assertion that present-day socialism in no way detracts from the theory ultimately amounts to intellectual shirking. It may be reassuring, but it only avoids the problem of deciding which components of the theory will sink with the wreck of socialism and which might still be salvaged.

What if the catastrophic economic failure of socialism today were due not only to a lack of democracy but also to the suppression of private ownership? Doesn't it seem these days that history itself has judged the duel between socialism and capitalism, and declared capitalism the winner? And isn't this winner now commanding from the mount: Thou shalt have no other social system besides me!?

My congratulations to anyone whose faith has not been shaken. But I'm afraid that those who don't feel doubts also won't be able to resist them in the long run. And those who do resist with eyes blindfolded and ears covered may well be saints, but they are not prophets.

Those who don't want to argue out of pure ignorance will have to come to terms with the following four propositions—for better or for worse:

1. We probably cannot ascribe the failure of this massive seventy-year experiment in socialism exclusively to Stalinism and the lack of democracy. What has happened appears to refute the utopian notion that masses of people in the industrial age can work creatively over long periods of time for a loftier purpose than self-interest.

2. Evidently we must reject the idea that socially undesirable tendencies like egoism, greed for private property, exploitation, aggression, racial hatred, and nationalism can be attributed to the relations of production under capitalism and can therefore be eliminated by changing those relations. Such "flaws" are clearly as human as the sense of justice, the notion of solidarity, and the willingness to help others—though both "good" and "bad" qualities may be weakened or strengthened through socialization.

3. The doctrine of socialism is not scientific but utopian. "Scientific socialism" distinguishes itself from other doctrines of salvation by claiming to describe objective laws of history. It asserts that "scientific insight" alone—not faith—is needed to enter into the earthly paradise of communism. Yet it requires terror and dictatorship to support its so-called laws of history, to show how humankind has inexorably moved toward a socialist utopia.

4. The socialist utopia is, without a doubt, a product of the contradictions of capitalism. The outrages of capitalism have not been resolved since Marx and Engels; in fact, they have worsened dramatically and on a global scale. Little is likely to remain of the "scientific" system called socialism; but of the anger and the criticism, the social and humanistic ideals that inspired Marx's revolutionary teachings, almost all. We have returned to the beginning, we need a new critique. Those who would formulate this radical critique of capitalism must first drop the false intellectual propriety that says, "You have to know the answer before you can criticize." Who was the wise man who gave us the proverb: "He who says 'I know' has already stopped thinking"?

THE END OF HISTORY

Francis Fukuyama (1952-), a State Department functionary, published "The End of History?" in 1989, advancing the thesis that all events of any historical consequence already have come and gone. Western liberal capitalism has triumphed over all other possible ways of organizing human society, and nothing remains to be done except the chores of maintenance.

The triumph of the West, of the Western *idea*, is evident first of all in the total exhaustion of viable systematic alternatives to Western liberalism. In the past decade, there have been unmistakable changes in the intellectual climate of the world's two largest communist countries, and the beginnings of significant reform movements in both. But this phenomenon extends beyond high politics and it can be seen also in the ineluctable spread of consumerist Western culture in such diverse contexts as the peasants' markets and color television sets now omnipresent throughout China, the cooperative restaurants and clothing stores opened in the past year in Moscow, the Beethoven piped into Japanese department stores, and the rock music enjoyed alike in Prague, Rangoon, and Tehran.

What we may be witnessing is not just the end of the Cold War, or the passing of a particular period of postwar history, but the end of history as such: that is, the end point of mankind's ideological evolution and the universalization of Western liberal democracy as the final form of human government. This is not to say that there will no longer be events to fill the pages of *Foreign Affairs's* yearly summaries of international relations, for the victory of liberalism has occurred primarily in the realm of ideas or consciousness and is as yet incomplete in the real or material world. But there are powerful reasons for believing that it is the ideal that will govern the material world *in the long run*.

The passing of Marxism-Leninism first from China and then from the Soviet Union will mean its death as a living ideology of world historical significance. For while there may be some isolated true believers left in places like Managua, Pyongyang, or Cambridge, Massachusetts, the fact that there is not a single large state in which it is a going concern undermines completely its pretensions to being in the vanguard of human history. And the death of this ideology means the growing "Common-Marketization" of international relations, and the diminution of the likelihood of large-scale conflict between states.

This does not by any means imply the end of international conflict *per se.* For the world at that point would be divided between a part that was historical and a part that was post-historical. Conflict between states still in history, and between those states and those at the end of history, would still be possible. There would still be a high and perhaps rising level of ethnic and nationalist violence, since those are impulses incompletely played out, even in parts of the post-historical world. Palestinians and Kurds, Sikhs and Tamils, Irish Catholics and Walloons, Armenians and Azeris, will continue to have their unresolved grievances. This implies that terrorism and wars of national liberation will continue to be an important item on the international agenda. But large-scale conflict must involve large states still caught in the grip of history, and they are what appear to be passing from the scene.

The end of history will be a very sad time. The struggle for recognition, the willingness to risk one's life for a purely abstract goal, the worldwide ideological struggle that called forth daring, courage, imagination, and idealism, will be replaced by economic calculation, the endless solving of technical problems, environmental concerns, and the satisfaction of sophisticated consumer demands. In the post-historical period there will be neither art nor philosophy, just the perpetual caretaking of the museum of human history. I can feel in myself, and see in others around me, a powerful nostalgia for the time when history existed. Such nostalgia, in fact, will continue to fuel competition and conflict even in the post-historical world for some time to come. Even though I recognize its inevitability, I have the most ambivalent feelings for the civilization that has been created in Europe since 1945, with its north Atlantic and Asian offshoots. Perhaps this very prospect of centuries of boredom at the end of history will serve to get history started once again.

[POLLING DATA]

From a Time/CNN *poll of 1000 adult Americans conducted on April 28 and 29, 1993, by Yankelevich Partners Inc.*

Will the second coming of Jesus Christ occur sometime around the year 2000?
      Yes   20%
      No   49%
      Not sure   31%

[NEWSSTAND BLURB]

Atlantic Monthly, *February 1994, hawking Robert D. Kaplan's article,* "The Coming Anarchy."

THE COMING ANARCHY: NATIONS BREAK UP UNDER THE TIDAL FLOW OF REFUGEES FROM ENVIRONMENTAL AND SOCIAL DISASTER. AS BORDERS CRUMBLE, ANOTHER TYPE OF BOUNDARY IS ERECTED—A WALL OF DISEASE. WARS ARE FOUGHT OVER SCARCE RESOURCES, ESPECIALLY WATER, AND WAR ITSELF BECOMES CONTINUOUS WITH CRIME, AS ARMED BANDS OF STATELESS MARAUDERS CLASH WITH THE PRIVATE SECURITY FORCES OF THE ELITES. A PREVIEW OF THE FIRST DECADES OF THE TWENTY-FIRST CENTURY.

[PRESIDENTIAL ASSESSMENT]

Bill Clinton's comments, quoted in the Boston Globe *July 20, 1994, after reading Kaplan's* "The Coming Anarchy." *Clinton talked about the article for weeks.*

. . . stunning article . . . makes you really imagine a future
that's like one of those Mel Gibson "Road Warrior" movies . . .

[BOOK TITLES]

A short selection of the 272 books currently in print, whose titles begin "The End of . . ."

NAME OF WORK (DATE)	AUTHOR
The End of Affluence (1975)	Paul Ehrlich and Anne H. Ehrlich
The End is Coming (1984) (Survivalist Series, No. 8)	Jerry Ahern
The End of Literary Theory (1987)	Stein H. Olsen
The End of the History of Art? (1987; Eng. trans.)	Hans Belting
The End of Beauty (1987)	Jorie Graham
The End of Ideology (1988; reprint)	Daniel Bell
The End of Nature (1989)	Bill McKibben
The End of History and the Last Man (1992)	Francis Fukuyama
The End of the Novel (1992; Eng. trans.)	Michael Kruger
The End of Acting: A Radical View (1992)	Richard Hornby
The End of Education (1992)	William Spanos
The End of Architecture? (1993)	Peter Noever (ed.)
The End of Manhood: *A Book for Men of Conscience* (1993)	John Stoltenberg
The End of Physics (1994)	David Lindley
The End of Work (1994)	Jeremy Rifkin
The End of Fame (1994)	B. Adams and C. Brooks
The End of Racism (1995)	Dinesh D'Souza
The End of the Nation-State (1995; Eng. trans.)	Jean-Marie Guehenno
The End of the Future: The Waning of the High-Tech World (1995)	Jean Gimpel
The End of Science (1996)	John Horgan
The Ends of the Earth: A Journey at the Dawn of the 21st Century (1996)	Robert D. Kaplan

[INDEX]

RAPTURE WATCH

Latest available information (November 1996) from the "Rapture Index," a site on the World Wide Web.

1 False Christs	3	26 Nuclear Nations	4
2 Satanism/Occult	3	27 World Unrest	5
3 New Age	4	28 Arms Build Up	5
4 Unemployment	1	29 Liberalism	5
5 Inflation	1	30 Peace Treaty	2
6 Interest Rates	1	31 Kings of the East	1
7 Economy	1	32 Mark of the Beast	4
8 Oil Supply/Price	4-1	33 Beast Government	2
9 Debts/Trade	3	34 Second Roman Empire	2
10 Depression/Crash	3	35 The Antichrist	2
11 Leadership	4-1	36 Volcanoes	5
12 Forward Momentum	4	37 Earthquakes	3+2
13 Apostasy	5	38 Hurricane/Tornado	5
14 Supernatural	1	39 Persia (Iran)	4
15 Moral Standards	4	40 Famine	5
16 Anti-Christian	2	41 Drought	3
17 Crime/Rate	1	42 Plagues	3+1
18 World Church	3	43 Climate	4-1
19 Globalism	3	44 Food Supply	5
20 Tribulation Temple	5	45 Drug Use	5
21 Anti-Semitism	4		
22 Israel Unrest	5	Rapture Index: 149	
23 Gog (Russia)	5	Net Change: unchanged	
24 Less Civil Rights	3	Current Index	
25 The False Prophet	2	14 Oct 1996	

Record High 164*	Record Low 50	1995 High 137	1996 High 149
Oct 26 90	Dec 12 93	1995 Low 100	1996 Low 111

*Record high occurred as the result of the Gulf War. As it stands now, there are two more major battles to be fought in the Middle East, the Gog [Russia] war and the battle of Armageddon. A host of other prophecy-related events like the peace treaty between the PLO and Israel have resulted directly from the Gulf War. The rise of the UN as a world policing force was another.

COMMENTS ON SELECTED CATEGORIES

1. *False Christs*: More reports about this Maitreya character—a secret world savior that few have seen.

2. *Satanism/Occult*: The number of psychic phone lines has upgraded this category.

12. *Forward Momentum*: (A measurement of the forward motion that events build up.) The Temple Mount issue is currently the strongest momentum building event to come along since the Israeli-PLO peace treaty.

13. *Apostasy*: The Barna Research group is reporting that church attendance, Bible reading, and Bible knowledge has declined sharply according to their latest survey.

18. *World Church*: The movement to join all religions into one. This has been a goal of the Devil for some time. By having all religions unified, he could more easily control their leadership.

20. *Tribulation Temple*: (2 Thes. 2:3-4; Dan. 9:27—If the Antichrist will sit in God's temple, it is logical to conclude the Temple must be rebuilt.) The Israeli government's willingness to defy Arab protests over the Holy site Tunnel raises the possibility that they may be willing to risk the same scorn over the rebuilding of the Jewish Temple.

23. *Gog* = Russia.

26. *Nuclear Nations*: This is what I call a courtesy downgrade. Whenever an event takes place that on paper seems to ease a prophetic situation, I will often oblige the action by downgrading the category—even though from prophecy we know that the opposite will occur—i.e., more nukes.

29. *Liberalism*: It's not just a part of the Democratic Party. Liberalism is what I would call the "true conspiracy." The liberal media is 100 percent controlled by the forces that bow to this humanistic ideology.

32. *Mark of the Beast*: Rev. 13:16—the economic system the Antichrist will implement. It will be compulsory, for all, to receive an implant in their right hand or forehead.

35. *The Antichrist*: This category rarely has a rating; the unrest in Israel has become a problem in search of a solution. Although there is no sign of the man with the solution, we know he must be near.

36. *Volcanoes*: A volcano in Iceland has started erupting. The eruption zone is located under a glacier, which is being melted by the heat causing flood worries.

37. *Earthquakes*: A 6.8 magnitude quake strikes the Middle East region.

40. *Famine*: Floods in China have prevented the summer rice crop from being planted. Earlier flooding prevented the spring rice from being planted.

42. *Plagues*: A new outbreak of the Ebola Virus in Gabon.

43 *Climate*: World weather has had very few notable events lately.

[INTERNET POSTING]

THE GATES OF HELL?

A message posted anonymously on the Internet in the fall of 1994.

Warning! Bill Gates (president of Microsoft) may be the next Antichrist.

Revelation 13:18 says, "Let anyone who has intelligence work out the number of the beast, for the number represents a man's name, and the numerical value of its letters is six hundred and sixty-six."

Bill Gates's full name is William Henry Gates III. Nowadays he is known as Bill Gates (III). By converting the letters of his current name to their ASCII values, you get the following:

BILLGATES3

66+73+76+76+71+65+84+69+83+3=666

Daniel 7:23 says, "The explanation he gave was this: 'The fourth beast signifies a fourth kingdom which will appear on earth. It will differ from the other kingdoms; it will devour the whole earth, treading it down and crushing it.'"

Current history knows three Antichrists: Adolf Hitler, Joseph Stalin, and the Pope. Is the fourth beast the Microsoft corporation, which represents the power of money?

[PRESS RELEASES]

The End Is Nearish!

From a series of press releases issued between August 1993 and October 1994 by Neal Chase, spokesman for Baha'is Under the Provisions of the Covenant, a religious sect based in Missoula, Montana.

RELEASE DATE: AUGUST 4, 1993

In our previous releases, we gave you the exact date that New York was to be bombed: November 26, 1992, the Day of the Covenant. That date, plus the prophesied season of three months (Daniel 7:12) brought us to February 26, 1993, the day, the minute, the hour, the second that the World Trade Center was bombed. We stated that this was just an OMEN of the big one yet to come.

Now we are giving the date for the big one. Saddam Hussein has vowed to take revenge on New York and the United Nations for what they did to his country. Ezekiel gives us THE VERY DAY that this will happen. In chapter 4, verse 5, he states that the destruction of the city will last 190 days, which, counting from the date of the bombing of the World Trade Center, brings us exactly to September 4, 1993, the day the UN building and all New York City will be nuked.

We have warned you. The blood of the people is not on our hands.

RELEASE DATE: SEPTEMBER 27, 1993

From the date of the World Trade Center bombing of February 26, 1993 (which we accurately predicted), there were exactly 190 days to September 4, 1993. Ezekiel then gives 40 more days in chapter 4, verse 6, which brings us to October 14, 1993, the day the UN building and all New York City will be destroyed by a thermonuclear bomb!

Noah sent out three releases telling the people the day of the flood to come. With the third and final release, the flood wiped out those who had scoffed at him. This release is the third release pertaining to the big one. This third release is the final blast, the warning trumpet.

The waiting is over.

RELEASE DATE: NOVEMBER 1, 1993

On March 23, 1994, the veils will be rent asunder with the fiery holocaust of New York City's millions of inhabitants! Forty days later, on May 2, 1994, will come the Battle of Armageddon, in which one third of mankind will be killed in one hour of thermonuclear war.

WE DIDN'T MAKE A MISTAKE when we wrote in our previous releases that New York would be destroyed on September 4 and October 14, 1993. We didn't make a mistake, not even a teeny eeny one!

The New Jerusalem Bible and the New English Bible both say, in Ezekiel 4, that the destruction of the city of New York will occur over a period of 190 days. But the King James Version and the Revised Standard Version give 390 days for that same verse of Ezekiel. We gave the earlier date because if we had given the later date of 390 days and all New York had been destroyed after 190 days—on September 4—or even 40 days after that—on October 14—then everyone would be dead and we would be to blame for having misguided the people.

There shall be no more delay! God never makes a promise he doesn't keep.

RELEASE DATE: APRIL 4, 1994

All the dates we have given in our past releases are correct dates given by God as contained in the Holy Scriptures. Not one of these dates was wrong; all of them pertain to the siege of the city of New York and the UN building which will come to an end on May 2, 1994.

Exactly 390 days after the World Trade Center bombing, on March 23, 1994, came the Edison Gas Explosion. [A gas pipeline exploded in Edison, New Jersey, on March 24, injuring about a hundred residents.] As reported by *The New York Times*, it was likened by eyewitnesses to a nuclear blast comparable to Nagasaki or Hiroshima. This woke up the people of that area, who are in IMMEDIATE DANGER, so that now they can leave the city by May 2, 1994, when the siege will be complete.

Ezekiel gives a total of 430 days for the siege of the city, one day for each year that the Israelites were in captivity in Egypt before the Exodus of Moses. Four hundred and thirty days added to the World Trade Center bombing of February 26, 1993, brings us exactly to May 2, 1994.

By now, all the people have been forewarned. We have done our job.

RELEASE DATE: OCTOBER 9, 1994

Exactly as we have been predicting, Saddam Hussein has now mobilized his forces to take his revenge for the Gulf War: full-scale thermonuclear destruction of the UN building and all New York City, scheduled to take place on November 26, 1994, give or take a week or two.

On May 2, 1994, there was the Lincoln Tunnel Explosion, which completed the days of the siege. [On May 5, a helicopter crashed near the New Jersey entrance to the Lincoln Tunnel and burst into flames, killing two.] In Revelation 8 it says that there will be "silence in heaven for about half an hour." The original Greek shows that in fact this half hour is half a year, or about 180 days. About 180 days from May 2, 1994, brings us to the significant Holy Day of November 26, 1994. The Bible does not say exactly 180 days but about that much time, with a week or two leeway, for the nuclear destruction of the UN building and New York City to take place.

We are the only ones in the entire world guiding the people to their safety, security, and salvation!

We have a 100 percent track record!

[DATES]

END TIMES

NAME	DATES LIVING	PREDICTED DATE FOR END OF THE WORLD
Zoroaster	After 1500 B.C.	Imminent
The Apostle Paul	Died c. 67 A.D.	Imminent
Matthew	1st century A.D.	Within a generation
Lactantius	c. 260 - 340 A. D.	Before 500 A.D.
Augustine	354 - 430 A.D.	Thought setting a date certain was impossible, but institutionalizes view of history as a cosmic week with "thousand year" days. He took these to be metaphorical, many of his readers did not.
The Venerable Bede	c. 673 - 735 A.D.	2048 + Like Augustine, Bede discouraged enthusiastic expectation of a specific date. In choosing his date, he intended to push off the world's terminus to a distant future, and put a stop to the heightened expectation that surrounded the year 800.
Joachim of Fiore	c. 1131 - 1201/02	Imminent
Christopher Columbus	c. 1451 - 1506	1650

NAME	DATES LIVING	PREDICTED DATE FOR END OF THE WORLD
Nostradamus	1503 - 1566	To begin sometime near 1827—the King of Terror arrives in July 1999
Isaac Newton	1642 - 1727	1866 (predicted in his youth) 2060 + (in his mature years)
William Whiston (Newton's successor at Cambridge)	1667 - 1752	1736 - 1866
Jonathan Edwards	1703 - 1758	c. 2000
William Miller (precursor to the Seventh-Day Adventists)	1782 - 1849	October 22, 1844
Charles Taze Russell (founder of the Jehovah's Witnesses)	1852 - 1916	1914
Jeane Dixon	1918 - 1997	1999
Hal Lindsey	1930? -	before 2050
Jerry Falwell	1933 -	before 2031

AFTERWORD

THE WRECK OF TIME (II)

The approaching end of the world strikes me like some
obvious but quite subtle scent—just as a traveler nearing
the sea feels the sea breeze before he sees the sea.

—Vladimir Solovyev

The careful reader might ask why no mention has been made of the flood that floated Noah's ark, or the scattering of Montezuma's feathered glory and Napoleon's defeat on the field at Waterloo. Or again, nearer our own time, why nothing was said of the assassination of President John F. Kennedy and the fall of Saigon, or the recent massacre of 500,000 Rwandans on the shores of Lake Tanganyika.

Fair questions, but a book of ten or even twenty times the present length could no more encompass the complete record of all the world's calamity than could a single dictionary contain all the world's names for grief. The annals of destruction bulge with reports of burning cities, and accounts of the primordial flood appear not only in the Bible and the Epic of Gilgamesh but also in Greek mythology (Zeus instructing Deucalion to build a large chest) as well as in stories told in India, Burma, Sarawak, and by the Papagos Indians in Arizona.

The better questions speak to the uses of history in an age beguiled by the joys of forgetfulness. Resident within the glass walls of the media, we live among the images of a legendary past ceaselessly dissolving into an eternal present. The time is always now, and the alarms of the moment (war in Bosnia, greed in Washington, crime in Moscow or Los Angeles) come and go like monstrous apparitions inexplicably drifting across the mirrors of the news. Narrative becomes montage; nothing necessarily follows from anything else, and chronological sequence gives way to the arranging of symbolic icons in mosaics like those made from the neon signs in Times Square. Closer in character to poetry than prose, the electronic media proceed by analogy—the face of a hungry Rwandan child standing as surrogate for the continent of Africa, a helicopter shot of an Iowa village green expressing the boundless store of small-town American virtue. The constant viewer learns to accept the images on the screen as metaphors, all of them weightless and without consequence, returning as surely as the sun—reworked and rearranged as other commercials, other press conferences, other football seasons—demanding nothing of the audience except the duty of ritual observance.

People unfamiliar with the world in time find themselves marooned in a perpetual and therefore terrifying present. Bereft of memory, we become, in Henry Adams' phrase, "nervous invalids," frightened by loud noises and forgetting how or why the door closes and the days pass. Not knowing where to find our place in the human story (in chapter 14 or on page 438) we become easy marks for the quack evangelists and political demagogues who promote the necessary cleansings of an earth that Isaiah—not unlike the more militant members of the Sierra Club—beheld as a foul sewer lying "polluted under its inhabitants." To the prophet secure in the knowledge that only the wicked shall perish, the promise of Armageddon is a consummation devoutly to be wished. When at last the lyre is stilled and the host of the damned falls into the hands of Jonathan Edwards' angry god, then Satan's constant associates and inseparable companions—variously identified over the course of the centuries as false priests, proud barons, profiteering capitalists and vile communists—shall gnaw their tongues in anguish. Let the Lord make manifest his bright vengeance and so loose upon the earth the redeeming flood or the purifying fire, and like Sylvester Stallone making good his escape from a cloud of Hollywood explosions, the faithful and the saved shall find their way home to Paradise.

The promise is false, and when confronted with the seers of all faiths and denominations who lately have been searching out the abyss of the millennium for the prospects of revolution, famine and war, we do well to remember that they conceive of history as a blueprint instead of a story, as if it might be possible to reduce the contingency of human experience to a rule of right conduct or a principle of mechanics certain to lead to a man-made future consistent in all its important particulars with the God-given Eden.

The prophets mistake the nature of the enterprise. History relieves our loneliness and teaches us that the story in the old books is also our own. Without history, we become orphans, deprived of our kinship with a larger whole and a wider self, with those who have gone before and those who will come after. The writers who speak only to the mysteries of the eternal now cheat us of our inheritance, breaking our connection to Mr. Tanimoto, who ferried Hiroshima's wounded across the river from Asano Park, and causing us to lose sight of Siegfried Sassoon in the Hindenburg Trench, "a single human being with my little stock of earthly experience in my head," discovering that a man can stand up against stupefying shell-fire and so find in himself "the invincible resistance of an animal or insect and an endurance which he might, in after days, forget or disbelieve."

The imaginative taking up of the experience of the past can be put through as many paces as a well-trained circus horse. Actively engaged, the study of history instills a sense of humor, wards off what Hamlet decried as "the slings and arrows of outrageous fortune," encourages a decent distrust of the simple answer and the false analogy, furnishes what Dionysius of Halicarnassus praised as "philosophy learned by example."

Were it not for the measure of history, I wouldn't know how to make sense of the newspapers, much less question the wisdom of what G. K. Chesterton once called "the small and arrogant oligarchy of those who merely happen to be walking around." When I'm told by the protectors of the nation's virtue that the shows of violence on network television have debased the once-innocent American mind, I remember that in the Iowa of the 1840s (i.e., the *fons et origo* of Dan Quayle's family values) prosperous farmers brought picnics and small children to public hangings.

At Washington conferences sponsored by the makers of diplomatic *realpolitik*, I listen to important newspaper columnists urge the sending of American troops to Bosnia because the Serbian bullies must be punished to discourage other bullies elsewhere in the world, and I think not only of the same important columnists making the same fierce remarks prior to the American expedition in Vietnam but also of the slaveholding southern gentry in Charleston in April 1861, drinking triumphal toasts to their certain victory on the night before the Confederate artillery fired on Fort Sumter. In Central Park some years ago I saw Pope John Paul II blessing the crowds gathered in the sheep meadow, but instead of thinking his message as pious and sweet as the greeting on a Hallmark card, I thought of Pope Innocent III preaching the Albigensian Crusade and remembered how the flock of the faithful was winnowed by the good shepherds of the Spanish Inquisition.

The number of people in the United States at the moment who believe in the literal truth of the biblical Book of Revelation exceeds the number of people who lived in all of medieval Christendom, and in a newspaper I notice that a voodoo priestess in New Orleans by the name of Sallie Ann Glassman seeks to rid the city of crack cocaine through the good offices of Ogoun La Flambeau, a god of war and fire, whom she had summoned from the forest with an offering of rum, gunpowder, and old graveyard dirt. At Harvard University a professor of psychiatry verifies the sighting of intergalactic aliens, and across all 24 time zones, the magi of the World Wide Web announce the coming of Gog or Magog.

The voices of experience counter the visions of transcendence, and although the reading and writing of history settles nothing (neither the grocer's bill nor the next election) it assumes the continuity of human feeling and thought and argues for the sense of community in the wastes of time. All things decay and go to what Lucretius called "the reef of destruction, outworn by the ancient lapse of years," but from the ruin of families and empires we preserve what we have found useful or beautiful or true, and on our way to death we have nothing else with which to build the future except the wreckage of the past.

L.H.L.

SOURCES

Albrecht Dürer, *The Four Horsemen of the Apocalypse,* 1497-1499. Gabinetto dei Disegni e delle Stampe, Florence. Courtesy of Scala/Art Resource, NY.

Stanzas from W. H. Auden, "Musée des Beaux Arts," from *W. H. Auden: Collected Poems,* by W. H. Auden, edited by Edward Mendelson (New York: Random House, 1976). Copyright © 1940 and renewed 1968 by W. H. Auden. Reprinted by permission of Random House, Inc.

Excerpt from *The Epic of Gilgamesh*, translated by N. K. Sandars (London: Penguin Classics 1960, second revised edition 1972). Copyright © 1960, 1964, 1972, by N. K. Sandars. Reproduced by permission of Penguin Books Ltd.

Tablet in *Gilgamesh*, translated by John Gardner and John Maier (New York: Alfred A. Knopf, 1984). Copyright © 1984 by the Estate of John Gardner and John Maier. Reprinted by permission of Alfred A. Knopf, Inc.

Genesis 19, The King James Version.

Excerpt from Plato, *Timaeus*, translated by R. G. Bury, Loeb Classical Library (Cambridge, Massachusetts: Harvard University Press, 1929). Reprinted by permission of the publishers and the Loeb Classical Library.

Excerpt from *The Aeneid of Virgil*, translated by Allen Mandelbaum (New York: Bantam Books, 1981). Translation copyright © 1971 by Allen Mandelbaum. Used by permission of Bantam Books, a division of Bantam Doubleday Dell Publishing Group, Inc.

Isaiah 24, The King James Version.

Excerpt from Thucydides, *The History of the Peloponnesian War*, translated by Sir Richard Livingstone (New York: Oxford University Press, 1943). Reprinted by permission of Oxford University Press.

Citation of Polybius in Appian, *Roman History*, translated by Horace White, Loeb Classical Library (New York: Macmillan, 1912).

Excerpt from Lucretius, *On the Nature of Things*, translated by W. H. D. Rouse, Loeb Classical Library (Cambridge, Massachusetts: Harvard University Press, 1975). Reprinted by permission of the publishers and the Loeb Classical Library.

Excerpt from Lucan, *The Civil War*, translated by S. H. Braund (New York: Oxford University Press, 1992). Reprinted by permission of Oxford University Press.

Mark 13, The King James Version.

Excerpt from Suetonius, *Works of Suetonius*, translated by J. C. Rolfe, Loeb Classical Library (New York: G. P. Putnam's Sons, 1924).

Excerpt from Josephus, *The Jewish War*, translated by G. A. Williamson (London: Penguin Classics 1959, revised edition 1970). Copyright © 1959, 1969 by G. A. Williamson. Reproduced by permission of Penguin Books Ltd.

"Herod's Temple" and "Herod's Temple Enclosure" from Josephus, *The Jewish War*, translated by G. A. Williamson (London: Penguin Classics 1959, revised edition 1970). Copyright © 1959, 1969 by G. A. Williamson. Reproduced by permission of Penguin Books Ltd.

Excerpt from Pliny, *Letters and Panegyricus*, translated by Betty Radice, Loeb Classical Library (Cambridge, Massachusetts: Harvard University Press, 1969). Reprinted by permission of the publishers and the Loeb Classical Library.

Francesco Paolo Maulucci Vivolo, *Pompeii: I Graffiti Figurati*.

Revelation 16, The King James Version.

Excerpt from Procopius, *History of the Wars*, translated by H. B. Dewing, Loeb Classical Library (Cambridge, Massachusetts: Harvard University Press, 1916).

Óengus of Clonenagh, pre-Viking Irish poem, translated by Frank O'Connor, in Frank O'Connor, *A Short History of Irish Literature*, (New York: G. P. Putnam's Sons, 1967). Copyright © 1967 by Harriet R. O'Donovan. Reprinted by arrangement with Writers House, Inc. as agent for the proprietor.

"The Viking Terror," translated by Brendan Kennelly in *The Penguin Book of Irish Verse*, edited by Brendan Kennelly (London: Penguin Books 1970, second edition 1981). Copyright © 1970, 1981 by Brendan Kennelly. Reproduced by permission of Penguin Books Ltd.

Excerpt from *The Chronicle of Fulcher of Chartres*, translated by Martha E. McGinty in *The First Crusade*, edited by Edward Peters (Philadelphia: University of Pennsylvania Press, 1971). Copyright © 1971 by the University of Pennsylvania Press. Reprinted with permission of the publisher.

Joachim of Fiore, "Letter to All the Faithful," reprinted from *Apocalyptic Spirituality*, translated by Bernard McGinn (New York: Paulist Press, 1979). Copyright © 1979 by Paulist Press. Used by permission of Paulist Press.

Excerpt from Guillaume de Tudèle, *Crusade Against the Albigensians*, translated by Joshua Phillips.

Excerpt from Giovanni Boccaccio, *The Decameron*, translated by Guido Waldman (Oxford: Oxford University Press, 1993). Reprinted by permission of Oxford University Press.

Excerpt from Ibn Khaldûn, *The Muqaddimah: An Introduction to History*, translated by Franz Rosenthal, abridged and edited by N. J. Dawood (Princeton: Princeton University Press, 1969). Copyright © 1969 by Princeton University Press. Reprinted by permission of Princeton University Press.

Excerpt from Ducas, *Decline and Fall of Byzantium to the Ottoman Turks*, translated by Harry J. Magoulias (Detroit: Wayne State University Press, 1975). Copyright © 1975 by Wayne State University Press. Reprinted by permission of the Wayne State University Press.

"Another Ballade," from François Villon, *Selected Poems*, edited and translated by Peter Dale (New York: Penguin Books, 1978). Copyright © by Peter Dale. Used by permission of Peter Dale.

Hieronymus Bosch, *The Seven Deadly Sins and the Four Last Things* (detail), late 15th century. Museo del Prado, Madrid, Spain. Courtesy of Scala/Art Resource, NY.

Leonardo da Vinci, *Study of Two Heads*, 1503. Museum of Fine Arts (Szepmuveszeti Muzeum), Budapest, Hungary. Courtesy of Scala/Art Resource, NY.

Leonardo da Vinci, *Drawing of Shouting Warrior*, 1503. Museum of Fine Arts (Szepmuveszeti Muzeum), Budapest, Hungary. Courtesy of Foto Marburg/Art Resource, NY.

Christopher Columbus, seal and preface, *Libro de las Profecías*, translated by Delno C. West and August Kling (Gainesville: University Press of Florida, 1991). Courtesy of University Press of Florida.

Excerpt from Bartolomé de Las Casas, *A Short Account of the Destruction of the Indies*, translated by Nigel Griffin (London: Penguin Classics, 1992). Translation copyright © 1992 by Nigel Griffin. Reproduced by permission of Penguin Books Ltd.

Excerpt from Luigi Guicciardini, *The Sack of Rome*, translated and edited by James H. Mc Gregor (New York: Italica Press, 1993). Used by permission.

Pieter Bruegel, the Elder, *The Triumph of Death*, 1568-1569. Museo del Prado, Madrid, Spain. Courtesy of Scala/Art Resource, NY.

William Shakespeare, *Richard II*, Act III, scene ii.

John Donne, "Holy Sonnet 174."

Martin Droeshout, *Death's Duell: or, A Consolation to the Soule, Against the Dying Life, and Living Death of the Body* (death mark engraving of John Donne), 1631. Courtesy of Corbis-Bettmann.

Anonymous, *King Charles his Speech, Made upon the Scaffold at Whitehall-Gate* (London, 1649).

Dispatch from Lisbon, *Gentleman's Magazine* (London: December 1775).

Excerpt from Voltaire, *Candide*, translated by Lowell Bair (New York: Bantam Books, 1959). Translation copyright © 1959 by Bantam Books, a division of Bantam Doubleday Dell Publishing Group, Inc. Used by permission of Bantam Books, a division of Bantam Doubleday Dell Publishing Group, Inc.

"Cornwallis' Report of the Surrender," and "Correspondence on, and the Articles of, the Capitulation," in Henry P. Johnston, *The Yorktown Campaign and the Surrender of Cornwallis, 1781* (New York: Harper and Brothers, 1881).

John E. N. Hearsey, *Marie Antoinette* (New York: E. P. Dutton, 1973).

"Decree of the Era" of the French Government. Convention nationale [France, 1792-95], "Calendrier de la République française, précédé du décret su l'ère . . . ," du 4 frimaire An 2, (Paris, Year 2, [1793]) Department of Special Collections, University of Chicago Library.

G. H. Lewes, *The Life of Maximilien Robespierre* (London: Chapman and Hall, 1849).

Edmund Burke, *Letters on a Regicide Peace* (London: F. and C. Rivington, 1796-97).

Thomas Malthus, "An Essay on the Principle of Population," (1798).

Francisco de Goya, *The Ravages of War*, 1810-1814, reprinted from *Goya: The Complete Etchings and Lithographs*, edited by Alfonso E. Pérez Sánchez and Julián Gállego (Munich, New York: Prestel-Verlag, 1995). Courtesy of Prestel-Verlag.

Evan Jones, "On the Trail of Tears," in *The Baptist Missionary Magazine* (September 1838 and April 1839).

Burton N. Harrison, "The Capture of Jefferson Davis," in *Century Magazine* (New York: November 1883).

Excerpts from *Mary Chesnut's Civil War*, edited by C. Vann Woodward (New Haven: Yale University Press, 1981). Copyright © 1981 by C. Vann Woodward, Sally Bland Metts, Barbara G. Carpenter, Sally Bland Johnson, and Katherine W. Herbert. Used by permission.

George Cary Eggleston, *A Rebel's Recollections* (New York: Hurd and Houghton, 1875).

Karl Marx, "Historical Tendency of Capitalist Accumulation," first published in *Das Kapital: Kritik der politischen Oekonomie* (Hamburg: Erster Band, 1867); printed according to the English edition, 1887, edited by Friedrich Engels.

Excerpt from Robert Sencourt, *The Life of Empress Eugénie* (New York: Charles Scribner's Sons, 1931). Copyright 1931 by Charles Scribner's Sons, copyright renewed. Reprinted with the permission of Scribner, a division of Simon & Schuster.

Archibald Forbes, "We want but a Nero to fiddle" (London: *The Daily News*, May 26, 1871).

James Mooney, *The Ghost-Dance Religion and the Sioux Outbreak of 1890* (1896).

C. P. Cavafy, "Waiting for the Barbarians," in *The Essential Cavafy*, translated by Edmund Keeley and Philip Sherrard (Princeton: Princeton University Press, 1967). Copyright © 1967 by Princeton University Press. Reprinted by permission of Princeton University Press.

Jack London, "San Francisco Is Gone!" in *Collier's* (May 5, 1906).

Siegfried Sassoon, *Memoirs of an Infantry Officer* (London: Faber and Faber, 1930). Reprinted by permission of George Sassoon.

Oswald Spengler, *The Decline of the West*, translated by Charles Francis Atkinson (New York: Knopf, 1939). Translation copyright 1926 by Alfred A. Knopf, Inc. Reprinted by permission of the publisher.

Excerpt from Harry Kessler, *In the Twenties: The Diaries of Harry Kessler*, translated by Charles Kessler (New York: Holt, Rinehart and Winston, 1971). Copyright © 1971 by Charles Kessler. Reprinted by permission of Henry Holt & Co., Inc.

"Talk of the Town," *The New Yorker*, November 2, 1929. Reprinted by permission; copyright 1929 The New Yorker Magazine, Inc. All rights reserved.

Excerpt from Sigmund Freud, *Civilization and Its Discontents*, translated by James Strachey (New York: Norton, 1961). Translation copyright © 1961 by James Strachey, renewed 1989 by Alix Strachey. Reprinted by permission of W. W. Norton & Company, Inc. Also by permission of Sigmund Freud Copyrights, The Institute of Psycho-Analysis, and The Hogarth Press to quote from *The Standard Edition of the Complete Psychological Works of Sigmund Freud*, translated and edited by James Strachey.

H. L. Mencken, "The End of an Era," originally printed in the *Baltimore Evening Sun* (September 14, 1931), reprinted in *A Second Mencken Chrestomathy* (New York: Knopf, 1994). Copyright © 1994 by the Estate of H. L. Mencken. Reprinted by permission of Alfred A. Knopf, Inc.

Pablo Picasso, *Guernica*, 1937. Museo del Prado, Madrid, Spain. Transparency copyright © ARS, NY. Courtesy Giraudon/Art Resource, NY.

Tadeusz Borowski, "This Way for the Gas, Ladies and Gentlemen," from *This Way for the Gas, Ladies and Gentlemen and Other Stories*, selected and translated by Barbara Vedder (New York: Penguin Books, 1967). Originally published in Poland: *Wydor Opowiadan*, 1959, original text copyright © 1959 by Maria Borowski. This translation copyright © 1967 by Penguin Books Ltd. Used by permission of Viking Penguin, a division of Penguin Books USA Inc., and in Canada, by permission of Penguin Books Ltd.

Excerpt from Primo Levi, *If This Is a Man (Survival in Auschwitz)*, translated by Stuart Woolf, translation copyright © 1959 by Orion Press, Inc., copyright © 1958 by Giulio Einaudi, Editore, SPA. Used by permission of Viking Penguin, a division of Penguin Books USA Inc.

Excerpt from John Hersey, *Hiroshima*. Copyright 1946 and renewed 1974 by John Hersey. Reprinted by permission of Alfred A. Knopf, Inc. Originally printed in *The New Yorker*.

William L. Laurence, "A thousand Old Faithful geysers rolled into one blast," *The New York Times*, September 9, 1945. Copyright 1945 by The New York Times Co. Reprinted by permission.

Hal Boyle, "Washington Under the Bomb," (*Collier's*, October 27, 1951).

Rachel Carson, "The Obligation to Endure," from *Silent Spring* (Boston: Houghton Mifflin, 1962). Copyright © 1962 by Rachel L. Carson. Copyright renewed 1990 by Roger Christie. Reprinted by permission of Houghton Mifflin Company. All rights reserved.

Haing S. Ngor, with Roger Warner, *A Cambodian Odyssey* (New York: Macmillan, 1987). Reprinted by permission of the Estate of Haing S. Ngor.

Adaptation from Peter Schneider, *The German Comedy: Scenes of Life After the Wall*, translated by Philip Boehm and Leigh Hafrey (New York: Farrar, Straus & Giroux, 1991). Translation copyright © 1991 by Farrar, Straus, & Giroux, Inc. Reprinted by permission of Farrar, Straus & Giroux, Inc.

Francis Fukuyama, *The End of History?* (New York: Macmillan, 1989). Copyright © 1989 by Francis Fukuyama. Reprinted by permission of International Creative Management, Inc. Originally printed in *The National Interest* (Summer 1989).

Excerpts from the Rapture Index on the World Wide Web: http://www.novia.net/~todd/